HEADWATERS

THE ADVENTURES, OBSESSION, AND EVOLUTION OF A FLY FISHERMAN

DYLAN TOMINE

ILLUSTRATIONS BY FRANCES B. ASHFORTH

patagonia

HEADWATERS

The Adventures, Obsession, and Evolution of a Fly Fisherman

Patagonia publishes a select list of titles on wilderness, wildlife, and out-door sports that inspire and restore a connection to the natural world.

Hardcover edition

Printed in the United States on Rolland Enviro 100 Satin FSC®certified 100 percent post-consumer-waste paper.

Editor – John Dutton
Art Director and Designer – Christina Speed
Artist – Frances B. Ashforth
Project Manager – Sonia Moore
Production – Rafael Dunn, Michaela Purcilly, and Tausha Greenblott
Publisher – Karla Olson

Hardcover ISBN 978-1-952338-07-6, E-Book ISBN 978-1-952338-08-3
Library of Congress Control Number 2021948566

Published by Patagonia Works

Versions of some of these stories have appeared in the following publi-cations: *Fish & Fly, Wild On The Fly, The Flyfish Journal, The Drake, Fly Fisherman, The Cleanest Line*, the Patagonia catalog, and the Sage catalog.

ENVIRONMENTAL BENEFITS STATEMENT

Patagonia saved the following resources by printing the pages of this book on process chlorine free paper made with 100% post-consumer waste versus paper made with virgin fiber.

TREES	WATER	ENERGY	SOLID WASTE	GREENHOUSE GASES
229	19,000	97	800	99,200
FULLY GROWN	GALLONS	MILLION BTU's	POUNDS	POUNDS

This is based on the current requirement of a total of 19,120 pounds of paper (119,500 sheets 25" x 38" 80# Enviro Satin Text).

Environmental impact estimates were made using the Environmental Paper Network Paper Calculator Version 4.0. For more information visit www.papercalculator.org.

FOR THE PLANET
MEMBER

FSC
www.fsc.org
MIX
Paper from responsible sources
FSC® C002589

*For Skyla and Weston, I hope you find something
to love the way fish and fishing found me.*

STORIES

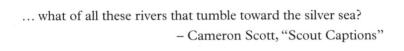

... what of all these rivers that tumble toward the silver sea?
                       – Cameron Scott, "Scout Captions"

FOREWORD

I learned to fish before I learned to read, but books—not blue-gill or trout—stoked my boyhood interest into the inferno that still burns red-hot inside this midlife angler. We lived eighteen miles from the nearest trout stream, which was too far for my BMX bike, and so I was forced to take my fishing where I could get it: in back issues of *Field & Stream*, and later from pages written by the likes of John Gierach, Ted Leeson, and Thomas McGuane.

Once I had a driver's license and a drift boat, fishing became a daily ritual of exploration and discovery, yet the reading habit stuck. After a day on the water, I'd often devote an hour or two to tying tomorrow's flies and then fall asleep with a fish story in hand. It was on one such night in my late twenties that I read an essay by a writer new to me, Dylan Tomine. It was called "State of the Steelhead," and it's collected here.

Something about Tomine's voice drew me in. During the years to come, when I found a new story of his in a magazine, I'd flip straight to that page and read it first, often leaning toward the prose as if it were a dry fly bobbing down a riffle.

Part of Tomine's charm on the page, then and now, is that he sounds like the ideal campfire guest. He's funny and profound, humble, and well traveled.

Back then, I read his stories to be swept up in the currents of his latest adventure. He was exploring rivers I could only dream of, and not as a dude who paid for his five days and six nights, but as a devotee of the watershed who camped on the moss or the couches of sympathetic locals. Of course, I'd had other writer crushes, but for the first time in my life, I worked up the courage to pen a fan letter.

To my surprise, Tomine responded. After a few months, our email thread spanned tens of thousands of words, spurred on by the realization that we grew up in the same small college town in Oregon, half a generation apart. We had fished the same little cutthroat creeks and admired the same local angling legends (praise be Andy Landforce). We decided we needed to fish together on the old waters. We did. It was awesome.

In the almost fourteen years since I penned that letter, I've remained a Tomine fan. I like to think I bought the very first copy of his book, *Closer to the Ground*. Both my editions are signed. I'm still reading Tomine now because he's a writer I've grown to trust.

Since the spark of our consciences, Tomine and I have shared a passion, a landscape, and its people. His new book delivers its audience to far corners of the planet; I can confirm the authenticity of his depiction of our shared rivers.

Headwaters is a book to reach for when you want to go fishing but can't. It's rich with the pleasures of angling: exploration, youthful obsession let off its leash, awe before fleeting beauty. In prose as fertile as a beaver pond, Tomine pays homage to the scaly abundance that still swam the rivers of the Pacific Northwest during the 1990s, and he bears witness to the steep decline in that abundance over the years since. Yes, this is a book that charts a fishing life, one man's movement from angling bum to fish conservationist, but it's more than that. Like a line cast over shadowed water, these pages come taut with hope for what happens next.

– John Larison, author of *Whiskey When We're Dry*,
Bellfountain, Oregon

INTRODUCTION

A dime-sized clump of mussel guts concealing a size-eight bait hook sinks into the murky depths. I lie on the splintery dock, head hanging over the edge and hands cupped around my face, watching it disappear. I am completely absorbed by the task at hand, which is to say, getting a bullhead or shiner or baby flounder to bite and stay attached. It's not easy. Most of the fish here are so small, our tiny bait won't fit into their mouths. My fishing partners, Skyla and Weston, are fifteen and twelve years old, respectively. We are killing time, waiting to see if the wind will quit enough to let us launch the boat and do some "real" fishing, but disappointment has turned into a nearly fanatical level of intensity. When Skyla rears back to set the hook and her rod tip bends into the slightest of curves, that old, familiar feeling surges through my stomach. Fish on!

After a lifetime of dragging a fly rod around the world in search of large and glamorous fish species, it's more than a little disorienting to discover that this moment on the old dock strikes me in the same spot as that twenty-pound steelhead on the Dean or the sight of giant trevally tearing into a school of bonefish. Maybe to a slightly lesser degree, but still, the feeling is there. And I am reminded that whatever ambiguity and doubt may cloud my day-to-day thoughts, there is one thing I know for sure: I was born to fish.

Fishing was never a sport, a pastime, or a hobby for me. It was, and continues to be, who I am. In a vast majority of photos taken of me as a kid, I am holding one kind of fish or another, smiling through the faded amber of old Kodachrome. My childhood memories all revolve around fish: watching my father hauling a burlap sack full of salmon across a riverside pasture; holding my grandfather's hand in a crowd gathered to see the sharks at Steinhart Aquarium; casting into a roaring coastal river while my mom waits for me in the car.

All this makes for a pretty strange kid. If I wasn't fishing, I was thinking about fishing. When I fell asleep, I dreamed about fishing. While I was careening around town on my bike with a fishing rod across the handlebars or holed up in my room pouring over the well-worn pages of an ancient Herter's catalog, my contemporaries worked on their jump shots and traded baseball cards. Later, when the more mature among my peers started delving into the mystery of girls, I was too busy trying to catch my first steelhead to notice. When I recall people saying I was "obsessed," it occurs to me now that they were probably being charitable.

As a young adult, my life revolved around a carefree fishing schedule, where the main concerns were water levels, weather, and scraping up enough cash for the next trip. Summers, I guided in Bristol Bay. In the off-season, I fished wherever and whenever, traveling from the Klamath up through the Deschutes, the Hoh, the Thompson, the Bella Coola, and on into Skeena Country, mostly on a mission to quench an insatiable thirst for steelhead.

Of course, I also needed a day-to-day fishery. For a long time, I found the comfort of home waters on the Skykomish River, where I probably spent close to seventy days a year. Most of those days were during the Sky's famous March/April catch-and-release wild steelhead season. It was fantastic fishing, filled with big, wild fish that chased down flies in classic water, and an opportunity to develop an intimate understanding of a single watershed. Better yet, it was just forty-five minutes from my home in Seattle. Those days, I worried very little about anything beyond my ability to catch fish, and lots of them.

In 2001, I received the proverbial wake-up call: My beloved Skykomish was closing for the spring season, an emergency ruling necessitated by the dwindling wild steelhead population. I'm ashamed to admit, this was the first time anything about conservation ever crossed my mind. But it hit me hard. As I write this, more than nineteen years later, the Sky has yet to reopen in March or April, and I miss it more than I can express. It's still open in December and January for hatchery steelhead, and there are usually a few wild fish mixed in, but I can hardly bring myself to fish the old, familiar places anymore. I'm not sure why. Maybe I just don't want to be the guy who shoots the last buffalo.

In the years since the Skykomish closed, I've had the great fortune to travel widely in search of fish. Christmas Island, Arctic Russia, the Outer Banks, Patagonia, Japan, Cuba, and countless days on the Skeena and other systems in British Columbia. The Bulkley, nearly a thousand miles from where I live, became my de facto home river. Somewhere along the way, I realized that nothing could fully replace the Skykomish in springtime for me, and I have been forced by circumstance—and a vague sense of guilt—to wade ever deeper into the issues surrounding wild-fish conservation.

I think the stories in this book, written across the better part of two decades and arranged more or less in chronological order, show a kind of arc in consciousness. My daughter, Skyla, was born around the time my first story was published, and Weston followed three years later. My fishing and writing have been informed by them and thoughts of their future ever since. Even when traveling, I find it's hard to fish anywhere now without thinking about how it used to be, or what the future might look like. I'm just not the same person I was back when I started writing these stories.

I'm not the same fisherman, either. Priorities change. I find myself looking forward to fishing trips as much for the company of good friends as I do the actual fish. There's a deeper appreciation for the natural and cultural history of a place, and more time spent watching the weather and birds. Great meals are often remembered as highlights of any trip. With kids I love being around, work to do, and decent fishing nearby, I spend more time closer to home now. Of course, I still feel the stoke of adventure whenever a trip starts coming together, but even that doesn't come without doubt.

What about the footprint left by my travels? Does advocacy for wild fish make up for the damage caused by planes, helicopters, jet boats, and trucks employed purely for recreation? Then there's the car and boat I drive at home, along with the electricity we use, the products we buy, the food we eat. ... Today, it's not just the Skykomish. The overall population of wild Puget Sound steelhead hovers below 4 percent of historical average. Many of the great fisheries I've traveled to and love are in peril from the ever-present forces of resource extraction. How complicit am I in all of this? I honestly don't know. But I understand clearly the irony pointed out by former Secretary of the Interior Sally Jewell when she talks about driving a gas-powered car to get to the oil-company protest.

Back on the dock, the wind is still blowing and our boat sits on the trailer. But the rising tide has brought in bigger bullheads—some pushing well into the four-inch class—and I watch the kids fish with growing intensity. When Weston lands and gently releases a nice, seven-inch mini-flounder, my adrenaline really kicks in. Before I know it, I'm rigging up a handline and pulling another mussel off the underside of the dock to join the fun. I want to feel the bite, that vital sensation of life on the line, and say, yet again, the best two-word sentence in the English language. Fish on!

Looking back through these stories, I feel overwhelming gratitude for all the people, places, and fish that I've been lucky enough to experience. What an amazing world we live in. I just hope the one Skyla and Weston inherit will be at least as good, if not better. There's plenty of work ahead to make it happen, but I think we have a shot.

Bainbridge Island, Washington

NOVEMBER 1969

I am bundled in blankets on my mom's lap in the shotgun seat of our faded yellow Toyota Corolla. It's chilly and damp, the windows coated with condensation. Rain drums steadily on the roof. My mom pauses from the story she's reading to me, wipes the window to look outside, and there, across an open pasture surrounded by dark forest, I can see my dad. He's a young man here, walking toward us, fishing rod in one hand, a burlap sack slung over his shoulder in the other. His old cotton porkpie hat droops with the weight of rainwater, his wool logger shirt is soaked. Jets of steam hang in the air with his every breath, yet he moves with a distinct bounce in his step. As he comes closer, his smile comes into focus, and I can see salmon tails sticking out of the gunnysack.

CONFESSIONS OF
A STEELHEAD BUM

Let me tell you how bad it's gotten: Ten days into a two-week fishing trip and nine hundred miles from home, I called my wife, who was eight months pregnant with our first child. Now, any sane person would object to that statement alone, but hey, I'm just getting started. I was sitting in my car watching dusk fall across the Bulkley River, excited to tell her about my day. When she answered, her voice sounded shaky and strained. "Someone broke into our house today," she said. And my first thought was—I swear—*good thing I have all my Spey rods with me here.* I'm not kidding.

Of course, I was relieved she was OK, and I asked all the rational questions and said comforting things, but that's not really the point, is it? And sure, I cut the trip short. Packed up all my gear that night, hooked up the boat, and headed home in the morning. But then again, the fishing was lousy anyway. Which, if we're asking real questions of ourselves here, was something else to consider on the seventeen-hour drive home.

In 1978, as we cast tiny flies from a rowboat on a small pond, Andy Landforce, the great Oregon steelhead guide, said to me, "Bluegills are the fish of the future." I was twelve years old at the time and already deep in the grips of steelhead mania. Steelhead are big, powerful, migratory rainbow trout that travel to the ocean and return to spawn in beautiful, fast-flowing rivers. They are among the most prized sport fish in the world. Bluegills, in contrast, inhabit murky, warm-water ponds, don't fight much, and average about five inches in length. Needless to say, I had no concept of why we were wasting time on a farm pond when there were steelhead to be caught in nearby rivers. I remember thinking he must be joking, because if bluegills were the fish of the future, it was a pretty bleak future indeed. When I think back to that summer afternoon and the statement that has somehow stuck with me, I wonder: Was Andy anticipating the sad state of steelhead populations we find ourselves with today, or did he mean it on a more personal level?

It's difficult to trace the exact beginning of an obsession. Can a single snowflake falling on a quiet slope trigger an avalanche? But it must have been quite early for me. I can vividly recall an event that occurred when I was still very small. My father, who, following my parents' divorce, lived in another state, came to visit and took me trout fishing. It was early spring and the weather was rotten. Knowing him better now, I'm sure there must have been a thousand things Dad would have rather done than stand out in the rain, but I had been looking forward to the fishing trip for weeks. And so we went. It rained all day, and yet we fished, me, too happy to notice my soaking clothes, and my dad, patiently casting for hour after wet hour.

Late in the afternoon, with any realistic hope of catching fish long gone, my dad suddenly hooked something that ran downstream with unbelievable fury. His little trout rod bent into the handle and the drag made a shrieking sound that pierced the noise of the rapids below. We fought that fish for more than an hour, through emotional highs and lows, down through the tailout and into the churning whitewater below. At one point, the line snagged on a boulder, and Dad handed me the rod and waded out chest-deep to free it. As the line came tight, I could feel the incredible strength of the fish pulling me downstream, and a hot surge of adrenaline shot through my body. When we finally landed that fish, a bright, fourteen-pound winter

steelhead, my dad lifted me up in the air in celebration. It was the first steelhead I ever felt on the line. The die was cast.

Who knew what that fish would mean to my future?

Throughout my childhood and early teen years, I was consumed by steelhead fishing. Literally. I ate, drank, read, thought, and dreamed steelhead. My single mother, conscious of her son's strange obsession, took me fishing every Sunday, rain or shine. Not that she would actually fish with me. As a graduate student with a full-time job, she was far too busy to fish. She spent those Sundays in the car, at one riverside turn-out or another, with textbooks and notepads spread on the dashboard, studying. My little brother would be wrapped in blankets with his stuffed animals and comic books in the back seat, waiting while I fished. I think the experience scarred him permanently—to this day he has not the slightest inclination to do anything even remotely "outdoorsy." Years later, when I returned to that rainy, western Oregon river, several people stopped me and asked, "Weren't you the kid whose mom waited for you in the car?"

And that's how it was. I fished—and my mom and brother waited—through a year of Sundays before I caught my first steelhead, and hundreds more after that. But the madness was firmly in place. And thus began a pattern that would repeat itself over and over again: my single-minded pursuit coupled with someone else's sacrifice.

It's been said that as you grow older, your thought process becomes less focused on the self, that you gain empathy, compassion, and a sense of responsibility to others. Collectively, these traits are frequently referred to as "growing up." Unless you're a steelhead bum. In which case, growing older merely means a widening circle of possibilities. Longer trips to faraway places, often involving the kind of equipment reserved for military conquests of small, developing countries. Airplanes, helicopters, four-wheelers, jet sleds, rafts, drift boats, all in service of one purpose: getting the steelhead bum to the steelhead. And we're not just talking about the home river anymore, either. The Oregon high desert, northern British Columbia, Idaho, Southeast Alaska, and even Russia come into play. After years of such lunacy, the rivers, the fish, and the people all begin to blur into one long, rain-soaked voyage.

Not long ago, up on the Skeena, we were driving along the river, searching for good water. By some miracle, my cell phone had service, and on a whim, I called my buddy Yvon (who, even more miraculously, was between adventures and actually at work) for advice. He's fished this river for years, and from his office in Ventura, California, he gave directions by memory to a spot that was "probably loaded with fish." He described a boulder-filled run above a huge set of rapids, and before he hung up, he casually added that it required a "short walk down a little hill." I guess I should have paid more attention to that last part. When one of the world's great climbers talks about a "short walk down a little hill," well, you ought to take notice. But no, the usual insanity took over and all I heard was "loaded with fish."

It was a short walk all right. After tiptoeing to the edge of the canyon-like precipice and eyeing the killer water down at the bottom, I felt a pang of concern about surviving the descent. My fishing partner, Nate, a considerably saner person than I, suggested looking for another spot. But the words "loaded with fish" bounced around in my steelhead-addled brain and I stepped over the edge. My feet flew out from under me, I landed on my ass, and I proceeded to bounce, slide, and fly down the slope like a pachinko ball, frantically trying to avoid breaking my Spey rod between tree trunks. Serious injury was more than a possibility. But as I careened through the devil's club, ricocheted off a boulder, and came to rest against the splintered end of a gigantic windfall cedar, I don't think I ever took my eyes off the water. At the bottom, bruised knee and twisted ankle in tow, I staggered to the water, made one cast, and hooked a gorgeous sixteen-pounder, which, unless I think about it deeply, is pretty much all I remember of the day.

The point is that this steelhead affliction, to any normal human being, is a personality defect at best, and something far more serious in a lot of cases. You might say one's priorities get a little out of whack.

My friend Carson once famously told his girlfriend that he was put on this Earth to fish, and that fishing would always come first, no matter what. Period. End of story. Not surprisingly, he's single now. But he does catch a lot of fish. And while normal people might shake their heads in pity, true steelhead bums feel more than a twinge of envy.

At a restaurant in Telkwa, British Columbia, a fishing acquaintance was telling the story of his near-death experience the previous day, which involved flipping his raft and swimming nearly a quarter mile submerged in icy rapids. All it took was a minor miscalculation with the oars and a fallen cottonwood blocking the main current somewhere on the lower Kispiox. He was obviously shaken up as he described the fear, hypothermia, and loss of his fly rods. Another angler, hearing the story, said without blinking, "Yeah, but was there any good water down there?"

Another friend and mentor of mine, Mike Kinney, attained mythical status by fishing the Stillaguamish River nearly every day for ten years. The knowledge he gained in that decade became the foundation for a legendary understanding of steelhead behavior and fly-fishing techniques. Of course, he had to raise his son in a one-room cabin without electricity or running water in order to do it, but as he says, "It wasn't too bad once you got used to it."

Then there's the story of Bill Schaadt, the Northern California angling icon, who, upon driving off a cliff on a predawn trip to his favorite steelhead pool, crawled from the smoking wreckage and limped to the water to fish. He returned to the totaled car only after dark when he could no longer see enough to fish. As the story goes, the water was dropping and clearing—ideal steelhead conditions—and fresh fish were coming in, which pretty much says it all.

So I'm not alone. But then, finding others in the same boat as you is hardly a definition of sanity. The fact that just about anyone can name at least half a dozen infamous serial killers demonstrates that even the most extreme lunatics have a peer group. In his wonderful book *The Habit of Rivers*, Ted Leeson writes that there are only two kinds of anglers—those who are born to it, and those who aren't. For those of us in the first group, whose earliest memories, and for that matter, most of the subsequent ones as well, revolve around fish and fishing, this business can spiral rapidly out of control.

The stories of wasted potential, lost careers, and broken marriages are rampant in steelhead circles, and often reduced in print—for humorous effect—to clichés like the stereotypical "fishing widow." I will, however, point out that these stories, if you happen to play a part in them, carry a little more impact than mere literary conventions. For my own part, the list is nearly endless. I narrowly avoided flunking out of college while dreaming of rivers, and missed my graduation ceremony completely, trading it for a floatplane trip in Southeast Alaska. There were the two promising career jobs left behind on short notice when the fishing got good, because rivers are rarely perfect on weekends. Hell, I had to quit my job as a fishing guide in Alaska because it was cutting into the prime seasons on the Deschutes and the Dean. Add to this the missed family gatherings, the bailed-on friends, the strained relationships, and what you see in the mirror is not a pretty reflection.

Don't get me wrong, I love my family and friends. It's just that when the river's right, the river's right. Although that's hardly a valid excuse for the time I was supposed to help my future wife move to a new apartment and instead spent the entire day on the Skykomish, or when I nearly got myself and a friend killed by a charging sow grizzly in the name of "one more cast." All of which proves nothing more than that I am most likely an asshole.

Once, out on the Olympic Peninsula, I became so absorbed in fishing, I completely failed to notice the passage of time. On a six-mile float, night caught us two miles short of the takeout. In a near panic, I raced downstream, rowing like a madman. If you've spent much time in a drift boat, you already know this is an obvious recipe for disaster. In our case, we ended up high-centered on a subsurface log in the middle of a steep, narrow chute. We teetered back and forth as the water roared past us in the darkness.

After much debate, and for lack of a better plan, we leaned hard to one side, felt the hydraulics grip the chine, and as the boat stood up on end and nearly capsized, we floated free. If it wasn't already apparent, it was now clear we couldn't make it to the boat ramp. Instead, we spent a long night in twenty-eight-degree weather, trying to huddle around our make-shift campfire. One of the guys slept so close to the fire that he was completely covered with ash and burning cinders. In the morning, his $500 Gore-Tex coat looked like Swiss cheese.

In addition to the fear of death by drowning or hypothermia, and a long, hungry, freezing night on some very hard rocks, we missed work the next day, and perhaps most importantly, caused our families incalculable worry when we didn't return home. But, and this is what I'm getting at here, in the morning we resumed fishing ("Hey, we're here, we might as well ..."), and with teeth chattering and stomachs rumbling, we were immediately into fish. Oh, we could have rowed out at dawn, called our families, and maybe even made it into work, but who could pass up first water?

You've probably seen that silly bumper sticker that says, "Work is for people who don't know how to fish." Well, for some of us, it's more than a silly bumper sticker.

According to the Mayo Clinic, a sociopath is someone who tends to *antagonize, manipulate, or treat others harshly or with callous indifference.* Focus on that last part, and the ground gets shakier. On my home river, there is a piece of water that's as close to a guarantee as you can get in steelhead fishing. If the conditions are right, chances are you will get a fish, often more than one. Problem is, it's hardly a secret, and it only works if you get there before the other maniacs can beat you to the spot.

This has devolved into a middle-of-the-night, headlamp-equipped foot race so extreme even I have given up. But a few years back, I happened on the run relatively early in the morning and was surprised to see it vacant. I parked the car and began to race wildly down the railroad tracks toward the coveted hole, all the while thanking the Fishing Gods for their beneficence.

About a hundred yards ahead I noticed what looked like a pile of clothes. As I drew closer, it became apparent that it was a person slumped on the side of the trail. As I got closer still, I became alarmed at the utter lack of movement displayed by the prostrate form. With a growing sense of dread verging on panic, I shouted for the guy to wake up. No response. When I reached him, I found a tattered, disheveled-looking old fellow who had clearly seen better days. And still no movement. None. So I responded the way health care professionals everywhere recommend: I found a stick and poked him in the neck. Hard.

Nothing. I poked again, even harder, and still he remained motionless. Shit. This was the long-feared yet inevitable headline come to life: "Local Angler Finds Dead Guy." Now I had a serious decision to make. By the time I hiked back into phone range and waited for the police, some inconsiderate slob would be in "my" run, most likely landing "my" fish. On the other hand, I rationalized, since the guy was already dead, what would another hour or two matter? As I stood there contemplating the concept of morality in general, and more specifically, how it might apply to me, I heard car doors slam back in the parking area. That sealed it. I was going fishing. Now, lest you think I'm totally heartless, I will mention that I fished through rather quickly and ineffectively, and didn't enjoy it much.

When I returned to the trail, I was shocked—and somewhat relieved—to discover the dead guy was gone, an empty vodka bottle the only proof of his presence. Later that day I saw him staggering around town with another bottle wrapped securely in a brown paper bag. I guess that absolves me of guilt. But still, if we're looking at intent, this story says something.

There was a time, shortly after my "career-killing" move to Steelhead Country, when I lived in a tiny studio apartment, pizza boxes and dirty dishes stacked in precarious towers. When you fish all day every day, who has time to clean house? Christmas was approaching and I was broke, another direct result of my addiction. What little savings I had was quickly dwindling away and being hoarded for gas money to get to and from the river. And my mom, the very same mom who sacrificed her every Sunday of my childhood to take me fishing, was arriving Christmas Day so that I wouldn't have to spend the holiday alone.

I fished with unusual fervor all week, hoping against hope that I could catch a fish for Christmas dinner. I somehow felt that Mom just wouldn't appreciate my standard fare of ramen noodles and pizza. The water was low that year, the fish hardly moving. My string of fishless days was well into double digits. Late in the day on Christmas Eve, with darkness falling, while desperately fishing through a treacherous, broken-water section of the river, a ten-pound hatchery steelhead took my fly. By some miracle, I landed it, and the potential Christmas-dinner disaster was averted. This may be the one case of redemption-by-fishing that I know of, although since fishing was the cause of the predicament in the first place, it probably doesn't count.

All this, you may be wondering, for what? A fish? For hour after hour, standing waist-deep in freezing water? For weeks spent enduring constant rainfall and dripping tents? For months thrown away on crazed quests to the middle of nowhere? All this for a pursuit in which success is defined by a single fish per day? Hey, I never claimed it made any sense. And I admit it's tough to explain.

What is it then that fuels this madness? Unfortunately, there is no simple answer. No single, defining explanation to satisfy friends and loved ones. In fact, I suspect that if you asked any number of serious steelheaders, you'd get an equal number of answers, though they'd probably come in the form of barely coherent mumbles. Ultimately, I can only attempt to answer for myself.

For me, it starts with the fish itself. The sleek, chrome beauty, luminous and explosive, carrying all the strength and fecundity of the sea to inland waters. In essence, steelhead fishing is an opportunity to encounter ocean fish in the kind of water usually associated with trout. And it's the spectacular places these fish inhabit as well, from steep-walled alpine rapids rushing beneath glaciers to the dark and mysterious coastal rainforest rivers, dripping with moss and the sweet scent of wet alders. From meandering tidewater stretches on the barren tundra to ice-cold streams cutting through the heat of red-rock canyons and sage-brush. These are all steelhead waters, and not coincidentally, places I love dearly. But as far as explanations go, I realize it falls a little short. Maybe the best reason I've heard came from a man who literally gave it all up, a true steelhead bum who lived out of his truck for years, endlessly driving from river to river. When someone asked him why, and how he could live such a life, his answer was simply, "I don't have a choice."

No matter how you look at it, one thing is becoming increasingly apparent: This steelhead business isn't getting any easier. In fact, it's become downright tough. Now, after decades of diminishing runs, my home river, the Skykomish, is closed to fishing during the prime season to protect what's left of our wild steelhead. Nobody seems to know for sure what's causing the decline, but it's hardly a surprise that it's occurred at a rate directly proportional to the influx of development that now paves the valley, and the massive numbers of hatchery steelhead dumped into the river. To the north, the mighty Skagit, which in the 1960s and '70s boasted annual *harvests* in the tens of thousands, now has a total wild spawning population of fewer than six thousand fish. Down south, on the Columbia, more Endangered Species Act-listed wild steelhead often perish as "bycatch" of the commercial spring Chinook gillnet fishery than the target species.

In any event, things aren't getting any easier for the steelhead bum these days. As Tom McGuane recently said, "It's getting to the point where you have to worry more about the fish than the fishing."

All of which leaves us where? On the long drive home from the Bulkley, thoughts of impending fatherhood, the sacrifices others have made for me, the spiraling steelhead populations, and the very nature of what it means to be a steelhead fisherman rumble around in my head. A few things seem clear. There is every possibility that if we continue on our current path, we may be the last generation of anglers to fish for wild steelhead. Those of us who care about such things will need to get involved in politics—as distasteful as that may seem to solitude-seeking steelhead bums—in order to have any chance of preserving what we love. There's really no other choice.

On a personal level, will I be willing to make the kind of sacrifices for my daughter that others made for me? I don't know, but I'm going to try. If bluegills are truly the fish of my future, whether for reasons of dwindling steelhead runs or family priorities, I say bring 'em on. I will happily spend an afternoon—or a hundred, for that matter, if she has a passion for it—with my daughter, on a quiet pond, fishing for bluegills.

Although it may be a bit late in the game, I now understand it's time for this steelhead bum to "grow up." And strangely, it feels pretty good. In a lot of ways, it's a relief to feel no worry over weather forecasts and river levels, no stress over rain falling on the roof, and no pressure to tie flies and clean lines in manic late-night sessions. My lips no longer tremble at words like *work* or *responsibility*. And I can quickly dismiss sudden trips based on unreliable reports of hot fishing in faraway places, which formerly would have sent me looking into the feasibility of a third mortgage. Of course, while I may not be exactly proud of all the craziness of the past twenty-five years, I wouldn't trade the experiences, the fish, or the people I've met on this quest for anything. As the old song goes, *What a long strange trip it's been.* For the first time in my life, the steelhead jones is quiet, and I'm content to be at home. It's a surprisingly relaxed and peaceful state of mind I've found.

But it'll probably pass.

JANUARY 1970

*In the dark exhibit halls of Steinhart Aquarium, I stand
close to my San Francisco grandpa, holding his rough,
calloused hand in awe as sharks circle through the brightly
lit tank. Earlier, at my insistence, we'd tried fishing from
Fort Point Pier in the shadow of the Golden Gate Bridge,
but the cold fog made my teeth chatter before we could catch
anything. The aquarium is Grandpa's backup plan. And
now I never want to leave. I will dream of these moments for
months, years. On our way out, already late for dinner, my
grandfather tells me to wait. I sit on a bench in the open entry
area, surrounded by strangers, but when I close my eyes, all
I see is fish. My grandfather returns and hands me a small
paper bag from the gift shop. I open it to find a tiger-shark
tooth the size of a quarter, its edge sharp and serrated. He
says it's to help me remember this day. As if I'd ever forget.*

TROUT FISHING AT THE END OF THE EARTH

The problem, as it turned out, was the Swedes' cheese. About twenty minutes into our three-hour, dirt-road drive from Murmansk to an abandoned Soviet military installation, the four of us were already casting sidelong glances at each other in the steamy van. The stern Russian driver looked back at us with suspicious eyes. Finally, someone broke down, "Man, is that you?" Denials all around. Up ahead, we could see the eight Swedish rafters in their van. They seemed to be looking out the back window at us a little too frequently, and it soon became clear they were laughing. Nobody in our van was laughing. In spite of the frigid air outside, someone opened a window. The large mound of bags that we'd volunteered to haul for the Swedes sat innocently between us. The road, if you can call it that, hammered away on our kidneys. At our first tundra "bathroom" break, the other van backed up to where we stood stretching our legs and swatting mosquitoes. One of the Swedes rolled down his window and said very seriously, "We want to thank you for helping us carry our gear." Then, as they roared away in a cloud of dust, he leaned out the window and yelled, "So, how you like our cheese?"

What does it mean to start a fishing trip on the butt end of a practical joke? Was it some kind of sign? We dug through the pile of rafting equipment, located the offending cheese, tossed it out the window, and tried to put the incident behind us. After another hour of bad road, thankfully with much-improved air quality, we arrived at a deserted army communications base. Disintegrating cinder-block buildings loomed out of the fog like a set from *The X-Files*. A distant mechanical drone approached, transforming into rotor slap as the hulking Soviet-era Mi-8 helicopter appeared. Now, at last, we were going fishing instead of just traveling.

But first, a moment to examine our aircraft: What the de Havilland Beaver is to Alaska, the Mi-8 is to the Russian Arctic—a hardy, reliable workhorse that, through the loving (and often miraculous) devotion of backwoods mechanics, somehow manages to defy the effects of time. Bigger than a school bus, grease-smeared, and battle-scarred, this particular bird had clearly seen better days. The giant rear cargo doors that once opened for Soviet troops in Afghanistan were now held shut—barely—by duct tape and bailing wire. Not metaphorical duct tape and bailing wire, but the real articles.

"Are those bullet holes?" somebody asked. I was too busy studying the frayed wires dangling from the ceiling to respond. Then, suddenly, we were screaming over the tundra in a heart-pounding, nose-down takeoff. Somewhere under the shriek of rotors, turbines, and bearings, I imagined *Ride of the Valkyries* pushing us forward to what we all hoped would be a waiting trout paradise.

• • •

Imagine Alaska fifty years ago, before jet boats and floatplanes descended en masse on Bristol Bay, and trophy rainbow trout lived and died without ever seeing a fly. Now, in your mind's eye, replace those huge rainbows with brown trout, and you begin to understand the potential of the Russian Arctic fishery. To be specific, we're talking about the Kharlovka Company's exclusive rights to two million acres of pristine wilderness tundra on the Kola Peninsula. Within this vast holding lie nearly two hundred thousand rivers, streams, lakes, and ponds, many of which have never been fished. Rumors of giant, football-shaped trout in Russia's far north have been circulating for years, but solid information was scarce. How and where to find the fish? What flies and techniques would work? Just how big do these fish really get?

To find the answers to these questions, the Kharlovka Company, famous for what may be the best big-fish Atlantic salmon camps in the world, decided to run an exploratory trout camp above the traditional salmon water on the Kharlovka River. The second week of July found a loose team of serious trout anglers—and me—assembled in a comfortable tent camp at the mouth of Kufshin Creek with a helicopter, a topo map, and two hundred thousand bodies of water to explore.

Outdoor photographer Tim Pask would lead the effort. As the first-ever Kharlovka Trout Program manager, Tim had been on the tundra for several weeks when we arrived, and was already looking a little frayed around the edges. A serious knee injury, the resulting painkillers, and the near-constant strain of getting things done in the wilderness had reduced his energy level to that of a normal human being. Those of us who have tried to keep up with Tim in the past secretly considered this a good thing. Joe "Rubber Legs" Roope, an Idaho trout guide, would be our technical guru. Jeff Thompson, a well-traveled Western trout addict, and me, a Washington steelhead bum, rounded out the group. Gordon Sim, Kharlovka Company's general manager, and Valentin Efremenkov, the famous Russian salmon guide, both old hands on the Kola, would lend their expertise as needed. The sheer magnitude of the task ahead was daunting—with so much water to cover, it was almost impossible to know where to begin. Hell, we couldn't even read the river names printed in Cyrillic letters on the Russian map. What we would find when we got to them, nobody knew. Perhaps it was the twenty-four-hour daylight, jet lag, or rocket-fuel Russian vodka, but the experience plays out in my memory like a slide show of vivid flashbacks.

• • •

At the boulder-studded outflow of a large lake, we hunker down over our gear as the helicopter roars away. When the rotor wash dissipates, a vast silence—almost like a ringing in the ears—envelops us. Actually, my ears are ringing, as I've forgotten my earplugs and Russian helicopters are known for their skull-crushing decibel level. But gradually, there is the realization of sound. A staggering number of plops, splashes, and gurgles melt together into a watery hum of background noise. When we stand to survey the river, we are witness to a feeding frenzy of huge trout gulping bugs. Shafts of pale, Arctic sunlight angle down through broken clouds, illuminating a blizzard of hatching insects. Three kinds of caddis, five sizes of stoneflies, uncountable varieties of mayflies, and midges so thick they're gathered in inch-thick piles that float down the foam lines. The streamside foliage, mostly chest-high rye and scrubby, weathered birch, crawls with bugs, and each gust of wind brings a hailstorm of tiny bodies pelting my jacket and waders and, unfortunately, my teeth.

"Which bugs are they eating?" That's the first question I ask myself. As a steelhead fisherman, I award myself a gold star for thinking like a real trout guy. But in this case, such thinking is ridiculously off base. The answer is, "All of them." In the short northern growing season, these trout cannot afford the luxury of selective feeding, so they tear into the smorgasbord with abandon.

Is the fishing easy? In comparison to the hypereducated fish of say, Silver Creek, yes. But "easy" is a relative term, and these browns aren't suckers. I crouch on a fallen log, hands shaking, casting wildly, my mind a blur of possibilities. Any skills I may possess rapidly dissolve in adrenaline. My casting sucks. I've completely fallen apart. But this isn't Silver Creek—not by a long shot—and my first reasonably drag-free drift is met with a confident slurp. Downstream, through a haze of insects, Tim is fighting a fish with Gordon standing by, net at the ready. When it jumps, I see a splash like someone tossed a springer spaniel into the stream.

● ● ●

Standing on the very edge of the tundra, with the Barents Sea crashing on the beach just downstream, we are fishing the estuary of a small river called Chegodaevka. We are here to chase down a rumor of sea-run browns, which are said to gather here in great numbers when the tide is high. The tide is not high. In fact, judging by the hundred-yard stretch of inch-deep riffle where the stream runs across the beach, it's dead low. Still, the long, curving pool just above us looks good, especially where the glacial-sand substrate is interrupted by a large boulder. And hey, these are sea-run fish—my comfort zone. Valentin selects a tiny #10 Green Highlander tied on a double hook and explains the cross-stream presentation used for sea trout and Atlantic salmon. To a West Coast steelhead fisherman, it's all wrong. "Mend the line *down*stream? Really?" As we proceed through the run, I have to fight the instinct to slow the fly down, while Valentin does everything he can to get me to speed it up. I am doubtful.

Then a fish takes. Hard. The little five-weight Spey rod buckles deep into the handle and a flashing bar of chrome bursts into the air. *"Samga!"* Valentin shouts—"salmon!" My knees suddenly go rubbery, and though it isn't large, I can't remember ever wanting to land a fish more. At the exact moment this thought passes through my mind, the line goes slack, and the electric, twisting, leaping presence is gone. Gone. As I strip in my now-lifeless line, I feel the air going out of me like an untied balloon.

On my next cast, I make what feels like a radical downstream mend. Have to get that fly moving. Pump the rod tip? No problem. Strip in line as it swings? Yep. I have seen the light, and my conversion is rewarded. A twin of the first fish crushes the fly and tries to bail out of the hole. At the shallow tailout he arcs back, passing us, and I can hear the line hiss as it cuts through the water. When the fish tires, I back onto the gravel with wobbly knees and shaking hands. Valentin reaches down and lifts the fish into the air. I'm completely blown away. It's a small salmon, dressed in brilliant silver, with sparse, perfectly defined black checks sprinkled across a deep-gray back. I have never seen a more beautiful fish in my life.

• • •

Funny thing about the Arctic: It's freakin' freezing. Even in July. Yesterday it was seventy-five degrees with a balmy south breeze, bugs hatching, and trout rising. Last night the wind shifted, blowing in off the Barents Sea with a low, black ceiling of roiling clouds and icy rain. I'm wearing everything I've got and my teeth still chatter. Gordon, Tim, and I are fishing our way down a small, boulder-filled stream that connects two enormous lakes. Trout are not rising. Anywhere. Searching for fish, we scramble down crust-covered snowbanks and bust through dense thickets of twisted, ancient birch trees. In the gloomy light, the trees have a spooky, surrealistic look about them, and their branches seem to reach out and tear at our clothing, making forward progress difficult at best. I catch myself looking over my shoulder rather frequently, though I'm unsure of what I expect to see.

At a bend in the river where the tea-stained water sluices between two granite boulders, I am absentmindedly swinging a big Alaskan mouse pattern that Joe gave me last night. He had used it to great effect the day before, landing a series of spectacular trout, but I'm fishing without conviction. As I turn to say something to Valentin, a six-pound brown leaps clear of the water a full two feet from the mouse and eats it on the way back in. I'm caught off guard, but somehow manage to land what will turn out to be the only fish I see all day. I consider it a major success, and further proof that it really is better to be lucky than good.

On the way back to camp, the chopper rocks and sways in gusting wind, and looking out across the endless tundra I'm struck by the complete lack of human impact on the land. There is not another soul for miles around. No roads, no buildings, no anything that most of us would find familiar. With the barren, treeless landscape and a sun that endlessly circles the horizon, I wonder how I would get my bearings should the others meet with an untimely demise, leaving me as the sole survivor. I quickly suppress this thought process, but resolve, merely as an "intellectual exercise," to pay more attention to the maps and our direction of travel from here on out.

• • •

Humpback whales. The huge, ovoid granite boulders, mottled with lichen and scattered across the valley floor, look just like humpback whales breaching the surface of the grassy tundra.

Through the middle of this amazing spectacle winds a small, unnamed, Arctic version of a spring creek. Unnamed, in this case, not to protect its location from other anglers, but because in this vast wilderness, many of the streams literally have no names. High above the creek, exotic-looking bean geese fly in loose formation, and below them, jaegers careen wildly in the light breeze.

The sunshine is back and with it, the bugs. Valentin's stocking cap is alive with mosquitoes, and hordes of tiny, pale mayflies float down the glassy surface of the creek. The fish are feeding steadily with quiet, delicate sips—a sharp contrast to the feeding frenzies we've encountered on other river systems. I start in boldly with the #6 Stimulator connected to my fly line with heavy 2X leader material that's worked so well on previous days. No dice. Not even a look. Maybe they want the #4 Chernobyl Ant, an American fly, named with ironic humor that in Russia seems to gain a bit more irony and a lot less humor. The trout, shocked by my rubber-legged, foam atrocity, quit rising altogether. This is going to be tougher than I thought.

As the fish slowly recover from my insulting bad manners, I focus on a single bank feeder that's rising in a steady rhythm below me. Reluctantly, I taper my leader down to 5X, with its wimpy four-pound breaking strength, and begin a series of humiliating refusals. In order, I try the following: Yellow Humpy, size #10; Light Cahill, size #12; PMD parachute, size #16; and a nearly microscopic Sulphur Comparadun. This last fly, which appears, at least to me, to be an exact replica of the naturals, elicits a brief, half-hearted look, and that's it. The fish continues its leisurely feeding.

We break for lunch and sit on the boulders, watching with amazement. In the crystalline water, we can see trout of all sizes, some of them absolutely gargantuan, feeding at a relaxed pace. Gordon uses the satellite phone to check on his family in Ireland—a rather odd moment that finds him listening to his son's laughter in Belfast while watching a nine-pound brown eat mayflies 250 miles above the Arctic Circle. Valentin unpacks foil-wrapped bundles of bread, sausage, and cheese, and we dive into our tundra lunch while concocting new strategies for these finicky trout. Not insignificantly, nobody eats the cheese.

When I return to the water, desperation sets in. My fish is still there and he's still not having anything to do with me. I rifle through my fly boxes, searching for some kind of answer. The emerger is shot down. I unspool cobweb-thin 7X leader and try the Comparadun again. Finally, I hang a #20 Pheasant Tail Nymph under a big dry fly—my bobber—with a foot of 7X tippet and toss it out there. I watch the big dry dance down the foam line and suddenly disappear. Victory at last! By Kola standards, it's hardly a remarkable fish, about four pounds, but I couldn't be happier.

What makes these fish, on this day, in this water, so selective? I've always assumed selective feeding is some kind of Pavlovian response to angling pressure, that the educated trout of our heavily fished home waters got that way because of us. Here, that's simply not the case. These fish have probably never even seen artificial flies before today. Clearly, this will require further thought. But for now, it's a humbling lesson that reminds me again of how little I know about trout.

• • •

Roast wild duck and French wine seem like absurd luxuries for a little tent camp on the barren, windswept tundra. But we aren't complaining. In fact, we're nearly comatose with warmth and satisfaction. The kerosene heater creaks in the corner of the cook tent as greasy hands reach for fat-smeared wineglasses to drain the last drops of Bordeaux. It's a scene right out of Russell Chatham's brilliant story *The Great Duck Misunderstanding*. Outside, the midnight sun breaks through a thick blanket of clouds that's enveloped us all day, bathing the camp in golden light. The wind calms to a whisper and I'm already looking forward to some serious shut-eye. It's been a long day on the water and the usual post-dinner bullshit session is winding down. Suddenly, Tim appears in the door of the dining tent with a demented look in his eyes. "Wader up, boys," he says. "Time to go fishing." The strain of leadership has finally gotten to him, or maybe he's just been in the outback too long. Tim's gone Colonel Kurtz on us. He charges down to the riverbank, laughing maniacally, and in the distance we hear the high-pitched whine of helicopter turbines starting up.

It's one o'clock in the morning and we're blazing low over the tundra at max speed, the helicopter banking hard to follow a long granite escarpment toward higher ground. Up front, Tim is crouched behind the pilot screaming instructions and gesturing wildly with his hands. The pilot ignores him. We push onward, ducking lower to avoid looming banks of fog, low enough that I can see blades of grass racing by in a blur below us. We crest a small rise and a series of small, connected lakes appears, set in an alien moonscape of rock and ice. This is our destination.

When the chopper powers down, we are greeted by absolute stillness and the soft, purple light of dusk. The lake's surface is a perfect silver mirror, reflecting an exact twin of the surrounding icefields and violet sky above. We are supposed to fish for char. Tim mutters something about "recon," and with bloodshot eyes bulging and body leaning forward at a forty-five-degree angle, marches off toward the next lake. Joe, Jeff, and I watch in stunned silence until Tim becomes a tiny speck on the horizon. The three of us are exhausted. We sit at the water's edge and look out at the lake while Joe recounts a long and entertaining story of his adventures as a Christmas Island lodge owner. We've already fished enough today. We're content to sit back, relax, and fully absorb our strange and beautiful surroundings. And then we see it. First, one rise, way out in the lake. Then another. Then one within casting range. So much for contentment and relaxation.

• • •

In the Russian Arctic, plans change every five minutes. You are at the mercy of the weather, helicopter maintenance (or lack thereof), and the vagaries of cross-cultural communication. And there are no two ways about it: Russia is a long way to go to fish for trout. Twelve time zones is a long way to go for anything. Did we land countless numbers of ten-pound browns every day? No. Are they there? Absolutely. But for me, a trip to the Kola trout water is about something more. It's a wild adventure to a place of mind-blowing beauty, an opportunity to fish water that few, if any, have ever fished. It's herds of reindeer scattering before you, and wolverines shambling across the tundra. It's Joe landing a forty-seven-inch pike on his four-weight in the blazing Arctic night, cracking a beer, and shrugging it off as a "pretty nice fish." It's singing along to *Hotel California* at two o'clock in the morning on a white-knuckle cab ride through the crumbling Soviet architecture of Murmansk. And yes, it's even about the smell of ripe Limburger on a long ride down a bad road.

Our group fished fifteen different rivers and streams. By my estimation, that leaves somewhere around 199,985 more bodies of water yet unfished and unexplored. In them live more huge browns than anyone will ever know. The Russians say some of these watersheds hold trout that grow to twenty-five pounds or more, and I believe them. Welcome to the final frontier.

SILVER LINING

The river is going out. Big time. Sure, it's been raining since the helicopter dropped us off six days ago and seventeen miles upriver, but only enough to ensure that everything we own is wet. A week of dripping tents, soggy sleeping bags, and wrinkled fingers isn't so bad when the river's green.

But now, this is different. The gentle drizzle we've grown accustomed to has transformed into a howling, spitting front that roared off the Pacific in the middle of the night. Not that I'd been sleeping anyway. Exhausted as I was, I had been in the grips of paranoid insomnia, fueled by the news we'd received yesterday. Steve, an old friend and guide for one of the lodges, had steered his jet boat near enough to shout, "Saw a big sow griz in here yesterday, with a wounded paw ... and cubs. I'd be careful." In broad daylight, we thought it was hilarious—a laughable guide tactic to keep us moving downstream, out of his prime water. And yet, we'd known Steve for years. He wouldn't try something that obvious, would he? Something to ponder in a dark tent as the wind picks up and branches snap in the distance.

In the morning, we bail out the raft and row across, knowing we have at most a one-day window to fish. Visibility is limited to the river corridor, as menacing, charcoal clouds obscure the soaring granite walls and Windex-blue glaciers that loom somewhere overhead. Quarter-sized raindrops blast a foot of spray over the water, and I understand we are fishing our last hours of the year on this river. By the time the river drops back into shape, our permits will be long expired.

We hike upstream in a mad scramble, driven by our new-found sense of urgency, then spend the day fishing our way back to the raft. The weather continues to deteriorate. We laugh stupidly over lame jokes, yelling, "It might be raining, but at least the wind's picking up," and in the midst of a particularly torrential downpour, "I don't think the really heavy stuff's going to come down for a while." Mostly, we cast with crazed intensity. The fishing is nothing short of magnificent. We are finding fish now in almost every run—explosive, flashing slabs of bright chrome pushing in from the sea on rising water. And still, the rain lashes at us. Time is running out in paradise.

In the dim, murky light of early evening, we are back at the raft, fishing the gravel bar across from camp. The river has lost its emerald-green color, tinged now with brown run-off and milky glacier-melt. Tomorrow it will be chocolate. As I work my way down into the sweet spot, something catches my eye across the river: a brief flicker of movement in the brush just upstream from our sadly drooping tent. I squint through the gloom and just make out a large, dark mass moving quickly toward camp. It's hard to be sure, but I could swear it's limping.

This is serious. We need to row over there right now and deal with the situation while there's still a last bit of daylight left. Make noise. Light the lantern. Get a fire going. Walking into camp after dark would be terrifying. A surge of fear grips my stomach.

Down in the tailout, just above the break, a fish surfaces in a slow head-and-tail roll. The width of its back is breathtaking. I take two steps downstream, push my loop through the gale, and fire. The upstream wind makes the mend easy and as my fly begins to swing, I know he's going to take. I just know it.

APRIL 1973

An Easter Sunday picnic, just my mom and dad and me. Warm and sunny. My parents spread a blanket on the sandy shore of a lake not far from home, but I am too excited to eat. I race to the water's edge and unwrap my new lure—a bright-yellow Hellbender, the first anything I ever ordered from a catalog, a lure I've been looking at, playing with, and dreaming about through the winter—tie it to my line, and heave it out past the submerged boulders that line the shore. On the third or fourth cast, something grabs the lure, pulling away hard. A three-pound smallmouth bass leaps into the air, then leaps again. I am shocked. In all my dreaming about this lure, I never considered that a fish would actually eat it. Somehow, I manage to horse the fish into the shallows, where my dad scoops it up and holds it aloft. "Alright!" he says. We put the fish on a stringer in shallow water and for the rest of the day I crouch beside it trying to memorize every detail of shape, color, and movement.

WAY DOWN SOUTH
TO THE OLD WEST

Here's the thing about getting airborne in a pickup truck: When it happens unexpectedly—and I'm talking about serious flight here, not some little bump-in-the-road, oopsy-daisy kind of hop—what you notice is the silence. One minute we're bouncing along a slight incline in the rough gravel road, yelling over the teeth-jarring clatter of tires on gravel, and then suddenly, the noise just stops. We are flying. Soaring. Hearing nothing but the celebrated Patagonian wind whipping through open windows. Seeing Klaus's knuckles whiten on the steering wheel as his maniacal grin turns into the oh-shit expression of disbelief. Watching the rolling prairie sail by in peaceful, quiet, slow motion. Then: *KABOOM!* Reality crashes back into my brain at the exact rate that two-and-a-half tons of Japanese steel comes down on the front bumper and tires.

We slide sideways and grind to a stop in a cloud of dust. I can still feel all my extremities. The six fly rods strapped to the hood appear to have survived. Tim and Sonya are still in the back seat. They seem to have switched positions, but they're still there. We look back at our tire marks in the dirt two-track and note how they disappear at the crest of the sudden drop and only reappear a hundred feet farther down the road. The half-dozen ostrich-like lesser rheas that we'd been chasing stop their comical dinosaur gait and look back at us with alarm. The truck's still running. Time to go fishing.

That's how it is here in the dry-grass and red-rock outback of far-southern Argentina—the Wild West lives on in full, wide-open glory. Whoever said, "If you want to see Montana a hundred years ago, go to Patagonia today," nailed it. This is a place where sheep and cattle reign supreme, and gauchos still ride herd on horses instead of four-wheelers. Where the midday supper consists of large chunks of big animals roasted over an open fire. Where you can fish all day without seeing another angler and walk for miles without stepping on pavement. The main difference, of course, is that these cowboys speak Spanish. And the rivers here hold gigantic sea-run browns that could swallow the average Montana trout in a single gulp. Then there's the brand-new, jacked-way-up-off-the-ground Toyota four-by-four we're using to fly across the landscape. So maybe it's not just like the Old West. But it's close.

I left Seattle's freezing February sleet storm, changed planes in a New York blizzard, then flew south through the night, across the Caribbean, over the steamy and vaguely frightening Amazon, and continued down, down, down, to finally land in summer—in Buenos Aires. Across from the airport, a warm, humid breeze blows whitecaps on the Río de la Plata's chocolate waters. Old men line the railing, casting heavy gear out into the murky waves and whispering among themselves about what I can only guess are the conditions and chances for success. With a couple of hours to kill before my next flight, I cross the boulevard to join them.

As I loiter and watch, it becomes clear these are serious anglers. What they lack in modern graphite and Gore-Tex, they make up for in stern concentration and determination. Through pantomime and bits of shared Spanish and English, I learn that these guys know what they're doing, too. Which is fishing, after all. Standing there in the dense, subtropical heat, I'm struck by the idea that these anglers, cultural differences aside, are not so different from the guy flinging #18s on the Henry's Fork. When a battered yellow rod with rusty guides jerks and bends over the railing, I have to suppress an urge to pick it up and set the hook. The rod's owner comes running and does exactly that, yelling in rapid-fire Spanish. The battle rages for tense minutes until finally, a bright-silver—dare I say beautiful—carp of some kind comes over the rail. Backslaps, high fives, and congratulatory shouts ensue. The man proudly holds his fish for me to inspect, and I feel we're sharing what Tom McGuane calls "the universal language of fishing."

A kid on an ancient Schwinn pedals up to sell sausages. I know this because of the intricate rack attached to the handlebars from which dangle a wide variety of, well, sausages, and a sign listing various prices. Somehow, through idiot-Spanish and wild gesticulation, I negotiate a purchase for lunch. I'm disappointed by the lack of condiments and a bun, but quite self-satisfied with my interaction. I take a bite and am greeted with a tangy, not altogether pleasant flavor, which I chalk up to local taste. Until I notice that the kid's next customer is not eating his sausages, but is cutting them up and using them to bait his hook. Turns out, the kid's business is the purchase and resale of spoiled meats, which are eagerly consumed by the local carp, catfish, and other bottom feeders. Not to mention a certain bewildered tourist.

I haul my heavy parka and gurgling stomach back to the airport in shame. The fearless global adventurer façade crumbles, leaving just another sweating, overdressed *turista* lost in a foreign airport. I bumble through the terminal, miraculously find my gate, and board a small jet for the short flight south.

Río Gallegos, Argentina—best known, if it's known at all outside of angling circles, as the site of Butch Cassidy and the Sundance Kid's final bank robbery. As legend has it, in

February 1905, desperate and on the run from Pinkerton detectives, Butch and Sundance, accompanied by the beautiful Etta Place, held up and successfully relieved the Río Gallegos bank of nearly $100,000. While their final resting place remains a mystery, some say the ghosts of Butch, Sundance, and Etta still roam the Río Gallegos countryside looking for one last score. And when you stand on the edge of town looking out into desolate dry plains and hear the wind whistling through telephone wires, it's pretty easy to believe the rumors.

But I'm not here for ghosts. I'm here on the very tip of South America, at the Estancia Las Buitreras (which I believe translates roughly, and somewhat unpromisingly, as "Ranch of the Vultures") Lodge, to fish for massive, tuna-shaped sea-run brown trout that return to the Río Gallegos after months of ocean gluttony. Perhaps because browns are an invasive species with little competition here, while most of the world's fisheries are in decline, this one is actually improving. Each season since the trout were first introduced here—back around the time Butch and Sundance were pulling off their heist—the fish come back bigger and more numerous than the year before. Twenty years ago, a fifteen-pound sea trout was an impressive catch in Patagonia. Today, nobody even blinks unless a fish is pushing twenty pounds, and trout in the thirty-pound range have been well documented over the last several years. This is perhaps the only place in the world where a statement like, "You shoulda been here ten years ago," can be followed up with a surprising and refreshing, "Yeah, there weren't as many fish and they were smaller then." Although sea-run browns have been here for nearly a century, the Río Gallegos has only recently achieved a level of renown approaching that of its more famous sister to the south, the Río Grande.

Having survived the flying-truck incident on the first morning of our stay, I feel happy to be alive, let alone fishing a gorgeous pool running against a steep gravel cut-bluff. Klaus, a kinetic expat Dane and fine fishing guide (driving skills aside), stands at my side and explains the fast, cross-current presentation these aggressive fish prefer. As it has in other places, my steelheader's impulse to slow the fly down proves counterproductive, and I struggle to fish effectively. Klaus grinds his teeth and heads upstream to hang out with Tim and Sonya. By noon, I still haven't touched a fish. The wind, though, is picking up. Now I can't cast and I can't fish. My happy-to-be-alive optimism rapidly devolves into pure, unmitigated aggravation.

As we get ready to head back to the estancia for lunch, Tim hooks a brilliant, silver-sided trout that leaps higher than our heads and surges downstream with its back half out of the water. I grimly pretend to be happy for him. When he lands it, we gather around the fish to admire its broad flanks and black, X-shaped spots. It's his fourth fish of the morning. Sonya has several as well. And me? Nada. Tonight will be my time, I try to convince myself, as a blast of wind pushing thirty knots snatches my "lucky" hat and sends it flying across the prairie.

After a midday *asado* of gargantuan proportions and several bottles of velvety Malbec, everyone retires to their rooms for a little siesta. I, however, am not sleepy. Jet lag, exhaustion, a full belly, and wine cannot stand up to the craving I have for my first sea-run brown. I lie on my bed plotting strategy, sticking barbed hooks into an effigy of Tim, and listening to sheep bleating in the corrals outside my window. Gusts of wind shake the house. When I finally drift off, I have a startlingly vivid dream in which Tim is riding a sheep and yelling, "It's OK, I'm fine … really, it's OK." Freud would have a field day. I give up on sleep and go downstairs for a casting lesson with Mattias, the lodge manager who, in his "real" life back in Sweden, works as an underhanded casting instructor. By that I mean he teaches the Scandinavian underhand technique for casting two-handed fly rods, not that he's sneaky or subversive. That he happens to be both is irrelevant.

The evening fishing session arrives, and it is *not* my time. Having learned just enough of Mattias's casting technique to ruin my old Spey stroke—yet not nearly enough to achieve anything even close to competency with the new method—I am utterly helpless. And now the wind is really starting to rip. Of course, I had heard all about the wind. Even thought I was ready for it. But nothing can prepare you for the eyeball-peeling, breath-stealing Patagonian wind. The kind of wind where you need to remember to park the truck facing into it, or it will tear the doors off when you open them. We take turns leaning into the gale at forty-five-degree angles and laughing insanely. "Don't worry," they told me when I was considering the trip, "the wind always blows downstream, and anyway, it's not as bad as you think." They were right. Tonight it's not as bad as I thought—it's a thousand times worse. And it's blowing upstream powerfully enough that the river is backing up and the spray blowing off three-foot whitecaps hits me squarely in the face. On the upside, the Río Gallegos hose-down washes away the sand lodged in my teeth and eyes. Welcome to Patagonia, have a nice day.

In the morning, with curling tentacles of mist floating off the water's surface, ten casts into the top of a swift, cobbled riffle called Wagon Wheel, I am redeemed. The wind has stopped, the air is crisp and clear, the sky is blue, and ... I have a fish on. Having resigned myself, in my wind-battered, fishless state last night, to the idea that I would not catch a single fish this trip—or for that matter, ever—the grab comes as a shock. I pull back and the fish detonates in a double cartwheel, sides flashing in the early morning sunlight. At that moment I leave my body just in time to see myself standing slack-jawed with an unimaginably stupid look on my face as line peels off the reel. When I return, the fish is in shallow water and as I twist the hook free, it shoots away, showering me with water.

I am now in The Zone. The wind stays calm. My casting improves. And even in the unseasonably low water, I am catching fish. In a deep, slow pool called El Puesto, I am fishing with an enthusiastic young Argentine guide named Diego, or "Pollo," as everyone here calls him. (In the local pronunciation, that's Po*sho*, just as the river's name sounds like Río Ga*she*gos. But fear not, fellow eighth-grade Spanish graduates, no matter how you pronounce it, *pollo* still means "chicken.") He points to the top of the run and after a few tips on the finer points of the sea-trout retrieve, he takes off in the truck to check on Sonya and Tim. In quick succession I hook and land an eight-pound fish, one around twelve, and then an enormous female that tapes out at thirty-eight inches. This fish is absolutely huge, so thick in the midsection that I can barely lift her back into deeper water, and as she swims into the current, I notice my hands are shaking.

A thoughtful man would sit down on the bank, calm down, dry off, and savor the moment. I, however, charge back into the water, stripping line off my reel, and begin casting before I'm even in position. A fish surfaces along the far bank and before I know it, I'm up to my armpits frantically trying to cast with both hands above my head. As I begin to lose the battle with buoyancy and start bouncing downstream, my flailing cast somehow manages to get the fly to the other side. The fish takes and I immediately begin a frenzied, one-handed backstroke to regain my footing.

The fish veers downstream, then leaves the water in a series of spiraling leaps. I'm so engrossed in the fight that I don't notice the truck pulling up on the gravel bar behind me, and am startled to see Pollo splashing toward me with the net, screaming happy Spanish. We land the fish, a big male with massive shoulders and a snook-like profile, then dance around celebrating like neither of us have ever caught a fish before. We can barely understand each other, but we're both having a whale of a time. So maybe there is something to the "universal language of fishing" thing ... well, let's not get carried away. Besides, I've just proved another favorite theory—it truly is better to be lucky than good.

On the way back to the lodge, we spot a group of caracaras— long-legged, eagle-like raptors—feeding on something atop a low hill. I will be the first to admit that I am not a "birder" or even much of a bird appreciator, but the avian life here is spectacular. You simply cannot watch a rhea jogging down the road, its back-end swinging wildly to and fro and its head swiveling on that long neck, without laughing. And to see strings of hot-orange flamingos winging overhead, or a pair of striking, long-tailed meadowlarks perched on a wire fence, is to somehow understand the power of this vast landscape. At this moment, Tim, a photographer, is intent on capturing close-up images of the caracaras. We pull to a stop and he slowly assembles his camera gear with exaggerated quiet, then shuffles across the road in a crouching run. The comedy that ensues is impossible to fully describe, other than to say that as he approaches from the back of the hill, the birds shuffle to the other side, just out of his vision. As he circles, they move just enough to stay out of sight. This continues for nearly half an hour, while those of us in the truck enjoy Tim's confusion and helpfully point to the other side of the hill whenever he peeks back at us for direction.

Back at Las Buitreras, the biggest piece of roast meat I have ever seen is now sitting on my plate. I can't determine exactly what cut it is, either, other than it's a significant fraction—like one-fourth to one-half—of an entire animal. Kansas City, Memphis, the Carolinas … they all claim bragging rights when it comes to barbecue, but you really ain't seen nothin' until you've eaten lunch in Argentina.

After the lamb and the whole chickens and the sausages (freshly made, thankfully) and the potatoes, and the homemade ice cream, we decide to bypass the usual post-meal food coma. Perhaps a little walk is in order. We ask the guides what's in the woods back behind the main house, but they all shrug nervously and appear to say they don't know. Tim and Sonya head up the narrow, overgrown trail into a small, dense stand of trees while Mattias masochistically attempts yet again to improve my casting. "Like this," he says. "See, it's simple." His body barely moves and a hundred feet of line rockets across the lawn. Yeah, it's simple. Like quantum physics.

Tim and Sonya are coming back down the trail now, walking briskly, and as they approach I see that Tim is looking back over his shoulder as he walks. "You gotta see this, man," he says, "back there in the woods." I'm not falling for it. "No, really, you gotta check this out, I'm serious." He appears to be serious. We head back up the trail until we can see a miniature stucco building, about four feet high, way back in the underbrush. As we approach, Tim urges me forward, but I notice he seems to be hanging back. And then I see it. On the tiny porch, next to jars filled with mildewed paper bills and coins, lies a human skull, and centered in the side of the skull is a tiny round hole. That's all I need to see, and with goose bumps rising on my arms, I sprint past Tim and Sonya for the house. Inquiries of the staff—What is it? Who is it? Etc.—yield no satisfactory answers, and we are left with a serious case of the creeps. Could this be where Butch Cassidy met his maker? The site of some forgotten revolutionary's untimely demise? On the other hand, I have to consider the possibility that this is some kind of elaborate practical joke Tim set up, but then I remember that he passed me going full tilt on the way out of the woods.

As the week proceeds, the weather cools and fresh fish continue entering the river. By Río Gallegos standards, though, fishing is on the slow side. Anglers who have fished here before are complaining about the number of fish, but I'm in hog heaven. These are simply magnificent fish, with speed, strength, and leaping ability to rival any game fish in the world, and we're hooking enough that it feels like plenty to me. The scenery is remarkable, the people warm and friendly, and with hundreds of sheep on this working ranch, the jokes plentiful. Note: Argentine sheep jokes bear a striking resemblance to those of Montana. Evidence, perhaps, of the existence of a universal language of sheep jokes.

On our last night here, I am fishing with Claudio, who, like Pollo, is another young, enthusiastic, and very good Argentine guide. Claudio drops me off at a broad, swift run, saying, "Just keep fishing down. I will pick you up before dark." I jump in and start fishing down, picking my way among the big rocks and steep bank. Standing belly-deep in the dark waters, I hook and land a nice fish as the sky fades to cobalt. Fish are rolling below me, so I continue downstream, fishing hard.

Suddenly, a horrifying, croaking roar echoes across the water. Hair on the back of my neck stands on end and a shiver courses up my spine. I look around frantically, but can't find the enormous predator that's obviously about to attack. I do, however, notice that it is now very dark. The chilling, prehistoric sound reverberates across the river again and I hear wingbeats overhead. I look up and see a pair of ibises, outlined against the starry sky, circling and croaking at each other. A sheepish (sorry, I couldn't resist) sense of relief washes over me. But even with the sound's source identified and clearly harmless, I feel an unexplainable urge to get out of the black, swirling water. I wade by feel, probing for rocks and sticks with my feet, and climb up onto the bank, relieved to be on dry land. Another fish jumps out in the run, but I'm done fishing now, and for the first time all week, I sit calmly and watch the river run by. I feel amazingly relaxed. At least for a little while.

Apparently, in Argentina, when someone says they're going to pick you up "before" dark, it actually means "long after"—like more than an hour. In fact, I sit in the pitch-black night going through the usual logical questions of someone teetering on the verge of freaking out. What if Claudio ran into the Danish Mario Andretti coming the other way on the road? Can I actually walk the fifteen miles back to camp? Do bears live in Argentina? Finally, just as I'm getting ready to start hoofing it, I see headlights arcing across the far canyon wall, and another twenty minutes later the truck itself comes bouncing into view.

The next morning, with all dread and imaginary carnivorous beasts having evaporated in daylight, we get the unexpected good news of a delayed flight, allowing us an extra fishing session. I hook and land another fat sea-run brown on a steelhead pattern swung slowly through a deep run. We devour another amazing meal, this time a surprising treat of fat-laden sea-trout sushi and miso soup, right here in the Patagonian boondocks. We politely refuse Klaus's offer to drive us into town. And we all glance more than once at the little stand of trees behind the lodge. Even with time to kill, nobody wanders up the path. Not even a little way.

LUCK

The old Subaru's water pump blows up just outside The Dalles. Our already failing plan to make Macks Canyon before dark is now officially shot, and the whole trip appears to be in jeopardy. Visions of a week spent camping on hot asphalt behind the gas station while waiting for parts swim through my heat-addled brain. At seven o'clock on an unseasonably sweltering September evening in the central Oregon desert, I feel as far from catching a steelhead on a fly as you would in Phoenix, Arizona. Heat shimmers off the asphalt as I step onto the road and stick out my thumb.

By ten o'clock, I have somehow located a slightly—OK, highly—sketchy, tweaked-out, late-night mechanic who's willing to work immediately. He tows the old Sube behind his dilapidated pickup truck, unlocks the garage at a local gas station, and tears into her. A few calls and he miraculously comes up with the exact water pump, although we consciously avoid inquiring about how he got it at this time of night. Why, we ask, would he go to such lengths for complete strangers? "Boys," he says, veins bulging on his sweat- and grease-streaked forehead, "my car broke down in this place ten years ago, and I'm still here. I'd hate to see it happen to you. Now get outta here and let me work."

Next door is a café billing itself as Home of the World's Biggest Burger. Not the best, nor the tastiest, but the biggest. We order three. The waitress smirks. Each contains: one beef patty the size of a Frisbee, half a dozen fried eggs, a ham steak, ten slices of bacon, three tomatoes, a head of lettuce, a half-pound each of cheddar, Swiss, and blue cheese, and about a quart of mayonnaise. Delicious. Between the three of us we max out having consumed exactly half of one. The waitress wraps the remaining two-and-a-half burgers in foil and stuffs them into three grocery bags. "Sweet," Carson says, "now we don't have to stop for supplies."

Which works out perfectly since by the time we hit the road again and roll through Maupin, the town is silent, shuttered, and deeply asleep. No groceries. No ice. No water. But what do we care? We are, once again, going steelhead fishing. Cool desert air, heavy with sage, flows through the open car windows.

Strangely, the campground is deserted. One of us says, "Sleep when you're dead," and we wader up under a pre-dawn sky that stretches from pale orange in the east, through various shades of blue overhead, to pure-black night in the west. The exhaustion and hassles of the previous twenty-four hours vanish as I tie on a Purple Peril in the faint beam of my headlamp, hands shaking in anticipation. Just before the sun breaks the horizon, I make my first mend and feel the fly start to swing.

By noon, we haven't touched a fish and our excitement collapses suddenly into fatigue. We drag ourselves back to the car, set up camp, and keel over to nap away the midday heat. When we get up, Carson discovers the red shoelaces from his wading boots are gone. Dave mentions that he probably just forgot to put them on in the first place. Carson says, "You don't wade the Deschutes for six hours without shoelaces and not miss them." The heat has us all on edge.

A fishless evening. Followed by another fishless morning. Followed by another fishless evening. And on and on for two more broiling, cloudless days. In the afternoons I tie flies until my bobbin and a spool of tinsel mysteriously disappear. Carson hobbles around in his laceless boots. Dave fishes demonically, as if he might conjure up a fish through sheer persistence. And through it all, we gnaw away at those two-and-a-half burgers.

On the third hot and extremely fishless day, an old-timer comes floating down in a battered wooden drift boat and rows over to talk. He tells us we're insane to be fishing and camping in this heat. Says he hasn't touched a fish in weeks and until the weather turns, it's hopeless. "No rain in the forecast," he says, "but when it comes, the fishing will be unbelievable."

We stagger back to camp. Our mood is compounded when I realize I can't find the car key I'd left on the driver's-side seat. After a thorough and fruitless search of the car, the tent, and all our gear, I tear a chunk off The World's Oldest Burger and try to ignore the now-translucent mayonnaise and crumbling bun.

"I think we should bail as soon as we figure out how to hot-wire the car," I say.

"Anyone seen my pack of gum?" Dave asks.

For lack of anything better to do and trying to fight back the rising panic of being stranded, I pop the hood. And there, sitting in the middle of a huge wreath of twigs, feathers, and gum wrappers woven together with red shoelaces and silver tinsel, sits my car key. Behind the key sits a fat, beady-eyed pack rat staring at me with obvious disdain.

We burst into laughter and don't stop until tears run down our faces. When we recover, I start loading gear, relieved and happy to be heading home.

"What are you doing?" Carson asks.

"Getting out of Dodge."

"Are you crazy?" he says, "I just got my lucky shoelaces back and we have all the good water to ourselves. Let's fish."

Logic wins out. I unpack the car, crawl into the tent, and fall into a dreamless sleep. Sometime during the night, a thick layer of clouds rolls in from the coast and by morning, heavy raindrops are pouring out of the sky through cool, sweet air. There's still half a burger left.

OCTOBER 1976

I have not thought about my parents' divorce or fitting in at my new school or missing my dad in more than an hour. I am standing knee-deep in moving water, impossibly skinny arms and legs shaking from the chill. My heart pounds as ocean-bright coho salmon shoot over the shallow riffle, glide into the pool, and disappear. I strip line from the battered Pflueger and cast with an anxious mixture of hope and doubt. The crude, orange hackle-tip streamer I tied without knowing the right way to do anything sails into the shadows and settles on the water. I wait, letting it sink, then begin my retrieve. A wake forms on the surface, following, and I hold my breath, nearly bursting with expectation. My fly stops and suddenly there is miraculous, moving, head-shaking resistance. The fish shatters the glassy surface and bolts downstream. When I finally land the hook-nosed buck coho, I tuck it under my arm and run all the way back to the car, where my mother and baby brother have been waiting for the better part of the day. "Mom!" I yell. "I finally got one!"

HUNTING GIANTS

There's really nothing you can do to prepare yourself.

Sure, you can sharpen hooks, double- and triple-check your knots, buy the biggest rod you can cast, practice throwing flies the size of a chicken into the wind until you think you're ready. But you aren't. Not by a long shot.

The first time you actually encounter a giant trevally on the flats, the experience will be so startling, so mind-blowing, you will inevitably grasp for absurd comparisons: Godzilla in downtown Tokyo; the young, devastatingly efficient Mike Tyson in the ring, or for that matter, the later, wild-eyed, ear-chewing version as well; a carnivorous fifty-five-gallon drum flying open-end forward onto the flats. ...

Shortly thereafter, as you watch a seventy-pound GT power up into knee-deep water and pulverize the fleeing reef fish in churning, vicious subsurface explosions, you will look down at the puny twelve-weight rod in your hand with sudden doubt. You are hunting grizzly bears with a slingshot. And it will occur to you just how far from Sir Izaak's English chalk streams fly fishing has come. You may also feel something else: fear.

You won't be the first angler to suddenly backpedal for the boat when confronted by a frenzied GT in full search-and-destroy mode. As the enormous slab makes a sudden half-turn and heads directly for the bonefish cowering behind your legs, you may wonder who's hunting whom.

And you haven't even made a cast yet. Or should I say *tried* to make a cast yet. Did I mention the first rule of hunting giants? Things go wrong. Let me repeat: Things. Go. Wrong.

On a full-moon flood tide, the great Christmas Island guide Timon Corrie stands next to you in the broiling sun, slapping the surface of the water with his hand. Unsatisfied, he grabs your eight-weight and starts churning the surface wildly. "Won't that scare the fish away?" you ask. He laughs.

Your brain cooks in the heat. Sweat drips down your casting arm. Your eyes burn from squinting into the glare. And then, suddenly, it's happening. An immense shadow charges up onto the flat, throwing a wake like a jet ski. Big fish. Enormous. *Giant.* It's the moment you've been waiting for all day, all week. Maybe all your life.

You let go of the fly and begin to work out the line you've so carefully coiled around the fingers of your left hand. Two false casts, and Timon shouts, "Now!" You reach back, stop the rod hard into the wind, feel the line straighten behind you, and as you make your haul, the fly bounces off the back of your head, hooks the line, and collapses in a heap at your feet. The giant, now full of two-pound bonefish, drifts over the edge of the reef and disappears. Things go wrong.

Knots you checked seven times unravel under pressure. Four-piece rods magically transform into six-piece rods. Fly lines get woven through coral heads and snap. Two hundred yards of gel-spun backing blows up into a knot the size of your head. Reels overheat, seize up, and explode. The mayo on that sandwich you left in the sun seemed OK when you ate it.

Or let's say you're actually landing a giant. Your first one ever. Amazingly, miraculously, nothing has gone wrong. (Of course, later you will understand to even think this thought is an open invitation to disaster.) As its enormous bulk tires in the shallows, you reach out to grab your prize and suddenly jerk your hand back. "Tim," you say to the photographer, a guy

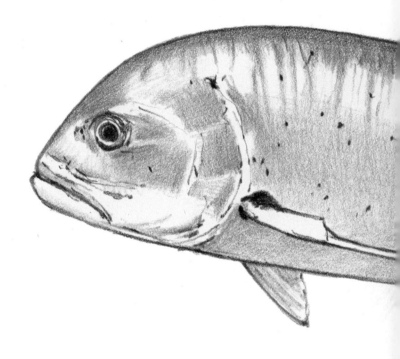

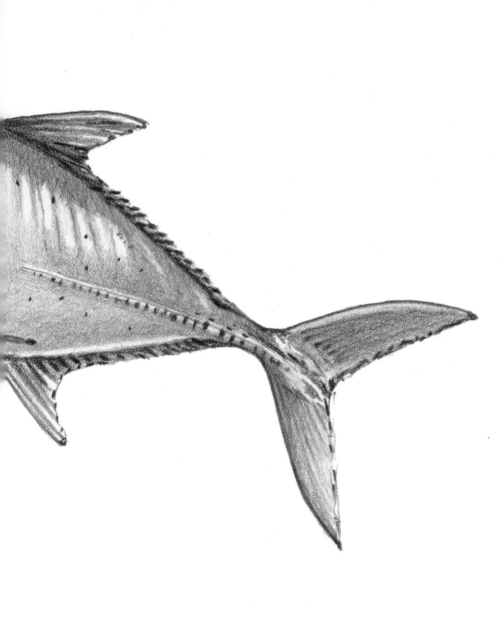

who's probably landed more giant trevally than nearly any other fly angler, "do these things bite?" He laughs, and demonstrates how to grab them ahead of the tail. "You just have to be careful because they have spines back there, but nothing to worry if you do it like ... AAAAAAAAAHHHHHHHHH!" Blood spurts from his fingers. Things go wrong.

Or maybe you're standing on a soft sand flat and Timon is explaining that the bonefish come to eat the two-foot-long silver sand worms that live here. The giants come to eat the bonefish. Then he says, "We eat the worms, too." You gulp. But wanting to be an enlightened traveler and part of the island food chain, not to mention one with your prey, you inquire further. "Sometimes raw," he continues, "but we also dry them like jerky. You can try the dried one."

The next morning, a small crowd of locals has gathered to watch you eat the worm. Something deep in your brain flashes back to a long-forgotten mezcal debacle, but you proceed anyway. This particular worm, in its salted, smoked state, appears to be relatively harmless. You close your eyes and gnaw off a small bit. "Oh," Timon says quietly, "I forgot, the first time you eat the worm, you will get red bumps on your. ..." Immediately, the small bite of leathery, dried worm flies out of your mouth like a missile. Much laughter (not yours) ensues. Things go wrong.

At some point in your quest for giants, you will have a good day. A great day even. This particular day has been epic. You have made decent casts. Your equipment has not undergone what corporate disclaimer lawyers refer to as "rapid unscheduled disassembly." You have swum across channels with your rod in your teeth to avoid being spooled. You have watched Timon dive into the coral heads to unhook your line and, miracle of miracles, found the fish still connected. You have gone two

for five and landed one pushing ninety pounds. *Ninety freakin'*
pounds! And you have photos to show your 7X-tippet-casting,
micro-midge-floating, ten-inch-trout-catching buddies back
home. You are on top of the world.

But all this has taken time. Lots of time. And now you are
racing the falling tide to get back across Nine Mile Flat before
all the water is gone. That, and it's getting dark. And there's
a complex maze of boat-eating coral heads and shallow channels between you and the comfort, safety, and drinking water of
camp. You suddenly regret even thinking that "top of the world"
bullshit. And then, when completely out of the blue, the outboard sputters, hacks, and comes to an abrupt stop, when the
silence is louder than anything you ever imagined, you understand: Things go wrong.

Of course, it's entirely possible that things could go right. You
may stalk, hook, and fight the biggest, most incredible fish any
wading angler has ever landed. Your tackle may hold up to the
strain. Your body might survive unscathed. Hell, you may even
find yourself smiling out into the sunshine and clear, blue South
Pacific distance, satisfied beyond belief. But don't count on it.

THE WORST GUIDE
IN THE WORLD

OK, I'm just going to come right out and say it: I sucked at guiding. Oh, my clients caught plenty of fish. But if I were a doctor, you might say I had a lousy bedside manner. Or what an old coach of mine often referred to as a "piss-poor attitude." The fact is, I could never stop thinking about whether or not various clients deserved to catch fish just because they could afford to travel and stay at an expensive lodge. That, and I was frequently impatient. And sarcastic. And irritable. But enough about my good days. I guess I thought guiding was about fish, and it turns out it's about people. No matter how dumb they might be.

I tried to be a nice guy. I would tell myself these people are on the trip of a lifetime, that they were too busy to learn how to actually fish, that blah, blah, blah. It's not like I'm a completely unsympathetic person. For example, when a client described his long-anticipated fishing trip with a famous Florida tarpon guide and how he found himself unceremoniously deposited back at the dock at ten o'clock in the morning for blowing two shots at big fish, I was filled with sympathy. For the guide.

What does it mean to be a fishing guide? I can't answer for anyone else, but this is what occurred to me about three weeks into my first season: If you take something that's inherently fun to do with people you like, and do it with people you don't like for money … well, you see where I'm going with this. Needless to say, I would have made an even lousier prostitute.

That thought haunted me through five summers. Especially while peeling the price stickers off thousands of dollars' worth of brand-new, top-of-the-line rods and reels and—after loading backing, connecting lines, and tying leaders—handing it all back to some rich dentist from Akron while he told me all about what a great angler he was. Did he deserve the fish we would catch?

Now, I don't want to make prejudiced statements or generalize ... OK, actually I do. What the hell. Here are a few things I learned: Doctors generally make the worst clients, followed by car dealers, and anyone from Texas. Women are the best clients—they actually listen—and will always outfish their expert husbands. Clients who really want to "whack a trophy" so they can "get it stuffed" always catch the biggest fish, no matter how hard you try to prevent it. Note to doctors, car dealers, Texans, expert husbands, and trophy whackers: I readily admit there are plenty of individual exceptions to the rules above, but if you're seriously offended by this paragraph, you aren't one of them.

Once, I had two doctors from Houston and a car dealer from Dallas and his wife as my foursome. Guess what happened? I spent an entire week staring at the back of the doctors' heads, trying to determine if it was possible, through sheer concentration and mental telepathy, to make a person's head explode. At the time, it seemed like a worthy research project.

The limit then was two king salmon per person for the week. By the end of the first day, they were limited out. This, despite numerous warnings from their guide before killing each client's second fish that should they land a bigger fish at any time for the rest of the week, it would be released. Of course, three days later, one of the docs hooks an immense fish—the biggest I had ever seen from that river. A giant slab of chrome that would have weighed close to sixty pounds. To avoid the inevitable conflict, I spent the entire hour-long fight working to help the fish escape. But no such luck. When the fish finally came to shore, I was asked, cajoled, and pleaded with. I was offered money. I was even threatened with bodily harm. And you know what? I can't even begin to describe the pleasure I felt when I twisted the hook loose and watched that fish swim away. Next day, the wife miraculously hooked one even larger, fought it with great efficiency, and happily released it without complaint.

What's the point of the story? I don't really know, other than it had to be a sign of something. Maybe that if all clients were women, I'd still be guiding? Or more likely that I was simply in the wrong line of work.

More signs: Secretly relishing clients' discomfort from bugs or lack of adequate rain gear. Covertly exacerbating husband-wife conflict when the woman hooks more fish than her spouse. Purposefully seeking out the most exposed, windiest spots for clients having trouble casting. Trying to make people's heads explode with brain waves ... but we already covered that one. Anyway, guilty as charged.

So why did I do it not just once, but for five summers? I mean, other than latent masochistic tendencies? Because, in all honesty, despite my conflicted thoughts about guiding, it was one of the best things I've ever done. It was an opportunity to be on the water every day, to intimately know the changing tides, river flows, and weather patterns. To live, eat, work, and fish with my best friends in the world, and yes, rare as they were, to enjoy some great moments with wonderful clients. Mostly though, it was because the fishing was unbelievably good, and I got to fish it every day of the season. Selfish reasons all, and in retrospect, I probably didn't *deserve* any of it.

What *did* I deserve, besides a swift kick in the ass? Probably the lesson that being a good fisherman qualifies you to guide about as much as an affinity for deep-fried chicken hearts makes you a thoracic surgeon. With this realization, and much to the relief of everyone concerned, I quit the business for good. Now I'm free to concentrate on the inherently fun-to-do-with-people-you-like part and leave the guiding to those who are actually good at it.

But if you're ever on a guided trip, happily flinging your flies from the front of the boat, and you suddenly feel a strange pressure building inside your skull, take a close look at the person on the oars. If he or she appears to be deeply focused on, say, the back of your head, with maybe a poorly hidden, demented grin forming, watch out. It's probably someone a lot like me. Your only hope, then, is to ask yourself this one simple question: Do I deserve this?

DECEMBER 1977

*I have finally settled into my new school, a new town,
this new life. I've made a few friends, caught some trout
and a couple of salmon. But what I want more than
anything, besides my dad, is to catch a steelhead. After a
year of Sundays without a steelhead, my mom called Andy
Landforce, the great Oregon guide, to inquire about a trip
for me. He was booked up, but said he'd call back if anyone
canceled. He called last night, and now, fifteen minutes into
a day I've looked forward to more than any other, my first
steelhead lies in the bottom of the boat. It is so beautiful
my heart feels like it's going to explode. When I reach into
my pocket to fill out my tag, I realize, with excruciating
embarrassment, that I hadn't bought one for this season. "It's
OK," Andy says patiently, "we'll just hike back to the car
and drive to town for a new one." Later, when he drops me
off at home with my two steelhead—a limit!—I try to pay
him with the money I saved from raking leaves and mowing
lawns. "Keep it," he says, "I'll call again. Be ready. And leave
your money at home—we'll just be friends going fishing."*

THE SEARCH FOR
ATLANTIC STEELHEAD

or How I Came to Love the Wind

It's not the wind blowing a hundred kilometers per hour. You can live with the wind. You can even fish in it. It's the rocks blowing a hundred kilometers per hour that gets you. On Argentina's Río Santa Cruz, it goes something like this: The wind starts cranking up, we see a red-brown cloud of haze way out on the horizon, and the next thing we know, our local boatman, Alber, is yelling with some urgency that it's about to get *"muy mal."* We reel up, pile into the boat, and try to make it to some kind of shelter before it hits. As we struggle forward against the gale in our ten-foot Zodiac, fighting three-foot whitecaps and vicious spindrift, we are suddenly engulfed by a stinging assortment of flying debris: BB-sized gravel and sand propelled at speeds high enough to give you a pretty solid idea of what Dick Cheney's hunting partner must have felt like.

We do not make it to shelter before it hits. In fact, we are caught out in the open river, driven by the wind up against a sheer cliff wall and the roiling, churning water at its base. Darkness is falling. Tim points behind me to the chaotic mess of the river ahead, now obscured by a combination of dusk, spray, and the aforementioned airborne rocks and sand.

"OK," he yells, "this is intense." Because we are facing each other, huddled in the bow of the raft, I reply by pointing behind him at the looming cliff wall and the sideways direction of the wind that is slowly pushing us toward it. "Holy shit," he says. Then the motor quits.

There is a fine line that separates exciting adventure from life-threatening calamity. In a surreal moment of detached clarity, I attempt to calculate where exactly we are in relation to this line as I watch Alber scrambling on hands and knees in the heaving boat, frantically trying to change out the clogged fuel line. I'm also trying to decide whether it would improve my chances of survival to abandon ship now and brave the thrashing water on my own—or wait and hope that Alber can get the motor going before we're smashed against the cliff.

The motor coughs, chugs, and miraculously springs back to life. Alber spits a mouthful of gasoline and two-cycle oil into the wind, raises his hand for a quick high five, and guns the throttle. The fine line is left in our wake, and we are now—at least for the time being—moving in the opposite direction of life-threatening calamity.

• • •

For a number of years, I'd been hearing about steelhead in Argentine Patagonia, but it seemed more like a novelty than an actual fishing trip. Atlantic steelhead? It hadn't ever occurred to me to actually go there. When photographer Tim Pask called to see if I was interested, I was pretty sure I had better things to do. But he, or, I should say, the pictures he sent, talked me into it. The photos, taken on a brief side trip to the Río Santa Cruz the previous year, showed steelhead that looked a lot more like huge Kamloops rainbows, with small heads, silvery sides, and amazing girth.

It seemed that Loop Adventures, which runs the sea-run brown-trout operation on Río Gallegos, was thinking about putting a program in place on the as-yet-unfished upper stretches of Río Santa Cruz. Our mission was to stay and fish from the proposed lodge site and find out if it was worth the investment. In other words, no guarantees—this would be a completely exploratory trip, fishing virtually unknown waters. To any self-respecting steelhead bum, this was the proverbial offer you can't refuse. Mission accepted.

The fact that sea-run rainbows exist in Río Santa Cruz is well documented. In fact, according to Dr. Thomas Quinn of the University of Washington and Dr. Miguel Pascual, his Argentine counterpart, the run appears to be large, healthy, and may even be increasing. So, the big question, of course, is how did they get there?

Based on genetic testing conducted by Dr. Pascual and others, Río Santa Cruz steelhead are the anadromous descendants of McCloud-strain rainbows imported to Argentina for aquaculture in the early 1900s. Over time, some of these rainbows escaped or were released into the river and found the Río Santa Cruz hospitable enough to live and reproduce in. Gradually, at some point, a majority of this "wild" population began migrating to salt water— in this case, the Atlantic Ocean—where they found incredibly rich nearshore waters teeming with baitfish and crustaceans. Today, the offspring of these original McCloud rainbows are evolving into a completely unique strain of steelhead.

Unlike most of our native West Coast steelhead, these fish don't have the need or impulse to travel far at sea, and most spend only four to five months a year in salt water before returning to the river to spawn and live for extended periods of time. The peak of the run occurs in March and April, the southern autumn, with large numbers of ocean-bright fish pouring into the river and traveling upstream.

Several tour companies already have sportfishing operations in and around the town of Piedra Buena, in the lower, more populated stretches of the river. But Loop wanted to find a better angling experience for their clients and was determined to search it out. Based on some brief float trips, local stories, and word that there was more interesting water (and no other anglers) a hundred miles above the river mouth, Loop's area of focus was centered around the enormous Estancia San Ramón. They just needed a few unsuspecting lab rats to venture into the unknown and report back.

. . .

Rising at the outlet of Lago Argentino, the country's largest lake, and fed by the Perito Moreno Glacier, Río Santa Cruz is, simply put, a monster. Maybe not Mississippi size, but close. Picture the Fraser, Skeena, or Sacramento, and you begin to understand what we're dealing with here. And, owing to its glacial origins, the Santa Cruz in ideal conditions runs a beautiful, milky, robin's-egg blue. Which is to say that if you think locating a steelhead in a river this big would be like finding the proverbial needle in a haystack, consider the limited visibility.

On our first day, as we gaze across an immense, featureless expanse of Río Santa Cruz, our twelve- and fourteen-foot Spey rods suddenly seem puny and inadequate. What we'd later come to think of as a mild thirty-knot wind whistles through the corrugated-tin pump shack where we would eat, sleep, and dock our boats. The North Americans—Tim, Kim Nakamura, Andy Turner, and me—stand in silence, daunted by the enormity of the task at hand. Claudio, the talented (and bilingual) Río Gallegos guide on loan to us as a translator, has nothing to translate; nobody is saying anything. We are a long, long way from the Stilly or the Dean. Río Santa Cruz makes even the mighty Skagit look like a ditch. Where do we start? What are we looking for? Are there even any fish here?

One other thing I forgot to mention: Remember how the Perito Moreno Glacier is the source of the Río Santa Cruz? Apparently, the slowly advancing glacier forms a giant ice dam way up in the Andes, and occasionally—say, two or three times a decade—the dam breaks, sending an enormous wall of water down the riverbed. It's a big deal when this happens, on par with volcanic eruptions and other large-scale natural disasters. Maybe you recall seeing this event on the nightly news. Want to guess when it last happened? Yep, that's right. So, as we prepare to fish it for the first time, the Río Santa Cruz is running, shall we say, a bit on the high side.

Fortunately, the water has dropped and cleared enough to make it fishable. Of course, fishable and catching fish are two separate concepts altogether, and our fears about the size of the river are confirmed as the gang goes empty-handed the first day. Aside from a six-inch rainbow (smolt?) I land on a five-inch string leech, we never have a grab. As my friend Steve Perih, the Canadian steelhead guide, might say, we got bagelled.

There's a saying in steelheading that the difference between zero and one is greater than the difference between one and any other number. With that in mind, we forge ahead, hoping for that one fish that might signal success. However, on the second day of fishing, with Tim and I in a boat driven by Santa Cruz legend Mario Zwetzig, and Andy and Kim with Mario's nephew Alber, an accomplished riverman in his own right, we are unable to determine the difference between zero and any other number. The wind is killing me. I struggle to cast the gigantic flies, mend my line, or even hold onto my Spey rod. The level of thrashing I achieve is unseemly at best.

At a sharp bend in the river, with the wind at our backs and likely looking water in front of us, Tim suddenly shouts,

"Fish on!" and starts backpedaling out of the water. His Spey rod doubles over, and I excitedly run up the bank to witness the miracle. After the better part of two fishless days, a sudden feeling of hope surges through my body. Tim leans back and braces for the run, but nothing happens. Out in the current, the fish boils and I see a quick flash of ... olive brown? I bite my lip, not ready to let the good feelings slip away so quickly. The fish rapidly tires and as it's pulled into the shallows, Mario says, *"Percha!"* Which I translate from Argentine Spanish to mean "wallarp." It looks exactly like a cross between a walleye and a carp, with spiny fins, brown scales, and bulging eyes—about as far from the sleek, silver-plated steelhead we're searching for as anything could be and still qualify as a fish. It occurs to me that *percha* could very well be Spanish for "shit." Or "deflator of all good feelings."

• • •

On the morning of our third day, we are surprised to find an utter and absolute lack of wind. After what we've been through the first few days, it's creepy calm out. Also, with cooler temperatures, the water has dropped and cleared to a level far superior to anything we've seen yet. Our spirits, though, are low. We've been beating the water to a froth from dawn to dark for two days with only a six-inch smolt and four-pound wallarp to show for it. I have fallen into that dark hole where nothing in my fly box looks good anymore, I've lost faith in my sink tips, and the spots that seemed so fishy before now appear hopeless. Did somebody say exploring was supposed to be fun? Doubt has raised its ugly, *percha*-shaped head and swallowed us whole.

Just below camp, we stop to fish a run that we've been fruitlessly pounding each day. Mario has assured us that they caught

fish here previously when setting up the boats. It's a long, beautiful run with a steep, gravelly bank and what passes for big rocks
in this country (about fist sized) scattered beneath the current.
With the weight of fishless days on our shoulders and a level
of enthusiasm usually reserved for washing dishes, we divide
the run in two and I step into the lower half. Without wind,
I'm surprised to find that I'm enjoying casting, and I concentrate on the easy double-Spey rhythm: cast, mend, step. For the
first time here, I feel like I'm actually fishing instead of fighting
the elements.

As I work my way closer to a partially submerged wire fence
(remember the glacier event?), the water slows to absolute perfect speed, and I can feel the fly swimming through bigger rocks.
I make another cast, mend, and when it starts to swing, I make
slow, steady strips to speed it up. On the third strip, the line is
suddenly ripped from my fingers, comes tight to the reel, and the
drag starts to shriek. Way out in the river a hole blows up in the
surface and sunlight flashes off the mirrored sides of a steelhead.
The reel is making a funny *bap-bap-bap* noise over the normal
drag sound, and I look down to see the blurred handle bouncing
off the first knuckle of my thumb.

Behind me, Tim is running down the bank with camera cases
in both hands, sliding to my side in an avalanche of loose rock.
"Big D! Alright! Don't lose him, man, we need pictures!" he
shouts. This brings me back to reality, and as I regain my senses,
I begin to stumble backward toward shore. The fish runs again
and leaps wildly, then screams downstream shaking its head.

When the fish tires, I work it slowly into the quiet water along
the bank, and finally reach out to cradle a luminous, immaculate
steelhead. She's nearly half-again thicker through the shoulders and flanks than any steelhead I've ever seen, with a small,

bullet-shaped head and exceptionally large eyes and fins—all traits we would later find to be shared by nearly all Santa Cruz fish. Her silver ocean coloring extends across her back and onto her tail, with a very light sprinkling of delicate black spots marking her back and head. An absolutely perfect fish. Tim takes some photos and I slip her back into the current, where she showers us with a rooster tail of glacial water and disappears. Amazing. I shake my head in disbelief and sit down on a rock to let the jitters fade away. This is what we came here for.

All I want is to wade right back in and start casting, but remembering my manners, I tell Tim to quit screwing around with his cameras and fish through. He's still checking exposures. I offer to fish it again myself and suddenly he's knee-deep in the pool working out line like a madman. And yes, three casts into the sweet spot another ocean-bright beauty takes his fly and shatters the surface of the river. When he lands it, we are nearly delirious with joy, dancing around like meth-addled circus monkeys.

Later in the day, we would each hook and land another spectacular fish in a run ten miles downstream. I would also, unfortunately, demonstrate the amazing acceleration of Patagonian wind when I single-handedly ruin the calm conditions by saying out loud: "I can't believe there's no wind." From the time I pronounce the *w* in wind to the end of the word, the real, physical wind itself has gone from zero to sixty knots. I mean, dead calm to hold-onto-your-hat, is-that-a-sheep-flying-by kind of wind in the split second it takes to speak a single syllable. Tim casts an accusing frown my way and shakes his head. Lesson learned, if a bit late.

But who cares? Now the fish are here and biting. Or we figured it out. Or the river has dropped to a fishable level. Or the

planets have aligned. The main thing is we are hooking fish, and not coincidentally, we struggle less in the wind, our food tastes better, life is good. Wind or no wind, I can hardly wait for tomorrow.

. . .

I'm not sure what makes some Argentines think it's a good idea to drink their morning yerba maté out of dried goat scrotums, but they do. And they don't just think it's a good idea, they think it's hilarious. Having been informed earlier that sharing the brew and the traditional single steel straw is an offer of friendship, I am well aware of the social obligations involved with the drinking of maté. So, when Alber, with his wild mane of hair, stern looks, and Metallica tattoos, offers me a sip, how can I refuse? Huddled behind a thorny calafate bush, seeking shelter from the gale and beat by a fishless, wind-thrashed morning, I am relieved to discover that maté doesn't taste too bad. Which is not in any way to imply that it tastes good. In fact, it's a lot like lawn clippings steeped in hot water. Only really bitter.

The funny part, at least to the locals, is that nobody mentions you're drinking out of a goat scrotum until *after* you've swallowed a few mouthfuls. Then, with tears of mirth dripping down his face, Alber goes into an elaborate pantomime describing in easily recognizable gestures just exactly what I'm drinking from. Ha-freakin'-ha. But it's been a tough morning, and the maté break is a good excuse to duck out of the wind and stop fighting it with a twelve-foot fly rod in my hands.

With the maté choked down and the laughter subsiding, I push my way through the wind back to the river and step out below a small rocky point. There is a distinct seam downstream from the point, and as I swim the big blue String Thing into soft water, a fish absolutely crushes it. The running line shoots out of my fingers, briefly snarls at the first guide, then is jerked free as the wind-chopped surface of the river erupts. I shout over my shoulder to Tim that I have a fish on, and hear some vague reply that sails by on the wind before I can catch it. The fish streaks out into the heavy current, pushing a wake like a Trident submarine, and the backing knot disappears into the milky river. By this time, I expect Tim to be running down the bank with camera in hand as usual, but he hasn't appeared. I yell again, "Hey Timski, I HAVE A FISH ON!" "I know," he hollers back, "so do I."

A steelhead double. That happens to me about as frequently as, well … never. Amazingly, the fish stay apart, and even more amazingly, they stay hooked and we somehow land them both at the same time. All I can say is pass the lucky goat scrotum, that maté flat-out works.

As the afternoon continues, the wind subsides, and we stay in the spot across from the steep, round-topped, pale-colored hills. "The Bucket" appears to be nearly half a mile long, as we find fish all along the muddy bank behind nearly every small point of rocks and down into the big pool at the bottom. It's here that we begin to understand that even half a world away, in a huge, nearly structureless river, these are still steelhead and the holding water is there if you look closely enough. Our confidence is on the rise, and we quit, satisfied and tired from fighting fish instead of the wind for once. "What will you call this place?" Alber asks as we climb into the boat for the ride back. Wait, we get to name it? That's right, we're quite possibly the first anglers to ever fish here, and probably the first to ever land a steelhead here. What a strange concept for a North American steelheader. After much discussion and thought (these things cannot be taken lightly, you know), we decide on White Elephants, or *Elefantes Blancos*, in honor of the hills and a famous story by a guy who loved to fish. All literary pretension aside, exploring has suddenly become a lot more fun.

· · ·

Patagonians have twenty-eight words for *wind*. OK, I lied. Like the mythical twenty-eight Eskimo words for *snow*, it's a satisfying fiction with logical underpinnings. During our short time on the Santa Cruz, we came up with at least twenty-eight words to describe the wind, all of them of the four-letter variety.

Which is to say, it's easy to let the wind get to you. On the day described at the beginning of this story, we parked Claudio's new four-wheel drive in the lee of the pump shack before setting out on our little adventure. After the harrowing events recounted previously, wherein Tim and I contributed to our survival by cowering and squealing for our lives like baby pigs, we returned to find Claudio's new and expensive truck sandblasted down to the primer where it faced the wind. Even the exterior rearview mirrors had their reflective surfaces ground away to an empty flat gray. And a fly rod left strapped to the side of our boat lost its shiny finish on the upwind side. So yeah, it can be windy. The kind of windy that allows you to amuse yourself by leaning into it to the point where you can reach out and touch the ground with your fingertips. Assuming, of course, you don't mind the small rocks bouncing off your face.

But if you accept it and spend enough time in it, you eventually get used to the wind. After a few days, you realize that if you just slow down and relax, you can still cast. You can still mend. And you can still fish. Really. And better yet, the Santa Cruz meanders back and forth enough that when you can't take facing into the wind anymore, you can cross to another spot and have the wind at your back. Which then means even a little roll cast tossed up into the jet stream results in a 120-foot cast that nearly yanks the rod out of your hands when it hits the reel. A couple days of Argentine downwind casting and you'll be checking your calendar to make sure you're free for the next Spey-casting contest.

On the few occasions when the wind just seems to be too much, you take a break. On one of those mornings, with the waves sending spray into our faces and grit filling our teeth, we walk away from the river into a scrubby arroyo, looking for a sheltered place to eat lunch. A hundred feet back from the water, we find a low bank where we can sit out of the wind and still watch the river. Perfect. Alber starts a small cookfire and begins grilling enormous quantities of beautiful Argentine steaks, green peppers, and bread. A bottle of Malbec is opened and we begin another riverside feast of epic proportions.

Tim, never one to just sit around and relax, disappears into the brush. The rest of us continue our gluttony. "Hey," he shouts from around the bend, "check this out." I put another steak on my plate. "I'm serious, come here," he says, above the roar of the wind. I pretend it's too windy to hear and pour myself another cup of wine. Given Tim's tendency toward practical jokes, I'm not taking the bait. After a long minute, Tim appears holding a nearly perfect stone spear point in his hands, and we all jump up. Spreading out around the arroyo, we discover that someone else had chosen this site to get out of the wind. In fact, we're sitting in some kind of long-abandoned indigenous— Tehuelche?—workshop, with hundreds of stone chips, partially formed arrowheads, spear points, and cutting tools. It's all so perfectly preserved that we actually find large rocks split open and can match the chips and arrowheads to the places from which they originated.

Hundreds if not thousands of years must have passed since these people sat here sheltering from the wind while they worked on their tools and watched the river. And yet, the hair stands up on the back of my neck with a feeling that they were just here. Like we must have passed them on the way in or something. Spooky. As I crouch in the dry dirt picking through another pile of rock flakes, I am overwhelmed by this powerful feeling of presence or vibration. Could spirits somehow linger here? Maybe it's just the Malbec.

Bowing to social obligations once again, I choke down a post-meal sip of maté, and as before, conditions and fishing miraculously improve. Of course, I'm stuffed to the point of being able to push into that hollow spot where your collarbones meet and feel pure Argentine beef. I can barely breathe. A strange sympathy for the ancient Romans and their throat-tickling feathers comes to mind. But I waddle out into the current anyway, and somehow manage to hook a fish. As I fight it, a full rainbow appears above the hills, and Tim goes completely sideways. Camera boxes and lens caps sail through the air. Threats are made, with strings of four-letter words that defy comprehension, to the effect that if I should lose this fish before he can get a photo, I will surely die an immediate and painful death. Fortunately, I'm so full of meat I can't react to anything he's saying, and instead slowly wear the fish down. Tim reels off several thousand photos, the fish showers us both with river water on release, and my untimely demise is once again averted. We raise our arms in triumph. Rather unimaginatively, we name the pool Rainbow Alley, and I begin rummaging through the ice chest, wondering if there are any more candy bars left.

The rest of our time on Río Santa Cruz continues in much the same vein. We explore, dodge the wind, eat huge meals, and catch fish every day. The river continues to drop and clear from its catastrophic glacier-dam incident, and fresh fish move up through the pools. We average two or three fish each most days, sometimes more, sometimes less, but we fish with increasing confidence and excitement to discover new runs. The fish are aggressive and bright, even a hundred miles from the sea, running from four to eighteen pounds, with an average of around ten. And for whatever reason, unlike most of our native North American steelhead, they seem to want the fly stripped through the swing. Needless to say, that produces some of the most mind-blowing strikes in steelhead fishing.

• • •

There are some things about Río Santa Cruz I may never get used to. It's just plain weird to look up and see flamingos gliding above a steelhead river. And it can be disorienting to witness dozens of tuxedo-wearing penguins waddling and standing around in what appears to be Eastern Montana sagebrush desert. The quantity and quality of Argentine beef and wine also takes a recalibration of the concept of "all you can eat," not to mention a few extra notches in the old wading belt. And the idea that you need to strip the fly in through the swing is certainly absurd to most dyed-in-the-wool steelhead veterans. But at the end of our trip, we are left to conclude that this is still steelhead fishing after all. Really, really good steelhead fishing, but steelhead fishing all the same. Even way down here where Christmas falls in the middle of summer, the fish still face upstream, they still hold in seams, soft water, and behind points, and until you hook one, you're never really sure if they're there or not.

Why, as several friends have asked, would anyone want to travel so far to fish a huge river in a place famous for wind, for fish that aren't necessarily any bigger or more numerous than you might find somewhere closer to home? Maybe it's because the Río Santa Cruz is an adventure unlike any other in fly fishing, with an opportunity to pioneer a section of river that's hardly been fished, in a breathtakingly isolated setting. There are literally hundreds of runs and pools on this river that remain untouched, and it would take a lifetime to fish and name them all. Or it could be the fish themselves, a unique run of introduced wild Atlantic steelhead that are just now in the process of evolving and filling their niche. While most, if not all, steelhead fisheries in the Pacific Northwest seem to be caught in a long and miserable downward spiral, the Río Santa Cruz is on the upswing. Remember, the first steelhead ever officially recorded here was only landed in 1985. Or how about solitude? In seven days of fishing, we never saw another boat on the water or another angler, anywhere. Try that on the Deschutes, Skagit, or Bulkley, or for that matter, anywhere else in North America. Or maybe it's the argument Tim makes: "Because it's just plain hard-core cool, that's why."

Whatever the reasons, I'm going back. Hopefully a lot. And in the meantime, should you happen across a guy on a Northwest steelhead river sipping yerba maté out of a dried goat scrotum, stop by, say hello, and have a sip—it would be impolite to refuse.

JUNE 1979

I couldn't sleep all night, tossing and turning, images of rising trout haunting my imagination. When the alarm finally sounds, I leap out of bed with relief and bounce through the dark house checking and rechecking my vest and fly boxes. My father, who now lives in a distant state, is taking me on a long-awaited fishing trip to the Metolius. As we drive through predawn night, gas-station signs and convenience-store neon streaking past in a blur, I chatter with manic energy: "Dad, will they be rising today?" "Dad, will it stop raining?" At the river, the fish are not rising, the rain doesn't stop, and we find the water so high I reluctantly accept an embarrassing piggyback ride across the first riffle. The rain continues all day and despite our best efforts, we remain fishless. In the evening, the weather breaks, and on the edge of a long, deep pool, we spot a single rising fish. "Go ahead," my father whispers. I cast, eyes locked onto the ripples of the rise, but keenly aware of his presence at my shoulder.

COMMITMENT

You know the look. Try explaining your steelhead jones to someone—a relative, coworker, or better yet, a potential spouse—and there it is: disdain, or worse, real concern. The less polite often feel a need to summarize, as if they didn't quite hear you or, more likely, to emphasize their disbelief, "Wait, so you stand in freezing water all day, in brutal weather, casting over and over ... and most of the time you don't even catch anything? Um ... wow." Then the look. The one that says you belong in a mental facility.

And now here you are again, standing in freezing water up to your waist, in brutal weather, getting ready to cast over and over, each time expecting a different result. Yes, you are acquainted with the pop-culture definition of insanity, thank you very much. This, after four fishless, dawn-to-dark days interrupted only by occasional breaks for the cold coffee, candy bars, and pepperoni sticks you bought at the gas station on the way out. Days so bleak that at times you wondered if these fish actually exist, or if you only imagined them.

A slurry of wet snow driven by a ferocious downstream wind pelts your face and stings your fingers. Dense, gray cloud cover, vaguely lightened by an invisible sun, obscures the surrounding mountains and fills the river valley. Pale, leafless alders jut from the bank behind you, the bare branches waving overhead in stronger gusts. This is spring, or what passes for it, on the Olympic Peninsula.

You come around with your loop, pause for it to line up, and launch for the far side. There's a subtle trough over there, tight to the bank, where the tumbling riffle falls away into deep, soft water. It takes a big mend and a downstream step or two to get the fly to fish. But if there's a steelhead in the river, that's where it'll hold.

This year, like too many of recent memory, the steelhead run is down. You lived through the precipitous decline of your Puget Sound home rivers, and this season on the OP dredges up old worries. Sol Duc, Bogie, Hoh, Queets—same story everywhere. Your mind roils with the work that needs to be done to save these fish. And yet, as your cast settles, you are still stoked, still holding your breath, knees shaking with anticipation. Or maybe it's the weather sapping heat from your core. Or insanity.

The fat part of your line catches fast water and the fly rockets across the bucket, accelerating downstream. Nope. Need a bigger mend. Maybe two. You fight your way back upstream, into the heavy current, and carefully inch out a little deeper to sharpen the angle of attack. Pebbles wash out from underfoot, joining the turbulent wake streaming out below your legs.

Another cast, a huge mend, another mend, and three sliding, bouncing steps downstream. The kind of steps where you aren't really sure if you'll be able to stop, or if you're going swimming. The line gradually gains tension, this time in a wide, open arc, with the fly swimming gently crosscurrent.

Then: Simultaneous explosions detonate in your brain, your heart, the surface of the river. Line peels off the reel in a furious blur, shooting away downstream. A hundred feet out and upstream, a fish vaults into the air. Your fish. Synapses fire, adrenaline pulses into veins, line slices through current. The fish greyhounds away, punching new holes in the river while the previous holes are still open. Heat surges out of your chest and down your arms, tingling frozen fingers.

The fish reverses course with a sharp downstream turn, a brief loss of tension—your heart stutters—then a long screaming run, punctuated by a cartwheeling leap that will remain frozen in your memory forever: a brilliant slash of silver suspended in a halo of sparkling water drops, illuminating the gray half-light.

Two more slower, shorter runs, then the fish veers in close, yielding to pressure now, its thick body curved into the S-shape of waning resistance. As it passes beneath a slick in the surface a window opens, revealing mottled, amber rocks and a yard-long fish twisting and turning in the current. Your heart thumps. A series of short, writhing turns and it glides into the shallows at your feet. You grip the broad wrist ahead of its tail, slip the hook out, and hold this incredible, radiant creature for a brief moment of wonder. When you let go, it shoots away like a speedboat, tail churning a wake of water and foam.

You are not cold, even though you are. You are not tired, even though you are. You are not hungry, even though you are. You feel better than you've felt in a long time, maybe ever. Insanity? If that's what this is, you'll take it. Try explaining that.

THE LITTLE THINGS

Steelhead season is going down the tubes. Six weeks into what will become the wettest winter in memory, the rivers are over their banks and gouging new channels with explosive fury. I have just canceled yet another fishing trip. Like last week's much-anticipated trip to the Olympic Peninsula, and countless other days on local rivers, this one is toast.

My three-year-old daughter and I had planned to go steelhead fishing together for the first time today. OK, I planned it, but as a kid who's enthusiastic about doing anything outside with Dad, she said yes. Instead, we sit by the woodstove reading *The Very Hungry Caterpillar* for the thousandth time and listen to rain lashing against the windows.

I am going insane.

A slight break in the weather. Not enough to bring the rivers into shape, but enough to send us out of the house and into a light but steady drizzle. We'll put on our rain gear and venture into the woods. It's not a fishing trip, but at least Skyla and I are going outside together.

Skyla dashes up the trail, splashing mud and sliding through a carpet of downed foliage. She kneels to examine the difference between maple and alder leaves. She throws fir cones into dripping ferns. She clambers up onto a fallen cedar log and careens down its length yelling, "It's a big tree slide!"

At the edge of a steep ravine, we can see the normally dry bottom now contains a tiny creek brought to temporary life by weeks of torrential rain.

"Daddy," she says, "let's go down there."

"Nah," I say with visions of us sliding down the precipitous hillside and the grueling slog back up. "It's too steep, and besides, what do you want to go down there for?"

"To go fishing in the stream!" she says.

I tell her we don't have fishing rods and there aren't any fish in there anyway. I tell her it's starting to rain harder and we should head home. I tell her we'll get muddy and wet.

Predictably, we scramble and skid down anyway. At stream level, we discover a perfect little river winding through a gravelly bed of miniature riffles, runs, and pools. Skyla hands me a bent willow stick and finds one for herself. "Here's your fly rod, Dad, and here's mine."

She crouches at water's edge, and with intense concentration, swishes the stick through the small pool. At last, a current-borne maple leaf folds itself around her stick, and she lifts it triumphantly for my inspection, shouting, "Fish on! I got one!"

We measure it. We admire it. We discuss it. Ultimately, we decide to release it.

"Daddy," she says, "now it's your turn to fish." We alternate for nearly an hour, landing dozens of leaves, deciding where the best spots are, naming the pools. We laugh and high-five. We forget to eat the lunch in our pack.

"Dad?" she says, folding her icy fingers into my hand. "I'm having a lot of fun fishing with you."

And suddenly, it occurs to me this may be one of the best fishing trips of my life.

MAY 1982

It's supposed to be a guided whitewater-rafting trip sponsored by the high school outdoor club. But when my mom drops me off, I have my own navy-surplus, two-man yellow life raft, a rowing frame cobbled together from two-by-fours, and a fly rod. Somewhat incredibly, the trip leader looks at my gear and says, "Go ahead, kid, knock yourself out." When we reach the river—the Deschutes—my classmates board huge gray commercial rafts, while a buddy and I climb into the tiny rubber ducky and shove off. We lag behind, losing sight of the big boats as I cast into eddies and behind rocks, rowing with one hand and fishing with the other. At a place called Oak Springs, I choose the river-right channel because the tailout looks fishy, and I'm surprised when the raft plummets into a torrent of whitewater and capsizes beneath an enormous standing wave. That night in camp, I pause in the midst of raucous teenage revelry to watch a trout rise and mourn the loss of my fly rod.

STATE OF THE STEELHEAD

Four feet deep. Rocks the size of bowling balls. Choppy on top. The big purple marabou settles into emerald-green water, comes tight, and starts swinging through the seam. I hold my breath and make a small inside mend. The fly slows briefly, swims crosscurrent into the soft water, and suddenly stops. The rod bends. The line pulls. And the river's surface shatters.

As my reel handle blurs, I hear the hiss of fly line shearing water and watch in awe as the biggest steelhead I've ever seen launches into the air and cartwheels away three, four, five times. When I come to my senses, there's only one thing to do: start running.

Twenty minutes later, heart pounding and sweaty, I'm holding the tiring fish on a tight line as it slips downstream into a chute of fast water. Unable to follow any farther, I clamp down on the spool and my fishing buddy leaps in chest-deep, plunges his arms into the icy water, and heroically comes up with an enormous slab of chrome. At forty-and-a-half by twenty-three inches, it's quite probably the largest steelhead I will ever land, and one of five we've hooked this morning in the same run.

The Dean? Russia? Some other exotic destination? Or maybe a complete steelhead fantasy? Hell no. This was the suburban Skykomish River, forty minutes from downtown Seattle, on March 14, 1997. That year, in the March–April catch-and-release season, I averaged almost two steelhead per trip. On swung flies. Fishing mostly in short three- or four-hour sessions before or after work. Unbelievable fishing, and even more unbelievable, it wasn't all that long ago.

Today, the fabulous March and April fishery on my beloved Sky is gone. The wild steelhead population in such a downward spiral that even the relatively low-impact catch-and-release season was completely shut down after the 2000 season. Heartbreaking? I can't even find words for how I feel about it. I moved to Seattle in 1993 to be closer to the fabled steelhead waters of Puget Sound. A city where I could work, and a great river with big fish, less than an hour away—it seemed too good to be true. Of course, it was. I had planned on a lifetime of learning and fishing the Skykomish. Instead, I arrived just in time to witness the beginning of the end.

That's only one river among hundreds of steelhead watersheds on the West Coast, right? What's the big deal? There are still plenty of fish to catch in other places, aren't there? And hey, if you aren't a steelheader, why should you get worked up about some river closing way out in Washington? Good questions all.

I would start with the fish themselves. Perfectly evolved to thrive in both marine and freshwater environments, wild steelhead carry the ocean's bounty inland as they migrate toward the places of their birth. And, as each watershed provides a different set of spawning and rearing conditions, it creates a unique race of steelhead. In the wild realm, there is no generic steelhead, only a range of fish with characteristics perfectly adapted to their specific rivers.

As anglers, we find ourselves seeking the small, free-rising "A-Run" steelhead of the high-desert Columbia Basin rivers; the "half-pounders" of Northern California and Southern Oregon; magnificent, heavy-bodied winter fish in the Olympic Peninsula rainforest and coastal Oregon rivers; the mind-blowingly powerful August steelhead above the falls on the Dean; the legendary autumn giants on the Skeena; the high-latitude chromers of Kamchatka and the Aleutians …

These fish range from fourteen inches to thirty pounds, from two to nine or more years old, from heavily spotted to nearly unmarked. And yet, they share several distinctive traits: a willingness to come to the swung fly; the speed and strength normally associated with saltwater fish; an individual beauty that possesses those who fish for them; and unfortunately, a future as cloudy as a glacial river after days of warm rain.

Why should we care? If you're a steelheader, the reasons are obvious. And if you are not, the depleted state of wild steelhead populations on the Pacific Coast serves as a powerful example of a valuable resource squandered and a lesson for anglers and fish managers everywhere. On a bigger scale, steelhead are an indicator species, the proverbial canary in the coal mine of population growth and human consumption. In other words, the health of wild steelhead is a direct reflection of the health of both our watersheds and marine environments. Steelhead can clearly survive without us—the question is, can we survive without them?

A curious thing happens when fish stocks decline: People who aren't aware of the old levels accept the new ones as normal. Over generations, societies adjust their expectations downward to match prevailing conditions.

Kennedy Warne,
National Geographic magazine

The very idea that steelhead are difficult to catch—the fish of a thousand casts—is a myth. Steelhead are actually very easy to catch. They aggressively take a variety of baits, lures, and flies. The problem is, there just aren't very many of them. Back on the Skykomish, during the eight years I fished it regularly, from

1993 to 2000, the average run size for the entire Snohomish system (Skykomish, Snoqualmie, and Pilchuck Rivers and their tributaries) was 6,356 fish per year. Spread out over several hundred miles of streams, that's not many. Compare that to the estimated 3,000 trout *per mile* on the Madison, and it's amazing we caught anything at all. But it was enough to provide challenging yet rewarding fishing, and, according to the Washington Department of Fish and Wildlife, enough to constitute a sustainable population. A look at some historical numbers, however, shows that this number did not, in fact, sustain itself; furthermore, we were fishing for crumbs.

It is estimated that Puget Sound wild winter-steelhead populations are now somewhere between 1.6 and 4 percent of the historic run size. Just to the north of the Skykomish lies the famed Stillaguamish River, immortalized by Roderick Haig-Brown and considered by many to be the birthplace of modern steelhead fly fishing. In 1895, the annual run of steelhead to this small, delicate stream came in between sixty thousand and ninety thousand fish. The most recent five-year average? Five hundred ninety-three wild steelhead per year. Since the closure of the Skykomish in 2001, the average return of spawning adult wild steelhead in the entire Snohomish system, of which the Sky is a tributary, has been hovering around three thousand.

How did this happen? The easiest and most correct answer is people. It's impossible to place the blame on any one specific factor, but there are plenty: poor logging practices resulting in heavy siltation (most of the famous pools on the Stillaguamish, once boulder strewn and heavily cobbled, now lie beneath a featureless bottom of sand and mud); exponential population growth and the resulting pavement, lawn chemicals, and septic waste; the industrialization of Puget Sound; sport and tribal fishing harvest managed by a philosophy of Maximum Sustainable Harvest (MSH), which fails to account for variations in ocean and stream rearing conditions; the mistaken belief that increased hatchery production could mitigate the loss of wild fish. The list goes on and on, but one fact remains the same: We were fishing for crumbs in the 1990s, and now even the crumbs are nearly gone.

> *Federal policy in both the United States and Canada is to extirpate steelhead—entirely because they are a pain in the ass that get in the way of fish farming, electricity production, commercial fishing, logging, development, and other resource extraction industries.*
>
> Yvon Chouinard
> Founder, Patagonia

That our governments are consciously trying to relieve themselves of the wild steelhead burden may ring of conspiracy theory, but the record speaks for itself. From the Bush administration's ridiculously off-base attempts (rejected in court) to count hatchery-produced steelhead as part of the overall wild steelhead populations to the Fisheries and Oceans Canada's (DFO) refusal to reduce commercial gill net fisheries in light of disastrously low returns of Skeena steelhead, we have witnessed repeated actions that lend credence to the theory.

The Skeena in the summer of 2007 is a prime example. The crown jewel of modern steelhead rivers, the Skeena is the mother river to legendary tributaries including the Kispiox, Babine, Bulkley, Morice, Sustut, Copper, and more. In recent times, by July 23, there will be an average of 4,368 wild summer steelhead in the Skeena system. In 2007, the count was 642. On August 16, the historical date for highest steelhead numbers in the Tyee test fishery, exactly zero were counted.

As early as mid-July that year, the alarmingly low numbers created a groundswell of concern from area anglers, guides, and lodges. Acting together and separately, these individuals mounted a campaign urging the DFO to alter or cut back on the scheduled commercial salmon gillnet fisheries. This, following 2006, a year when, despite warnings from their own biologists and the British Columbia Ministry of Environment and Climate Change Strategy regarding extremely low returns of steelhead, DFO allowed an intensive salmon net fishery and the resulting bycatch of depressed early steelhead stocks. DFO's response in 2007? No action taken whatsoever.

Why is this happening again in steelhead paradise of all places? It's the direct result of a "surplus" crop of two to three million sockeye salmon created in the artificial, government-built spawning channels of Babine Lake. These fish, produced purely for the small, four-hundred-boat commercial fleet's benefit, just happen to return to the Skeena at the same time as steelhead, coho, and other dwindling Skeena stocks. The result? Lots of dead steelhead found in lethal gill nets. All this for a fishery that paid a mere ninety cents per pound for sockeye and about five cents per pound for pink salmon.

Why are we subsidizing the broken part of this fishery, the commercial gillnetting, to the detriment of the only part of this fishery, the recreational side, that makes economic sense?

Bruce Hill
Headwaters Initiative

A 2008 study by Counterpoint Consulting shows the Skeena River sportfishing industry brings more than $52 million a year into the local economy. On the other hand, the average gross income of a British Columbia North Coast gillnetter during the time covered by the study was $8,000—about the value of two or three sport-caught-and-released wild steelhead. Exactly how many steelhead perished as bycatch to earn that $8,000 we'll never know for sure, but it's a significantly high-enough number that on the rare occasion when the nets are out of the water, steelhead escapement skyrockets. And this doesn't even take into account Skeena steelhead killed in the British Columbian and Alaskan salmon seine fisheries—many observers believe the number is as high as or even higher than those caught in gill nets. Again, in this commercial fishery, we have a low-income, high-negative-impact industry that kills thousands of steelhead and depressed salmon stocks, while the sportfishing sector provides large amounts of income with very little impact. And yet, our decision makers can't seem to do the math.

Think that's a Canadian problem? Think again. It isn't any better in the United States. On the Columbia River, a tiny fleet of gillnetters is allowed to target hatchery spring Chinook in the lower river. Unfortunately, as on the Skeena, other fish have the great misfortune to return in the same time frame. A recent year saw more endangered wild winter steelhead taken as bycatch than the targeted salmon.

Even more maddening is the cost to taxpayers to produce those hatchery spring Chinook. According to the Independent Economic Analysis Board (IEAB) of the Northwest Power and Conservation Council, at one point, a harvested adult spring Chinook from the Upper Columbia Basin's Entiat hatchery cost citizens $68,031 to produce. Yes, you read that correctly:

$68,031 for a single fish. No fuzzy math or cooked stats here: The IEAB simply took the total annual operating and maintenance cost of this hatchery and divided that by the number of harvested adult fish produced there. Amazingly, this ridiculous number doesn't even take into account the cost of lost electrical production when power generation is reduced to assist downstream juvenile migration or the expense of trapping, barging, and trucking the juveniles around the dams.

If a typical, hatchery-produced Columbia River spring Chinook weighs twelve pounds, that Entiat fish cost you nearly $5,700 a pound, the gillnetter probably made $7 or $8 a pound at the dock, and then you were offered the opportunity to pay $17 a pound for it again at the supermarket. And at the same time, large numbers of endangered wild winter steelhead perished in the process.

Farther south and not so very long ago, California was a steelhead mecca of fish-filled streams and unimaginably productive fishing. The home of early steelhead fly-fishing pioneers such as Bill Schaadt and Jim Pray, coastal California was the place to be in the 1950s and '60s. Movie stars came to catch steelhead, national magazines devoted cover stories to this phenomenal fishery, and the annual records were dominated by fly-caught California steelhead. If you're a true glutton for punishment, read Russell Chatham's beautiful book *The Angler's Coast* and see what the good old days were really like. Keep a box of tissues nearby.

In the 1960s, the Russian River averaged fifty thousand wild steelhead per year. Today, a good year sees seven thousand. As agriculture, development, industrialization, and other human factors have come to dominate the California landscape, the steelhead have predictably responded by disappearing. The numbers are staggering. The Carmel River, a small Central Coast watershed, once hosted twenty thousand steelhead each year. In more recent times, the run has fallen to as low as fifteen wild steelhead. In 1961, the mighty Sacramento–San Joaquin river system had forty thousand spawning steelhead. Today, the annual fish count at the Red Bluff Diversion Dam on the Sacramento River, which carries the bulk of this once-prolific system's steelhead population, averages fourteen hundred.

California obviously has the most intense population issues on the coast, and has seen the most catastrophic losses of wild steelhead. But management of these precious fish would be absolutely hilarious if the results weren't so sad. Even the mass-produced hatchery fish of the American River are hardly coming back. Despite enormous numbers of juveniles released each year, which used to result in a run of up to nineteen thousand fish in the 1970s, returns are now less than one thousand fish. The Ventura River, which once had a run of five thousand, now gets a return as low as fifty fish per year. As concerned locals petitioned to have the remnants of this run listed under the Endangered Species Act, the feds showed up claiming a need to obtain DNA samples to determine that Ventura River steelhead were in fact a distinct species. How many do you need, they were asked. "Fifty," was the reply. The situation deteriorated into a standoff between armed State Fish and Wildlife officers protecting the fish from federal employees who needed to "take" fish in order to protect them.

In Oregon, where population and development have only more recently become factors, the primary problem affecting wild steelhead seems to be genetic pollution from the massive coastal hatchery program. There are certainly logging-practice issues and the resulting spawning habitat loss, as well as a long history of high recreational-harvest rates, but according to the National Oceanographic and Atmospheric Administration (NOAA), hatcheries are the major reason eighteen of the twenty-one distinct Oregon Coast wild steelhead stocks are now listed under the Endangered Species Act as either "depressed" or "of special concern."

So what about the healthy runs of the far north, where wilderness rivers attract anglers from around the world to fish for larger numbers of wild steelhead? Well, the Situk River in Southeast Alaska, a small drainage famous for its incredibly productive steelhead fishery, certainly qualifies. Compared to other, more accessible rivers, recent average runs of twelve thousand three hundred fish makes it a veritable bonanza for traveling anglers. However, a quick check of historical numbers shows that once again, we are fishing for crumbs. In 1952, the Situk had a typical run of between twenty-five thousand and thirty thousand wild winter steelhead. Today's "bonanza" is really less than half of what it once was.

On the Skeena, beyond the intensive and unsustainable gillnet bycatch and the indifference, or worse, from the DFO outlined earlier, there's currently a vast array of potentially disastrous threats to wild steelhead circling this watershed. Despite the recent ban on North Coast open-water net pens, industrial fish farm corporations—with their proven track record of waste pollution, chemicals, and deadly sea-lice infestations, which easily spread to migrating wild fish, thereby decimating natural runs—are still fighting to place facilities near the mouth of the Skeena. (As a side note, it's a well-documented fact that salmon farms dramatically damage wild fish runs, but has anyone noticed what a self-fulfilling market strategy this is? As wild runs decline, the value of farmed fish will certainly rise.) Royal Dutch Shell is pushing to exploit coalbed methane reserves in the Sacred Headwaters, while other corporations seek to extract molybdenum, copper, and other precious metals, all of which would prove disastrous for the watershed. A pipeline carrying millions of gallons of toxic petroleum products is planned to run through the avalanche- and slide-prone Skeena corridor. Rail cars loaded with Indonesian petroleum by-products to be used as solvents rumble perilously upriver bound for the tar-sand oil fields of Alberta. And timber companies have their sights on vast tracts of forest protecting critical spawning habitat.

That such damaging, yet profitable, industries are even on the table for what may be the most valuable steelhead watershed in the world is mind-boggling. It also demonstrates the power of the almighty dollar and what people fighting to preserve this fishery are up against. Not surprisingly, very few believe government, if left to its own devices, will make any decisions here to benefit salmon or steelhead.

> *In our fathers' generation, they witnessed the*
> *complete collapse of the California steelhead*
> *fishery. In our generation, it was the famed rivers*
> *of Puget Sound. What's next? We're currently*
> *standing on the edge of the cliff and time is*
> *running out. If we're going to do anything to save*
> *wild steelhead, we have to do it now.*
>
> Dr. Nathan Mantua, Research Scientist
> NOAA Southwest Fisheries Science Center

Yes, we are fishing for crumbs. We have been for some time. But while these paltry numbers may provide acceptable fishing, the fact is, even the crumbs of our wild steelhead runs are fast disappearing. On Washington's remote Olympic Peninsula, a region generally considered to be one of the last strongholds of healthy wild steelhead runs in the Lower 48, the Quinault, Clearwater, Sol Duc, and Bogachiel Rivers each receive fewer than fifty wild summer steelhead in a given season. In biological terms, these fish are "functionally extinct." The Hoh River, mostly flowing through a national park's pristine rainforest environment, is, as of 2006, still managed as a catch-and-kill sport fishery for wild winter steelhead, with an escapement goal of 2,400 fish. I use the term *managed* loosely here. In the 2002–03 season, when a total run of 3,583 steelhead returned, the tribal and state managers allowed a combined sport and tribal harvest of 1,967 steelhead. In other words, more than half the run was harvested, resulting in an escapement of only 1,616 spawners—almost 800 fish short of the minimum goal. Maybe the feds don't have the corner on that extinction is-good-for-business conspiracy theory.

When fish managers talk about Maximum Sustainable Yield (MSY) or Maximum Sustainable Harvest, what we witnessed on the Hoh is pretty much par for the course. This obviously flawed management philosophy assumes a natural surplus of fish, and places belief in the idea that an agency can calculate the total number of fish required to sustain the run and the escapement goal, and also accurately estimate a given year's run size. By subtracting the former from the latter, they arrive at the number of fish available for harvest. While that might work in statistics class, here's the real-world problem: Nature doesn't operate according to computer models or statistics. This strategy, sadly still in place in Washington, doesn't adequately account for variable ocean conditions, flooding, drought, loss of habitat in rearing streams, or the longer-term challenges posed by climate change, and is frequently based on flawed escapement goals to begin with. How does anyone know it only takes twenty-four hundred spawning steelhead to sustain the Hoh River run? They told us the sixty-five hundred fish escapement goal on the Snohomish was sustainable and now we have less than half that number.

In its national assessment of wild steelhead runs, NOAA divided the remaining West Coast steelhead populations into fifteen Evolutionary Significant Units, or ESUs. Eleven of those fifteen ESUs are currently either listed under the Endangered Species Act or under review for ESA listing. In Washington State alone, every one of the seven ESUs is either ESA-listed, chronically under-escaped, or experiencing recent and rapid population declines. And yet, as of 2007, the Washington Department of Fish and Wildlife still considers sport harvest of wild steelhead perfectly acceptable on the handful of Olympic Peninsula rivers they consider healthy. God forbid we should let any surplus fish survive to spawn anywhere. In Canada, as we've touched on earlier, things are hardly better.

The fact is, steelhead are under attack at every level: from federal policies favoring commercial, unsustainable fisheries, mining, and forest harvest practices to bungled state management operating under a philosophy of MSH, to local municipalities' sanctioning of development and commercialization. Suburban sprawl engulfs our river valleys. Forestland is cut to build houses and make toilet paper. Modern agriculture requires increasing amounts of water, while dam operators fight to generate more electricity—all at the expense of natural, fish-producing streamflow. To mitigate these losses, we've come to rely on hatcheries, which we are now learning may contribute to wild fish declines as much as all the other factors combined. All this, and we're only beginning to see the effects of global

by a coalition of First Nations and local nonprofits, the BC government finally agreed with their citizens and implemented the new policy in 2008.

When possible, we need to provide alternatives to the status quo. If we look, there are some surprisingly simple solutions to a number of the challenges we face. For example, in places like the Columbia, Fraser, and Skeena Rivers, where commercial salmon gill-net fisheries intercept a high number of steelhead, live-capture fish traps or pound nets would allow safe release of fish from depressed stocks, while simultaneously increasing the quality (and thereby the value) of the targeted fish. Everybody wins.

We can also boycott farmed salmon from open-water net pens and explain to restaurants and markets that serve or sell it why this product is so damaging to wild salmon and steelhead. Turns out, most people have no idea about the harm it causes, and, when shown the facts, will happily stop buying or selling farmed salmon.

We should encourage—no, demand—that outdoor gear manufacturers actively give back to preserve the resources they depend upon, and support those that do with our dollars. We can eat local, organic food. Stop watering and fertilizing our lawns. Walk, pedal, or paddle whenever possible. In drought-prone regions, even not flushing when you pee helps.

The most valuable thing we can do, though, is to get directly involved. Of course, I understand most of us don't have the time or resources to understand all the issues or wage a personal political campaign. That's where grassroots organizations like Wild Fish Conservancy, Wild Steelhead Coalition, and Native Fish Society come into play. These groups are hard at work doing everything from political lobbying and litigation to scientific research, stream restoration, and funding steelhead-related projects. They provide the regular angler with the voice and clout of a larger organization, and distribute information to their members about issues requiring action. As distasteful as politics and joining organizations may be to many anglers, it is, as author and steelhead aficionado Tom McGuane reminds us, "now past the time where we can just go out and fish without worrying about the resource." That's pretty much what we've been doing, and look where it got us.

If you fish for steelhead or dream of someday fishing for them, if the numbers and issues in this story concern you, if you'd like to believe that we'll have fishable numbers of steelhead for the rest of our lives and our children's ... the answer is simple: get involved. For that matter, if you're passionate about trout or stripers or bass or salmon or tarpon, I urge you to learn from what's happened to our steelhead and get involved with the preservation of your fishery. As steelheaders know all too well, when it goes, it goes fast.

On my office wall is a photo of that huge Skykomish steelhead. The picture isn't old or faded. But it feels like a lifetime since I last fished a spring season on the Sky. I can't even begin to tell you how much I miss it. My hope is that we can work together as concerned anglers and citizens and someday set the stage for these magnificent fish to return in truly healthy numbers. I plan to be there when they do.

Postscript 2022

After two decades without a spring fishery on the Skykomish, the number of wild steelhead continues to languish and the fishery remains closed. I still feel the pain of missing my favorite river and fish every time March rolls around, and more than that, my distress over the fact that it isn't improving continues to grow.

Today, wild steelhead populations find themselves in significantly more peril than when this story was first published in 2007, or when it was updated and republished in 2010. The reasons are the same as outlined earlier, but recently, more ominous developments make the fight for wild steelhead more critical than ever. Human population along the West Coast continues its explosive growth, with more and more development expanding into rural and suburban regions. River valleys are filling with new homes, shopping centers, roads, and traffic, resulting in worsening run-off issues and more toxic pollutants entering streams.

Meanwhile, our reliance on hatcheries continues, filling the Pacific Ocean with inbred, domesticated juvenile hatchery salmon from hatcheries in North America and Asia. The climate crisis is upon us, too, causing higher stream temperatures and lower flows in summer, more scouring floods in the winter, and tougher conditions in the ocean. It is under these kinds of challenging environmental changes that wild fish, with their diverse life histories and genetics, and traits adapted to survive in adverse conditions, provide the only real hope of survival. And yet we continue to invest in the failed hatchery system.

However, the years since this story was first published did not pass without some hopeful developments as well. In 2016, the state of Washington effectively banned sport harvest of wild steelhead statewide. After long battles led by First Nations and supported by countless conservation groups, Royal Dutch Shell's plans for coalbed methane extraction in the Sacred Headwaters of the Skeena, Nass, and Stikine Rivers were foiled. Many of the same groups came together to stop the Enbridge Pipeline and the building of a massive liquefied natural gas facility at Lelu Island in the Skeena River delta. Outspoken citizens, led by Wild Fish Conservancy, forced legislation banning Atlantic salmon open-water net pens in Puget Sound. When the net-pen salmon farm located just off the island we live on was towed to the marine salvage yard this past winter, the kids and I cheered. To me, these are all examples of the power of an informed and activated public, and inspiration for the battles that lie ahead.

MARCH 1986

*Before the results of my disastrous final exams are posted
and shortly after breaking up with a girl I thought I'd seen
a future with, I leave campus with two buddies and head
south, down the Central Valley, through the smog-choked
traffic of Los Angeles, across the border and farther. We push
on through the night, dodging gaunt cows, crazed drivers,
and two police shakedowns. In the morning, we set up camp
on an empty, curving beach just outside Loreto. We fish for
days without success, subsisting on clams and the ten-pound
sack of potatoes we'd brought. Finally, using pantomime
Spanish, I convince a local fisherman to take us out to the
dark blue water. Bait bursts into the air and I hook a small
tuna on my first cast. When it finally comes to the boat,
it's bigger than expected, possibly matching the size of our
now-diminished potato sack. In my excitement, I recall road
signs ahead of large curves on the highway that read, "*curva
peligrosa,*" point to the fish, and say to the boatman with
pride, "*Muy peligroso!" Mysteriously, the boatman breaks
into belly-shaking laughter. Later, back at school, I discover
that* peligrosa *means "dangerous."*

CRASH

October 29, 2008. Evidence: A spiraling stock market sheds three hundred points a day with no bottom in sight. Rock-solid financial institutions disappear in a puff of cartoon smoke. Tampa Bay—*Tampafrickinbay!*—plays in the World Series. Historically low river levels bring what had been the best steelhead season in years to a skidding halt. A brutally early winter settles into the Skeena Country. Even better, Tim's got giardia.

The world is coming to an end. All signs point to yes. And we are doing what any sensible humans would to prepare for impending doom: *fishing*.

But things are going downhill fast. As the Dow plummets, so too does Tim's health—up and down, day to day, hour to hour, but overall, trending downward. Steeply. In fact, he seems intent on wearing out his felts running wildly from river to bushes, hunched over like the proverbial monkey humping a coconut. This the result of an unfortunate incident on the Babine a few weeks earlier, when a fishing buddy whom I shall not name here—OK, it was Justin Crump—used Tim's water bottle to wash down his raft, left it half full of river water, and forgot to mention it. Apparently, Tim was pretty thirsty that night.

The unseasonable winter deepens, and we struggle with frozen lines, chattering teeth, inch-thick ice at the put-in. Water temps drop and the river shrinks in its bed beneath skeletal, leafless cottonwoods. It's getting tougher to climb out of bed each day.

We thought we were outsmarting them all, way back in the summer, when we made plans to fish late this year. Let 'em have the peak-season crowds and high water. We'll follow everyone and bat cleanup. We'll show them. Ha! But as the early and midseason reports rolled in, they were uniformly good. Too good. Ominously good. Perfect water conditions, lifetime trips, double-digit days, huge fish, blah, blah, blah ... shit.

Echoes of giddy phone calls from weeks earlier haunt us as we fish through the gloomy light and bitter wind. *The fish still have to be here ... don't they?* We move farther upstream, searching. We're showing 'em, alright. Days pass and blur together, notable only for the absence of other anglers, and for that matter, all signs of life. *Nothing* is moving. Except Tim, on his increasingly urgent charges out of the water and into the woods. I tell him he should wear two pairs of socks in case he runs out of paper. He doesn't laugh.

Late afternoon on yet another day in our seemingly endless decline, I am fishing mechanically through another empty run, hope gone and mind wandering. Gradually, though, something wears through to my consciousness ... something familiar ... a strange, hollow thumping sound, like a small rock bouncing off a wooden barrel half full of water.

I look for the source and am startled to see a raven near the top of a tall fir, bobbing its head and calling to others soaring above. *Life.*

Then another realization—for the first time in days, I am not cold. In fact, there is a warm breeze on my cheek, and it smells faintly of the ocean.

With darkness falling, Tim drops me off at the head of a long stretch of choppy water and takes the boat to the other side. As I step into the top, a raindrop falls. And then another. And another. In the meadow behind Tim, I can see the dusky shapes of deer moving.

"Fish on," Tim yells, and his line comes tight, then just as suddenly falls slack. His shoulders slump, he looks at his fly and resumes casting. I begin fishing with renewed intensity, willing the fly to swim slowly through the boulder seams and small current changes. A fish crushes it on the hard swing and I fumble in disbelief as line peels out and then … nothing. Nothing. An empty feeling settles in my stomach.

I check my hook and keep fishing down. The water is getting better with each downstream step, the fly swimming cleanly across. Another grab. The fish makes a short run, then reverses direction and … nothing. Fish off. Tim yells from across the water, but I can't tell what he's saying. I squeeze my eyes shut and feel my brain churn. He yells again, and I'm pretty sure he's saying we need to go. I ignore him. It's getting dark fast now.

Desperation. On my seventh "last cast," the fly stops again and I feel a heavy headshake. Water boils and the fish bolts for the far side, my line arcing out into the gathering dusk. Somewhere out there I hear the fish jump and it sounds very big and very far away.

By the time Tim brings the boat across and walks down, I have the big buck in close, still bulling around the shallows, but clearly tiring. When I lean on the fish, it tips over and glides into shore. I remove the hook and hold him briefly in the soft water before he steadies himself and powers back into the current. My hands are shaking. Tim slaps me on the back and grins. He hasn't been to the bushes since lunch.

Success. Victory. All accumulated doubts evaporate, replaced by a dizzying sense of hope and optimism. Tim starts the motor and we triumphantly barrel upstream. "We are not cold," we shout. The world will not be ending as previously scheduled. Tomorrow, we will catch fish until our arms fall off. We laugh out loud, smiling, yelling, stomping our feet on the floorboards as we careen through the night, wind whipping our faces. And a hundred yards from the boat ramp, with throttle wide open, we smash into a boulder so hard it blows the outboard over the transom and sends us flying into darkness.

A RECIPE FOR
CADDIS CARBONARA

Ten miles up the old railroad grade it occurs to me that I am not a mountain biker. I know this because my overloaded, top-heavy backpack is pushing my neck forward at a ridiculous angle and every other part of my body feels like it's going to explode. That I'm bucking a thirty-knot headwind, it's a hundred degrees, and my water bottle is empty only add to the enjoyment. I'm pretty sure the borrowed bike, clearly designed for a seven-year-old girl, isn't helping, either. My vocabulary has been reduced to a constant stream of four-letter words, not that anyone can hear. The rest of the gang is miles ahead. Probably fishing already. Another string of four-letter words.

Down the slope to my right, shimmering in the heat, flows the blue and incongruously cool waters of the Deschutes River. An oasis in the Sahara, only better, as this oasis holds steelhead. I stand up and start pounding the pedals with renewed vigor. Sweat streams into my eyes and that clanking sound turns out to be my aluminum rod case smashing into the back of my helmet with each strenuous pedal revolution. I knew there was a reason for wearing a helmet.

Suddenly, Corkie and Hazel, Jeff's retriever and heeler duo, are running full tilt up the rocky sidehill to meet me, and when I strain enough to get my chin off my chest and actually look forward, I can see tents set up on a sagebrush flat next to the river. As I coast into camp, I feel as though I've just summited Everest. Without oxygen. On a tricycle. In a hurricane.

The wind is howling now, carrying with it a wide range of small projectiles and an abrasive haze of grit. The crew is not fishing. In fact, they are mostly sitting on the ground in the lee of whatever cover they can find, fiddling with gear. I fall off the hated bike in agony and the weight of the pack drags me backward onto the ground, where I struggle like an overturned turtle, arms and legs flailing. "Don't worry," Molly says looking down at me, "the wind only blows in the afternoons here. It'll settle in the evening."

If anything, the wind picks up steam throughout the day and as darkness falls, really starts to pummel us. A thin, splintered sheet of plywood careens by on the wind. With sudden inspiration, we chase after it and by holding it edge-into-the-gale, manage to drag it back and prop it between trees to make a windbreak.

In the eddy of our makeshift shelter, we boil water for spaghetti and watch with dismay as dozens of big, fat, crunchy October caddis spin out of the breeze and fall into our pasta. There are too many to pick out, so we eat caddis carbonara for dinner in the hurricane. Good to have some protein after the ride in, somebody says.

In the morning, I awake to the sound of flapping, snapping nylon and the keening whistle of air moving rapidly around tent poles. My eyes, nostrils, and mouth are all rimmed with a fine crust of sand, and I understand that we won't be fishing today.

Hours later and the steelhead are still safely beneath the churning, white-capped surface of the river, we're still huddled behind our sheet of plywood, and time has slowed to a crawl.

"You know what I really love about steelhead fishing?" Dave asks.

"Steelhead?"

"The hills look like gorillas," Jeff says to nobody in particular. "You know, in profile."

I look at the surrounding canyon walls. I look harder. I squint through my grit-crusted eyes … and yes, the pale, steeply sloped hillsides take on a vaguely simian countenance, and sure, the short, horizontal lines of dark, exposed basalt make a kind of inscrutable, cartoon-ape sort of brow. Or am I just going insane from the wind?

"Well, at least we have the ride out to look forward to," Molly says. I look at her, searching for even the slightest hint of irony or sarcasm, but just as I suspect, there is none. Her smile is genuine. Optimistic, even.

"Hey," Jeff says, "I think it's letting up. We'll be fishing tonight for sure." Another blast of wind lifts a corner of the nearest tent, pulls the stakes from the rocky ground, and launches it like a giant blue tumbleweed across the desert floor.

APRIL 1992

*Perilously stacked pizza boxes and unpaid bills pile up on
the counter of my small apartment. My once-promising
career has been traded in for winter steelhead on the fly, and
now my brain churns day and night on river levels, rain
forecasts, names of places like Thunderbird, I.R.S., Buck
Island. … Since I moved here last month, I've hooked three
fish in forty days of fishing, including a huge buck that
cleaned me out on Easter Sunday. But I have yet to land
one on my new home river. And now, this morning, I am
running out of time. There's a job interview at 10:00, and
it's an hour drive back to the city. At 8:55, on what has to
be my twenty-fifth "last cast" into a riffle called Two Bit, a
fish smashes the purple marabou and streaks downstream.
I chase it, stumbling, reeling wildly, hands shaking, and blood
pounding in my ears. When the fish finally comes to shore,
I shout in triumph, release it, and without even glancing at
my watch, head back to the top to fish through again.*

WHY CAN'T FLY
FISHERMEN BE WATERMEN?

In Hawaiian surfing tradition, the ideal, the goal, and perhaps the ultimate honor, is to be called a *water*man. Not just a good surfer, but a waterman. This means knowing how to paddle a canoe on the open sea, skin-dive, spearfish. ... It means understanding tides, currents, and wind, and how they affect shellfish collecting, surf conditions, sailing ... in other words, a deep, well-rounded, and personal relationship with the sea.

Sadly, this is not the case in sportfishing circles. We have somehow evolved into separate and divisive religions—Muslims, Jews, and Christians all fighting over the Holy Land of fish. For a fly angler to be caught trolling or cutting bait is equated to sin. Admitting to enjoying a fish dinner now and then is even worse. Fly fishing has somehow become a "clean" activity, one that fastidiously avoids the roots of angling as a blood sport, and before that, a survival strategy. Gear anglers frequently accuse fly fishers of being snobs or elitists, and in many cases, they aren't far off base.

So, I propose a paradigm shift for my fellow fly anglers. Let's all aspire to broaden our horizons and learn more about the waters and fish we love. Either find out or remember how to thread a worm on a hook and feel the excitement of watching a bobber dip and slide under the surface. Toss some jigs in the surf, mooch a herring, or rig a flasher behind downriggers. Dip some smelt, put out the crab or crawdad traps, and by all means, where resources and laws allow, eat what you catch.

Why, you may ask, would we want to do these things if we're already happy with our own little world? There are many reasons. First, in these days when politics and the scramble to preserve teetering fish populations are becoming a reality for all responsible anglers, the sportfishing lobby has been at a great disadvantage. While the commercial fishermen, cattle ranchers, farmers, resource extraction corporations, aquaculture, and timber and development industries each have a single clear mandate (more fish, more water, more latitude for destruction), we have been fragmented by infighting. To understand each other and find the common ground—our passion for fish and the waters they inhabit—is to gather much-needed strength in the political arena.

Beyond that, I think there's also a real issue of ethics and morality involved. Over the last few decades, as the concept of catch and release has gone from a fringe movement to dogma, fly fishermen have laid claim to moral high ground. Believe me, as a longtime practitioner of "letting 'em go," I can see how attractive that high ground is, and fully understand how easy it is to look down on "meat fishermen." The concept of fishing as pure sport, of not eating what you catch, is clearly a necessary management tool in a world of growing human population and shrinking fish habitat. But moral high ground?

For my generation of fly anglers, catch and release has evolved beyond a management tool into something of a sacred mantra. Leaving the fish in the water preserves the resource, making it the right thing to do. Period. But not so fast. In many Native American cultures, the very idea that man would choose to recreate at the expense of another living creature is not just frivolous, it's moral turpitude. That explosive cartwheeling leap? The drag-burning run? Entertainment for you and me, but to the fish, a highly stressful battle for life itself. This isn't a question of whether or not fish feel pain; what I'm talking about is purely on us as anglers. Is catch and release necessary? Absolutely. Is it moral or ethical? When I really think about it, I'm not so sure anymore.

While I have yet to find any easy answers to this dilemma, I understand more clearly than ever that there's also another reason for expanding our horizons as anglers: It's just plain fun. And the last time I checked, that was pretty much the point of going fishing, right? A seasoned, fish-a-day steelheader will find delight in dipping a bucketful of smelt. The hardy striper chaser, in gearing down for winter flounder or pulling a string of crab pots. The 6X-match-the-hatch trout pro, in landing a mess of bluegills. How did I learn this? From my four-year-old daughter, whose pride and delight in catching nearly anything is raised exponentially by the simple act of eating what she's caught.

Now, am I advocating giving up the quest for our so-called glamour species, or eating everything we catch? No. But I am suggesting that we at least take a moment to consider what we're doing, and try spending a little time outside our usual pursuits. As new experiences accumulate, so too will our understanding and appreciation of both our waters and the other people who care about them. From there, a generation of watermen of both genders can rise above the petty infighting and achieve a new level of political power and solidarity. And in the process, we'll have a hell of a lot of fun. See you on the water.

HIDDEN GOLD IN
THE DEEP BLUE SEA

Sarah Gardner squints into the morning light, searching for an opening in the breakers. On the radio, the familiar, monotone robot voice says there's weather coming, a nor'easter that'll blow these shoals up into a nightmare. But for now, a few hours of grace, and somewhere out there, the mother lode. If we can just make it out of the bay and into the ocean.

A brief lull to port reveals a narrow slot of green water surrounded by the chaos of waves breaking over shifting sand banks only inches deep. Captain Sarah turns the wheel and puts the hammer down, jumping onto step and banking hard into a sharp dogleg turn. Here she pauses for a moment amid exploding waves throwing spray higher than her head, then spots the next opening and guns it. Carefully now, she picks her way across the Cape Lookout Shoals, and in minutes, flies out the other side into the wide-open sea.

"We've always known they were here," she says, scanning the surface with predatory intensity, "but finding them consistently is a whole other story." She's talking about redfish, or red drum, as they're known locally. But these aren't the skinny-water puppy drum or marsh cruisers. These are monsters. Fifty- and sixty-pounders. Big enough to pull like a Peterbilt. Big enough to break records. Big enough to put a little fear into you. The true giants here are fish of the open ocean—spooky, elusive, unpredictable. And big.

"Finding them was just the beginning," she continues. "Then we had to figure out how to get close without spooking them, and then we realized we needed new flies and new lines. Oh,

and the weather's always an issue. And crossing the shoals …"
Nobody said developing an entirely new fishery would be easy.

A fifty-pound fish with a tail the size of a broom swims fast
even when lazily cruising along. These fish move. So you need
industrial-strength flies and lines that get down quick. And you
need to be ready to cast to them on short notice. From a moving
boat. In the wind. One shot, and then they're gone. That's the
not-so-relaxing news Captain Sarah lays out before we've even
started fishing.

How do you find something hidden beneath the surface of
a huge, featureless ocean? For starters, it isn't featureless to the
practiced eye. Sarah climbs up on top of the console, steering
with her foot, staring holes into the sea from her precarious perch,
looking for impossibly subtle signs—a slight change in surface
texture, a black-backed gull or two, the brief flash of a leaping
spinner shark—somewhere out there in the infinite expanse.

An hour passes. And another. The wind shifts under darkening skies and the soft, easy swells grow sharper with building
chop. Weather's coming. But on the new breeze, a faint scent,
something unexpected yet vaguely familiar … cucumbers,
maybe. Or watermelon. "Do you smell that?" Sarah calls down
from the console. "That's bait being eaten by reds."

With a quick, calculating glance back at the shoals, she
scrambles down from the console, turns the bow into the wind,
and follows her nose. Up ahead, two large birds, starkly white
against the charcoal sky, wheel around and dive. Gannets.
Redfish birds. "Get ready," she says, throttling down smoothly
in the building seas.

Behind us, surf crashes against the shoals, driving shards of
foam into the air. Time is short. As we coast into range of the
birds, the water around us flattens in a glassy slick, and beyond

that, endless rows of whitecaps stretch to the horizon. A glint of gold flashes through the waves and suddenly, there they are—a field of enormous copper submarines moving silently forward. Bigger than you can imagine. Big enough to put a little fear into you.

"One shot," Captain Sarah yells over the wind. "Get ready … get ready … OK … Now!"

warming, with its changing weather patterns, shrinking glaciers, catastrophic flood events, and higher summertime stream temperatures. Is it any wonder our fish are in trouble?

To quote Bill Murray in *Stripes*, "and then ... depression set in." I know, the numbers are staggering. The causes, seemingly insurmountable. The outlook, bleak. But there are reasons for hope, first and foremost of which is that wild steelhead are incredibly tough, resilient fish. As the glaciers retreated thousands of years ago, steelhead spread out, adapted, and colonized a wide range of disparate environments from high-desert sage country to coastal rainforest, from winding tundra streams to broad valley rivers. When Mount Saint Helens erupted in 1980, sending a boiling mass of superheated ash down the Toutle River, for all intents and purposes, the river as we knew it ceased to exist. To see it shortly after this catastrophic event was to witness a thin trickle of water winding through a wasteland of broken stumps and volcanic mud. And yet, within a few short years, the wild steelhead were back, recolonizing and adapting to their harsh new environment. As Dr. Nathan Mantua says, "If we just give them half a chance, the fish will respond."

So how do we give them that half a chance? Just as the threats to wild steelhead survival exist on every level, so too do the possible solutions. On a broad scale, since our governments seem to respond best to money, we need to remind the people we've entrusted with the management of our fish about the financial benefits of healthy runs and the resulting tourist and sportfishing dollars. We need to fight hidden subsidies and government sanctioning of resource extraction industries. We need to vote, petition, and write letters. Does it work? Absolutely. Just look at the ban on open-water salmon farms for the north coast of British Columbia mentioned earlier. After years of hard work

AUGUST 1995

*For days now, I've been waiting for the big silvers to come
in from Bristol Bay. It's my week off at the lodge where I'm
guiding, and my dad has come on a once-in-a-lifetime trip
to visit and fish with me. That the silvers are not cooperating
matters little to him, but I feel an urgent need for everything
to be perfect. Day after day we chase the tides across the
river's broad estuary flats, searching, but finding only pink
and chum salmon. Then, tonight, on the way back in, with
rain blowing sideways and darkness falling, I see a fish roll
out of the corner of my eye. Probably just more pinks. But
I veer over, cut the motor, and drop anchor. The sudden quiet
echoes across endless open tundra. We crouch together on
the bow, watching. A dorsal fin silently creases the rain-
pocked surface. Then another. And another. Silvers. Standing
at my dad's shoulder, filled with anticipation, I whisper,
"Go ahead."*

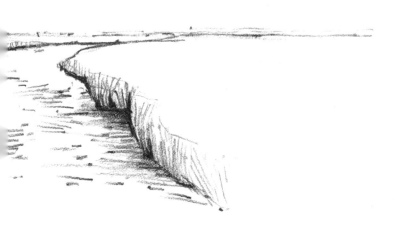

THE HIGH COST
OF KOLA CHROME

"You can rappel, right?" Gordon's static-obscured voice crackles from the camp radio in broken snippets. Between his Scottish burr and electronic interference, I have no idea what he's saying.

"What's that?" I shout into the receiver.

"Rappel ... like rock climbing ..." Static. "... not a bad hike, but there is one vertical face ... you'll have to rope up for ... doable, though."

"Have you done it?" I ask.

"What? ... no, no ... but I look at it all the time from the helicopter."

I have no reply.

"Just start walking downstream after dinner," he says. More static. "... meet you below the waterfalls about four in the morning ... don't fish till I get there ... and stay out of sight."

"What?"

"... stay out of sight or ... the patrol guy will shoot you."

"I don't know, Gordon. ..."

"Listen, lad ... do you want to fish for salmon or not? Just don't forget the rope."

The radio goes silent. Conversation over. Guess I'm going rock climbing. I mean, how hard can it be? I've seen plenty of people—some who clearly look dumber than me—descending vertical rock walls with ropes. I can figure it out. Right?

I scramble around camp throwing everything I can think of into my pack: waders, boots, extra reel, about thirty-five feet of marginal-looking rope that until this moment was bracing the cook tent—who's going to miss that?—against the wind. It looks marginal enough that I consider how much weight a fly line might support, and the merits of braiding three together. When I start strapping a heavy Spey rod onto my pack, the full stoke hits me: *I'm going salmon fishing.*

At dinner, I'm too jacked (or freaked) to eat, my imagination alternating between images of flashing, silver-sided Atlantic salmon and me sliding down a precipitous cliff, alone in the remote Russian Arctic. At night. With tent rope. I'm finally choking down soup when the cook comes out and says, "Gordon call again. Tomorrow no good. You stay here." It's off. A gut-punch of disappointment, but somewhere in there, I admit, a little relief creeps in as well.

I resign myself to one more final day of trout fishing and head for my pup tent to get a head start on dreading the long trip home.

• • •

What kind of jerk resigns himself to one more day fishing in what is, by all measures, a trout paradise? Me. I'm just going to say it: I am not a trout fisherman. There's too much small stuff involved, too many details, and to be honest, it's too hard. While I often enjoy trout fishing at home, my lack of success with it serves as a regular reminder that I am a steelhead guy. Have been my whole life. And somewhere in the heart of every steelheader lies a deep craving for only one other fish: Atlantic salmon. *That's* why I signed up for this exploratory trout expedition—the long-shot, I-know-a-guy-who-knows-a-guy chance that I might somehow, once I was here, weasel my way into fishing the famous salmon water. I wanted a salmon so bad, I would have endured almost anything to catch one. Which is pretty much what I did. Sure, I came to Russia on a trout expedition, but I did not come here to go trout fishing.

. . .

After thirty-five hours of planes and airports, six mildly toxic airport restaurant meals, and zero hours of sleep, I somehow arrived in Murmansk, Russia, by way of New York City, Paris, Amsterdam, and Stockholm. There are surely easier ways to get there, I just didn't find any of them. Instead, I settled for the red-eye, jet-lag express that left me with a pounding headache and the distinct taste of sweaty socks in my mouth.

At the Murmansk airport, I joined a couple of equally bedraggled, shabby-looking fish bums who were actually looking forward to the trout fishing. We then boarded one of several buses already occupied by dozens of tweed and waxed-cotton types on their way to the high-rent salmon camps. They looked extraordinarily well rested, fed, and relaxed, the obvious perks of owning your own jet.

I should point out here that the company sponsoring our exploratory trout expedition to the Russian Arctic is well known for what many consider the finest salmon camps in the world. One of these camps happens to be located a long hike, and short rappel, from where our trout camp was based. Though we traveled distinctly different paths to reach the Kola Peninsula, trout and salmon anglers alike would be sharing transportation from here on out.

On the three-hour, kidney-busting, dirt-road bus ride across barren tundra to the heliport, I ignored my trout brothers and sat with the *Lifestyles of the Rich and Famous* crowd, hoping to vicariously live their salmon experiences or maybe pick up some insider-trading tips. Also, in my travel-addled brain, I had this insane fantasy that one of them would take pity on me and invite me to go salmon fishing. My seatmate, a distinguished injection-molded-plastic magnate from London, regaled me with stories of fifty-pound salmon coming to the fly on this river, and cited incredible numbers of fish landed per day. "It's the greatest salmon river in the world … assuming, of course, you like extremely large, ocean-bright fish and lots of them. Absolutely tip-top, old chap." He actually said "old chap." But I was going trout fishing. I felt a sudden urge to throw up on his Harris Tweed.

We waited at the makeshift heliport, a deteriorating Soviet navy communications installation that had once been so top secret, it never appeared on any maps. A cold, gray fog settled over the enormous field of antenna wires. The kind of fog you might think helicopters would have a tough time flying in. Five hours of alternately sitting on the bus, jumping up and down to keep warm, and looking at my watch passed before anyone confirmed what we already knew: No flying today. Instead, we would ride the Incredible Springless Wonder back to Murmansk, losing, at least in the salmon crowd's case, nearly two grand's worth of fishing, to spend the night in a crumbling, potentially radioactive city. Mysteriously, a cheer went up from the crowd.

• • •

Beneath a malevolent brown sky and the decomposing architecture of a city best known for its sunken and leaking Soviet nuclear submarine fleet, we arrived at "the best hotel in town." The once-grand structure was now smog stained and tattered, The Plaza after forty years of atomic winter. Was this all that remained of the Evil Empire? The godless commie threat that once sent us scurrying beneath our desks in grade-school bomb drills and fueled my childhood nightmares? Outside, vendors hawking bootleg Madonna CDs and cheap T-shirts watched us unload with wolfish grins.

We checked in and I went up to my room, which featured, among other things, walls so close together I could touch my fingertips to both sides, and a bed designed for your average four-year-old, covered by a blanket that was surely made from my high-school prom date's blue taffeta dress. I was bummed beyond belief: wiped, depressed, jet-lagged, sleep-deprived, dehydrated, disoriented, hungry, exhausted, and beat. I think that about covers it.

From down the hall, the global glitterati were checking into their rooms and I could hear more hooting, hollering, and general good cheer than you'd get from a third-grade field trip to Disneyland. They were not bummed in the least. Where was the disappointment at missing a day of peak-season fishing on the greatest salmon river in the world? What about the dismal rooms and micro-beds? I mean, this was a crowd that normally calls the concierge about a speck of lint on the Egyptian cotton at The Ritz.

Hunger overcame exhaustion and I staggered downstairs looking to score some grub. In the lobby, a small kiosk advertising money exchange and a wide selection of made-in-Taiwan Russian nesting dolls had drawn a crowd. In fact, a great number of my fellow anglers were standing two abreast in a line that snaked across the room. Thinking it was some kind of dinner reservation deal, I headed for the back of the line when a booming voice called out to me: "Son, get right on over here. Come on now!"

If John Wayne and Foghorn Leghorn had a baby, and that baby grew up to be a wealthy, salmon-addicted oil baron, the gentleman calling out to me is pretty much what you'd get. The Texan. I had stood next to him at the heliport and wondered aloud how he'd traveled so far without crushing his crisp, ten-gallon Stetson. He'd said flying private had its benefits. He had also espoused a general distaste for all things trout, and I hadn't had the heart to tell him why I was here. To him, we were kindred Americans among the Eurotrash elite, joined in our nationality and love of what he referred to as "salmons."

And now he was looking out for his fellow American. Who was I to refuse a little help and patriotic good will? I cut in line to join him, and in the crowd's buoyant glee and general frat-house atmosphere, nobody said a word. As we drew closer to the kiosk window, it became apparent that people weren't making dinner reservations. Or changing money. Or buying nesting dolls. But I couldn't tell what exactly they were doing. When it was my turn, the stocky, middle-aged woman behind the counter said, "How many?"

"Uh ... how many what?"

"How many you want?" she yelled.

"Uh ... what are we talking about here?"

"Blue pill!" she shouted with derision, opening her fist to reveal a handful of grubby, pale-blue tablets. Viagra?

• • •

I quickly came to the conclusion that blue pills were the last thing I needed. I retreated to my room, collapsed onto the minuscule bed with my feet dangling over the end, and tried not to slide off the royal-blue satin. Maybe I was a little slow on the uptake, but I hadn't yet figured out what was going on. I blame jet lag.

As I settled in for the night, I discovered another amazing feature of my hotel room: It was uniquely situated to take full advantage of the booming disco immediately below and a bowling alley, of all things, on the floor above. Nothing like throbbing, full-Dolby, stereophonic surround sound, techno dance, and rumbling bowling balls punctuated by the occasional ten-pin strike to encourage sleep. A frantic search through my gear for another Ambien or twenty was interrupted by a knock at the door.

A tough-looking, thick-necked man I recognized as the bell captain—all Pat Riley hair, two-day stubble, and bad teeth—stood in the hall. "I have girl for you," he stated. Three equally tough-looking women stepped into the doorway behind him and suddenly, it all made sense. Ah-frickin'-ha! Based on shape, dental structure, and facial hair, I was pretty sure the women were somehow related to the bell captain, although it was difficult to tell what relation, exactly, that might be.

"Um ... no thanks," I said. He didn't move.

"I have girl for you," he repeated.

"Right, yeah, I see that, but ... um, I'm kind of, er ... busy tonight." Brilliant. He didn't move again. I handed him a ten-spot. No reaction. I handed him a twenty and he finally stepped back into the hall, grumbling and glowering. I shut the door in relief.

The night passed at an excruciatingly slow pace as I drifted in and out of consciousness, chased in fitful dreams by leering cowboys and my high-school prom date, all to the rhythm of disco and bowling. Through the haze, I seem to recall hearing a synthesizer version of *Hotel California*. Or maybe that was my prom dream? The midnight sun blazed through curtains and eyelids alike, further illuminating my misery. The bell captain returned on several occasions, banging on the door and promising, "I have different girl for you," and each time I saw they were the same girls in different outfits, looking gradually more disheveled as the night wore on. I vaguely wondered how they were passing the time between trips to my door, then quickly tried to push such thoughts from my mind.

In the morning, we were treated to a gourmet breakfast featuring poached salmon, which was broiled, and baloney sandwiches. It took three gulps from a large glass of water before I realized it was, in fact, straight vodka. I gratefully drained the rest without pause.

. . .

The helicopter, when it finally arrived, was a little more frayed around the edges than you'd probably want to see. In fact, it didn't appear to have been serviced, repaired, or even washed since its days fighting mujahideen guerrillas out of Kabul. Bullet holes, dangling wires, and a thick coating of soot were the most outstanding features, but Harris Tweed, fresh from his blue-pill and vodka-fueled "night fishing" expedition, was in good cheer. As we boarded the decrepit Soviet warbird, ducking under more wires and reaching for the rack of earmuffs, he clapped me on the shoulder, winked, and said, "Oh, she's a good one alright." I wasn't quite sure what he was referring to.

After a flight of some undetermined duration—between my vodka Big Gulp breakfast and a major dose of heli-fear, who could keep track of time?—we circled low over a broad, rocky stretch of tea-stained river and set down in front of a luxurious compound. A stunning young blonde woman opened the door from the outside and welcomed us in beautifully accented English. Flags fluttered in the breeze atop each tidy, immaculately kept cabin, and as I peered through the porthole, I could see large salmon porpoising in the home pool. Sweet! I grabbed my gear and headed for the exit.

At the door, the copilot put a hairy hand on my chest. "You stay," he said, "this is salmon camp." I stumbled toward my seat on the now-empty bench, and the Texan glanced back at me with

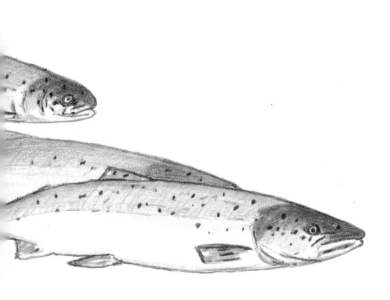

raised eyebrows. I shrugged sheepishly and mouthed the word *trout* under the roar of revving turbines. He shot me a look of pure disgust.

Fifteen minutes later the chopper set down again on another rock outcropping along the same tea-stained river, in front of seven tiny pup tents, a yurt, and a picnic table made of driftwood. No flags. No pretty girls. No porpoising fish. The falls below us were heavy. enough to block any migrating salmon and preserve this stretch of water as effectively trout only.

· · ·

The primary objective of this trip, from our host's perspective, was to verify rumors of mammoth brown trout in the upper reaches of the Kola Peninsula's famed salmon rivers. If we found good fishing, they could expand operations beyond the salmon lodges and start catering to trout anglers as well. But from my perspective, as mentioned earlier, the only objective of the trip was to somehow poach the salmon water. Period.

On our second night in Trout Land, Gordon, the mild-mannered, seemingly all-around nice guy who manages the salmon camp, choppered up to check on us. In real life, he's a tough-as-nails, Scottish-born policeman commanding a tactical peacekeeping force in Northern Ireland, but you'd never know it. Here in Russia, moonlighting on his summer vacation, Gordon's only mission was making sure the salmon anglers were happy, and we trout fishermen were, well … alive. Thus, the visit. Or maybe he just felt like slumming?

He arrived at dinnertime—but didn't eat anything, I noticed—and at one point, he covertly pulled me aside and whispered, "Listen, I got the call from our friend—I know what you want. I'm going to try to make it happen, but it won't be easy. Just be ready." OK, Tony Soprano. Then he jumped into his helicopter and zoomed off, back to the coveted salmon water and a plateful of caviar, no doubt. My hopes soared.

But for the next six days, I suffered through what was apparently trout-fishing nirvana. We spread out in smaller yet equally battle-scarred helicopters and flailed away at various headwater streams, spring creeks, and alpine lakes. The trout guys were ecstatic. Big, and I have to admit, beautiful, trout came to hand nearly everywhere we tried. Midges, hoppers, Hare's Ears, Humpies, mice, and Woolly Buggers were all deployed with deadly effect. And just as the trout were consuming our flies with reckless abandon, the mosquitoes were doing the same to us humans on an epic scale. I mean epic. As in seeing more bugs than skin on the back of your hand and actually getting worried about blood loss. But the trout fishing was good. I guess.

We hiked, tramped, and busted brush through some of the most breathtaking landscapes imaginable, from the granite and ice of high-altitude tributaries to gorgeous, spooky birch thickets and sedge-lined springs. Only I was so tormented by the salmon jones, I could barely bring myself to notice anything at all, let alone enjoy it. The phrase "so close and yet so far" stuck in my brain like a bad advertising jingle.

Oh, I matched the hatch, dead-drifted, and hopper-and-droppered my way through the days. A couple of times I even caught myself almost having fun. But I came to dread the evening radio reports from salmon camp. Each night it was "(insert film producer's name here) got one seventeen kilos at The Falls," and "(insert famous author's name here) had eleven fish to fifteen kilos." Based on what we were hearing, I was not only within rifle shot of the greatest salmon river in the world, but had somehow arrived in the middle of the greatest run ever. Meanwhile, my fellow trout guys were toasting five-pounders and tying microscopic caddis patterns for the next day. Not me. I was plotting, scheming, coveting, and when nobody was looking, tying Green Highlanders.

• • •

Morning of our last day. I have survived the previous night's crushing, ready-to-rappel, almost-but-not-quite salmon fishing letdown by telling myself that at least after today, I can return home and let go of this frantic salmon obsession. I just have to make it through one more day with grace and enthusiasm, and nobody will ever know the difference. I can do it. Really.

I'm climbing into the chopper with four-weight in hand and smile forcibly implanted on my face when the same copilot who stopped me from disembarking at the salmon camp again plants his hairy hand on my chest. "You stay," he says. What? Have they discovered what an ungrateful dick I am? That I'm an imposter in trout gear? "You go salmon fishing. Wait for Gordon here." Unbelievable. It's on.

Gordon lands minutes later in his helicopter, and having joyfully dumped all my trout stuff in a pile and re-geared, I climb aboard with Valentin, one of the guides on loan from the salmon camp. What he'd done to be banished to a week of exploratory trout fishing, I never found out, but Valentin is nearly as happy as I am to be headed downstream.

As we lift off, Gordon furtively elbows the pilot in the ribs and smirks, then they both laugh—seemingly in my direction. It suddenly occurs to me that maybe this had been the plan all along. Was I really ever expected to hike and climb my way to the salmon water? Or was I the gullible, salmon-obsessed chump in Gordon's version of a snipe hunt? But that's cool. This chump is going salmon fishing, and not much else matters anymore. Over the hammering rotors and shrieking engines, Gordon yells into my ear, "We're going to fish The Falls. But I had to tell the paying clients you're a famous photographer doing a big photo shoot for Patagonia. Play the part."

After a short flight, the helicopter banks hard enough that by looking out the side window, I can now see straight down into the river. Here, the open tundra appears to have simply sheared off and fallen, forcing the broad river into a narrow, precipitous canyon waterfall—the salmon blocker. Immediately below the falls, a deep tank of a pool flows between steep rock walls, and the smooth surface is broken by hundreds, if not thousands, of boiling, waking, leaping salmon. Oh. My. God.

Valentin points excitedly at the river. "*Samga!*" he says. Salmon.

Gordon points excitedly at three people on the rocks. "Paying clients!" he says. "Be cool."

As the helicopter settles and powers down, the three people approach, waving, and I throw the door open, jump out, and start shooting pictures in a crouching run like some Vietnam-era combat photojournalist. I am the famous photographer. In retrospect, it probably would have been slightly more convincing had I not been using a disposable cardboard point-and-shoot, but hey, you gotta work with what you have.

The paying clients—a distinguished, silver-haired, English husband-and-wife team, fully outfitted in matching Barbour waxed cotton and wellies—are impressed. Their guide is too. I can tell. They have interrupted their riverside tea service to welcome us.

I reel off a few more shots. The woman eyes my camera suspiciously (or maybe that's just my paranoia?) and says, "You must be the photographer from Patagonia. How lovely to meet you."

"Yep, big photo shoot." I say. She looks at me closely.

"I must ask you …" uh-oh, my cover's blown for sure, "… in what part of Patagonia do you live?"

I mumble something about the "southern part" in relief and try to restrain myself from running to the river. The couple and their guide return to their tea.

Gordon says we don't have much time, the paying clients will want to fish their water again soon. He also says this is the best pool on the river, and he'll go fish some "lesser water" while I have at it. Valentin says there is no way down to the river's edge, that we will fish it from the cliff top—about twenty feet above the water. The entire run of fish is stacked up here, waiting for the flows to drop enough so they can make it over the falls. For now, they are trapped. The proverbial fish in a barrel. It's so unfair, it would be illegal to fish a hole like this at home. I am about to crush.

Not. With shaking hands and adrenaline pounding through my heart, I make my first cast. The line settles, and at Valentin's urging, I make a downstream mend and feel it start to swing. I can't see the tiny Green Highlander, but back about where I imagine it is, three large gray shapes materialize and follow the arc of my line. I tense for the big pull, but it never comes. I try a faster swing. More torpedoes chasing and still no grabs. I try slower. I retrieve the fly in short strips. I cast more upstream, then down. Switch flies. Switch again. And eventually, the fish lose interest and ignore my presentations completely.

The clock ticks in my head, measuring the little time I have slipping away. I feel the eyes of the paying clients on my back, and track, by feel, a bead of sweat dripping down the side of my face.

From the "lesser water" below, I hear Gordon's voice echo over the roar of the falls, "There's another fish!" He is obscured by a rock outcropping, but a big silver salmon jumps and sunlight glints off a tight fly line. OK, I see how this works. Chumped again.

Now what? Valentin looks nervously over his shoulder at the paying clients. They're still drinking tea and eating watercress sandwiches. He looks upstream and down like a man contemplating a mad dash across eight lanes of superhighway, clearly weighing the situation and potential consequences. "OK," he says, "we try one more place."

We hike downstream to a fast tailout funneling into a steep, glassy chute on the far side. Halfway across the river, a rock stands clear of the surface, which Valentin points to, indicating we have to wade out there to fish. We start to cross and the force of the current about folds me over at the knees. I hear my studs scraping downstream over slick bedrock. Valentin grabs my arm, and in a semi-bear hug, we stagger to the rock.

The chute does not look like a spot. For whitewater kayaking, sure, but for fish? Not so much. I cast across and steelhead instinct takes over—I immediately make a huge upstream mend in a futile attempt to slow the fly, but the current bellies the line and whips the fly around anyway. "Faster," Valentin says, "downstream mend." I'm incredulous. "No way," I mutter under my breath. In his deep Slavic accent, Valentin replies, "Way."

I do as I'm told. The small fly careens across the current, skips to the surface, and a large V-wake appears behind it. And another. And then three more. All tracking the fly at closing speed. When my line reaches maximum velocity, the lead wake accelerates and takes with a ferocious back-out-of-the-water strike. Then the fish is in the air, a twisting bolt of silver and black. A second later, it's airborne again. Fish, fly line, and backing streak upstream at a furious rate and, in a remarkable display of angling prowess, I react by promptly slipping off the rock and plunging sideways into the heavy current. Valentin grabs the hood of my jacket, hauls me back up, and miraculously, the fish is still on.

Three more runs of shortening duration and when the fish swims past our rock, Valentin puts it in the net. I lean over to remove the hook and icy water streams out of my waders and vest pockets, but I hardly notice the chill. I lift the fish and elation washes over us. I look at the gorgeous, almost-translucent silver sides and sharply defined, black X-shaped spots, and then it's gone. Valentin and I do a little dance on the rock and he shouts, "We did it! We did it!"

Before Valentin even has the net rinsed, I'm already making my downstream mend. Again, multiple fish pursue the fly and one hammers it. And again, before the net is rinsed, I have yet another one on. Time warps. But gradually, reality encroaches. While I fight my fifth fish, a big buck that runs downstream into the churning whitewater, I see a man dressed in black commando gear with an AK-47 slung over his shoulder watching from the far bank. "Anti-poaching patrol," Valentin says quietly. Fortunately, I'm not a poacher. Oh, wait a minute … I glance behind us and see the English couple staring daggers at me as well. "Paying clients," Valentin says. It's time to go.

• • •

Somewhere over the Atlantic, sandwiched between a three hundred-pound Iowa corn farmer plotting an international get-rich-quick biofuel scheme and a globetrotting trustafarian who clearly considers showering a fashion don't, I finally have time to reflect on my experience. Could I come home and work really, really hard to eventually amass the necessary wealth for a totally legit salmon trip of my own? Doubtful. But was it worth it? Would I endure it all again for three hours of truly phenomenal salmon fishing? Probably not. But make it four and I'm booking a ticket tomorrow. After all, there's still plenty of trout water that needs to be explored in the Russian Arctic. ...

Meanwhile, in Belfast, a cop with a Scottish accent sits in a pub, laughing his ass off every time he tells the story. "Tent rope!" he roars over and over again with tears streaming down his face. "Tent rope!" Bastard.

JANUARY 1998

It's too early, really, to expect a wild steelhead on the Sauk River, but I'm eager to show Mike, my steelhead fly-fishing mentor, how much I've learned since we last fished together. "OK, I'll follow you and watch," he says. I step into the gray-green glacial waters, making long casts and compound mends in the tricky current, showing off. I glance upstream with pride, only to see Mike silently playing a fish from the very spot I just covered. When the brilliant bright female is released, we resume fishing, and minutes later, I glance upstream to see him hook another one, again, from water I just fished. Or thought I'd fished. As I reel up to watch the fight, I can feel my brain starting to melt. Another gorgeous female, even brighter than the first. "Mike," I say, "you might as well just fish through, I'll follow you and watch." "Nah," he says, "You keep fishing first." "Why?" I ask. "Because it's so much more satisfying to catch fish behind you."

TROUBLE IN PARADISE

The dream is always the same. Mist clings to steep, heavily forested slopes descending to the music of moving water. The river runs a slightly milky, emerald green with glacial tint, choppy over cobbled bottom, then glides downward, smoothly heeding the pull of gravity. Somewhere out there, moving invisibly against the flow like chrome ghosts, swim steelhead.

This is the mighty Hoh River, crown jewel of the Olympic Peninsula, a dream for all who feel the jones of wild fish and the swung fly. And while many consider the OP the last stronghold of healthy wild steelhead in the Lower 48, there is trouble brewing here. Even the pristine Hoh, its headwaters fully protected by Olympic National Park, is hanging by a thread. In fact, wild Hoh River winter-steelhead runs have fallen below escapement goals—the management target for minimum number of spawners required to sustain the population—in four of the last seven years.

In 2009, the incredibly productive "steelhead factory" of the Quillayute system, made up of the Sol Duc, Bogachiel, Calawah, and Dickey Rivers, was 20 percent below its wild winter-steelhead escapement goal. Wild summer steelhead in this watershed, as well as those of the Quinault, are teetering on the brink of extinction, with frequently fewer than fifty fish returning to each stream. The fish we love are no longer swimming upstream—they're circling the drain.

How can this be, in a remote and lightly populated region, with no dams, urban development, suburban sprawl, major industrial facilities, or agricultural water issues?

The problems start with an arrogant notion that we humans can somehow do better than Mother Nature. Despite the best available science clearly demonstrating the negative impact hatchery fish have on wild steelhead populations, state and federal agencies continue to spend millions of dollars on hatchery production here. This is potentially the lowest return on investment of any state expenditure—the fish come back in abysmally low numbers, they race to the hatcheries en masse, provide little sportfishing value in the rivers, and have a devastating impact on wild steelhead.

The harmful effects of hatchery fish occur at nearly every stage of life. The mass migration of hatchery steelhead smolts outcompetes wild fish for available resources, and as we are learning with the current IHN virus outbreak, they may also be vectors for harmful pathogens. After decades of nonselective fisheries targeting hatchery adults, the early December–January component of the wild steelhead runs have been decimated as bycatch. Even worse, unharvested adult hatchery fish interbreed with the remaining wild steelhead, introducing faulty genes and weakening the population. The study by NOAA scientists on the Oregon coast only confirms what we already knew: genetic pollution from hatchery programs is the primary cause of declining wild steelhead runs.

And remember, we—the taxpaying citizens—are paying for these results. Hard to believe at a time when severely reduced state budgets are forcing school closures and drastic cutbacks on critical services across the board.

Why do we continue to waste money on hatcheries? Harvest. Which, on the OP, occurs in two different forms: sport and tribal. For sport anglers, hatchery fish provide a guilt-free—at least compared to bonking a wild fish on the head—opportunity to kill steelhead. And that's pretty much it. These small, identically shaped "brats" or "cookie cutters," as they're derisively known, quickly ascend area rivers for a few weeks each December, where they famously ignore anything other than bait, and fight very little.

In contrast, wild fish—honed to perfection in the exacting crucible of evolution—return over a period of six to eight months, attain great size and vitality, aggressively chase a variety of lures and flies, and cost taxpayers nothing. But a small group of OP guides and businesspeople—at one time led by the former mayor of Forks—citing "economic hardship" and "loss of tourism dollars," has managed to stop any kind of hatchery reform or statewide wild steelhead–release laws. As of 2010, despite dangerously declining numbers, it is still legal to kill wild steelhead on several Olympic Peninsula rivers.

I wonder what kind of economic hardship they'll experience when there are no steelhead left at all? In contrast, the Skeena watershed in British Columbia has a healthy, hatchery-free sport fishery with mandatory wild steelhead release, which brings more than $50 million a year to the local economy. Think of what that kind of money could do for little old Forks, Washington.

While the sport angling community may find itself divided over these issues, tribal harvest is even more complex. Here, the state of Washington's relationship with individual, sovereign nations exists within the context of the Boldt Decision, which, in part, says that tribes are entitled to 50 percent of the harvestable number of fish. As you might guess, even negotiating how to define "harvestable number" in any given year is difficult, to say the least.

Further complicating the issue is a legal concept known as "foregone opportunity," which means that if one party decides to pass on harvesting their share—say, for conservation purposes—the other party is allowed to claim it. I can't think of a better recipe for hard feelings and a gold-rush-style, "gotta get mine" attitude.

These conditions have, predictably, created years of finger pointing and distrust between sport anglers and tribal nations. Hardly an environment conducive to solving the steelhead crisis. But we have to get beyond this. There's simply no other choice left. And if we can somehow find new ways within the Boldt construct to work together for a common good, I believe we can save our wild steelhead, and more.

Many American anglers, given the fractured politics and infighting to which they've grown accustomed, are surprised to find that the most important steelhead-conservation victories in British Columbia have been achieved through united efforts from all fish-user groups: the ban on North Coast British Columbia fish farms; Royal Dutch Shell's hiatus on coalbed methane extraction in the Sacred Headwaters; stopping logging in the Kitlope watershed; the successful protest of the Enbridge Pipeline. These battles were led by First Nations with support from sport and even commercial anglers. Amazing what can be accomplished when we all work together.

How do we get there on the Olympic Peninsula? I feel confident either scientific proof or pure economics—and taxpayer outrage—can eventually take care of the hatcheries. For sport harvest, we need to clean our own house before we can effectively negotiate with other user groups, which is to say, recreational anglers need to stop killing wild steelhead. And with tribal harvest, I am hopeful that the urgency of our current situation can force us to build a more cooperative, mutually beneficial relationship. I know none of this will be easy, that it will involve sacrifice by everyone, that it requires radical shifts in how we all think. But I believe we can do it. Am I dreaming? Maybe. But then, I've been dreaming of rivers filled with steelhead my whole life.

Postscript 2022

Since this story was published, the downward spiral of wild steelhead on the Olympic Peninsula has continued. While these fish are portrayed in an increasingly glamorous light by many anglers around the world, the current situation is not so bright. In the 2020–21 winter season, preseason forecasts predicted every river system on the entire Washington coast would either barely meet or fall below minimum escapement goals. The lone standout, the Quillayute system, which features the only river that isn't planted with hatchery steelhead, was projected to come in at nearly twice the escapement goal. Citizens can draw their own conclusions here, but the fact that the only river with anything close to a healthy wild steelhead population is also the only river without hatchery fish seems to make the case pretty clearly.

There's also been some incremental progress made to protect wild fish here: In 2015, after years of acrimony, recreational harvest of wild steelhead was finally closed on the Olympic Peninsula. The catastrophically low returns during the 2020–21 season resulted in a coastwide ban on fishing from boats—statistics show that boat anglers catch five times as many fish as bank fishermen—and eventually forced the state to make emergency closures on all but two major OP river systems. At the same time, tribal fisheries voluntarily reduced their harvest to minimal levels.

While these small signs of concern and the resulting cooperation are encouraging, they are also what Amy Cordalis of

Northern California's Yurok Tribe refers to as "putting Band-Aids on a gaping wound." To truly recover harvestable numbers of wild salmon and steelhead, we need to finally address and accept the fact that hatcheries may be the limiting factor that's preventing healthy wild fish populations on the Olympic Peninsula.

WRATH

The aerodynamics of a nine-foot graphite fly rod, when launched reel-first into the sky, bear a striking resemblance to those of an Exocet surface-to-surface missile. Which is to say, it can, with seemingly very little effort, travel well beyond recovery range. How do I know this? Let's just say such knowledge isn't easy to come by, and it might have had something to do with the fish of a lifetime and a seen-but-disregarded wind knot. Turns out, all that aerospace-grade aluminum and carbon fiber used in modern fishing equipment works pretty well for flight, too.

Pissed. Torqued. Sideways. Ballistic. Apeshit. The Red Ass. Full Tasmanian. Call it what you want, but close examination of river rage reveals two important truths: One, a fury-fueled meltdown rarely increases angling productivity, and two, for 100 percent of observers—discounting those related by blood or marriage who may feel embarrassment—it will be hilarious. I don't care who you are, if you blow a gasket and shatter that $700 fly rod over your knee in frustration, it's freakin' funny.

Someone once said 90 percent of all humor is based on other people's misfortune. I can't disagree.

Sources: Lost fish, as noted above. Arriving streamside to discover some key piece of equipment is sitting by the door at home "so you won't forget it." Being impaled by a hook cast by someone other than yourself. Being impaled by a hook cast by you. Driving off with your treasured (and irreplaceable) Bogdan reel on top of the car. Getting low-holed just as you reach the Bucket. ...

Of course, this list is purely hypothetical and has no relation to any direct, personal experience. But it should be noted that the effects of the listed events are maximized when more than one occur in rapid succession. Call it the Law of Compounding Aggravations, wherein the likelihood of a normally calm, peaceful angler transforming into a frothing, demented tornado of anger rises exponentially as a factor of number, frequency, and elapsed time between incidents.

For example, let's say—again, purely hypothetically—our hero has driven for two hours to reach a river at the peak of the salmon fly hatch. By some miracle, he hits it perfectly. Huge bugs spatter his windshield as he closes in on his honey hole. Unloading the trunk, he discovers he's forgotten his wading boots. Bummer. But no problem, he'll just slip and slide a bit in his sneakers. All quiet on the Western Front.

As he fishes down toward the sweet spot, he's distracted from the feeding frenzy by movement in the brush downstream. He watches in dismay as another angler steps into the river immediately below him. "Hey douchebag!" he yells. But the Low-Holer gives him the side-of-the-face and starts casting. Our hero's blood pressure rises. But … no problem. He's too stoked to let it get to him—an epic day is at hand, and he'll just slip and slide down to the next run.

In the hole below, our intrepid angler focuses on an enormous trout systematically destroying big stoneflies in the near seam. As he wades into position, that tenuous skein of traction between rock and sneaker sole gives way to algae, resulting in a momentary wild flailing of arms and legs, followed by the *thunk* of elbow, shoulder blade, and back of the head meeting cobble. Water pours into waders as pain registers and a scream is stifled. A certain pounding in the ears occurs, unrelated to injury or soaking. Our hero glances around to make sure nobody witnessed the fall, sees that his fish is still rising—perhaps a bit farther out now, but still rising—and collects himself. No problem. He staggers to his feet and moves into position, already stripping line.

As he makes his haul, nerves tingling with anticipation, a sudden gust of upstream wind drives the #4 orange-foam, rubber-legged bug into his neck. He feels the sting and his grasp on composure slipping away like Air Jordans on algae-coated basalt. And yet, he somehow maintains. Of course, there's the minor detail of a hook he forgot to de-barb in his haste (the blood pressure ticks upward yet again), but the fish is still rising and he clips the leader, leaving his new neck jewelry in place. After he ties on a new fly, he notices a small knot in the tippet but decides to deal with it later. Hey, 4X is tough.

He casts and the fly is pulverized by the biggest rainbow he's ever seen. Line rips out into the current, the fish blowing holes in the surface as it streaks across the river. Unseen, the tiny, formerly insignificant knot pulls ever tighter. He works the fish into the shallows and he can see it's bigger than he ever imagined … the fish of a lifetime. And two feet from the net, with victory almost in reach, the knot finally wears through, the tippet parts, and the massive fish fades from sight.

At that very moment, the hated trespasser from above comes around the corner chasing his own huge trout hooked in our hero's favorite spot. Upon landing it, he looks up, stupidly expecting congratulations, but is instead treated to something even better. Later, when remembering this day, the Low-Holer will cherish—even more than the lifetime fish he caught—an indelible image of the graceful, arcing flight of a nine-foot graphite fly rod against the evening sky.

GLUTTONY

When someone tells me they caught and
released eighty-five trout today, I disapprove.
– Tom McGuane

The question, I suppose, is how much do we really need? If we take the word *need* literally, the answer is, or should be, none. Not that I completely buy into the whole "it's just great to be out on the water" ethic, either. I like to catch fish as much as the next guy. Probably more. But the fact is, we aren't exactly out there trying to feed our families for the winter or, for that matter, an evening. Hell, I can't even name a single fishing buddy who would admit to knowing what a trout tastes like.

Even at its cleanest, most barbless, keep-'em-wet, catch-and-release best, fly fishing is still a blood sport. And while we anglers may be responsible for all manner of stream restoration, habitat preservation, and other beneficial deeds, it's tough to argue that hooking, fighting, and releasing a fish is in any way good for that particular fish. In short, no matter how careful we are, there is mortality involved. And a single angler can make a big impact.

A few years back, toward the end of a long day spent searching for early winter steelhead, I happened to catch a beautiful, sea-run bull trout. Upon releasing it, I cast again and caught another one. The next cast, another. And so on. Greed overtook me and I stayed in that pool catching fish after fish. Several were released with blood seeping from their mouths, but I persisted, pushed on by some inner compulsion for more.

Later, I stopped by my steelhead mentor's riverside home to relate my good fortune. "Mike," I yelled, barreling into the kitchen, "I caught a shitload of big dollies today." He frowned—not the reaction I was looking for. "Yeah," he said, "they keg up in a few pools this time of year, and if you just hook one or two and move on, you can catch them there all winter. But if you really hammer 'em, they won't be there again for the rest of the year." Oh.

Perhaps not coincidentally, I never caught another fish of any kind from that pool ever again. Karma, I guess. And a tough lesson learned.

How much do we need? Is more really the answer? Consider this: What puts more pressure on a fish population, a kill fishery where you stop fishing upon filling your two-fish limit, or the guy who catches and releases eighty-five fish with a 5 percent mortality rate? Oversimplified, I know, but you see my point.

Maybe, just possibly, some of those catch-and-kill, bait-slinging meat fishermen aren't so barbaric after all. And maybe, just possibly, some of us fly fishers ought to start thinking a little more about what we're actually doing.

Is catch and release necessary to manage our shrinking re-sources? For sure. But it shouldn't be a license to hook and fight every fish we possibly can just because we're letting them go.

When I first started guiding in Alaska, one of the senior guides told me, "Big number days are not good. If a client catches thirty fish, all he remembers is the number. But if he catches one, he'll remember and appreciate every detail of that fish." I didn't believe it then, but I do now. I've seen it happen over and over again to clients, friends, and yes, me.

So, how much do we need? For that matter, what is it that truly defines a great day on the water? In keeping with the new spirit of austerity brought about by recent economic conditions, I believe less really can be the new more. As in, it's OK to stop fishing when you know you could catch more. Really. Let's take the time to remember and appreciate every detail of that one fish. I'm working on it, but if you're already there, more power to you. It's taken me a long time to learn, but I'm starting to understand that catch and release is not without its casualties. Among them has all too frequently been our sense of perspective.

MARCH 2001

*Opening day of the catch-and-release wild steelhead season
on the Skykomish, my home river. My traditional kick-
off to two solid months of daily fishing and nights filled
with crazed fly tying, gear drying, lunch making, weather
forecasts, water levels, and phone reports. A day, a season, a
pursuit I plan my life around. But this year, I stand on the
porch at noon, looking at the lush green of new spring foliage,
feeling lost. An emergency closure to protect the dwindling
remnant of this once-great steelhead run means there will
be no opening day, no season, and, potentially, no more fish.
I don't know what to do with myself. In need of sympathy,
I call my buddy Nate, a longtime wild-fish advocate with
whom I've spent the last ten opening days, and tell him I
need to do something, that I didn't know how bad things
were, that I'm ready to … get involved. "It's about time," he
says. "Nobody can afford to just go fishing without working
to protect the fish anymore."*

OPERATION DITCH PICKLE

She steps quickly in front of us and stops. Standing there in the sweltering heat, sweat-soaked swimsuit straps cutting deeply into tattooed and sunburned shoulder flesh, a red-faced baby in one arm and the leash to a snarling Rottweiler in the other. "You the feather guys?" she asks. "Y'all got something to weigh?" It's tough to tell if she's taunting or inquiring. We look around for help. "No," someone says, "they're just hauling that bag of fish around for exercise." Hoots and hollers from the peanut gallery. She smiles. Laughs even. "Well, come on, honey. The weigh station's right over here."

Maps may show the Mason-Dixon Line goes no farther west than the Ohio River, but I'm here to tell you the maps are wrong. The line actually resurfaces again just north of the Sacramento–San Joaquin Delta. Sure, it's in California, but this is not the West. Aside from the occasional palm tree, the Delta is more southern-fried than sushi. More bayou than beach. More hillbilly than Hollywood. And as such, that beloved fish of the South, the murky-water-swimming, spiny-finned, gluttonous, pot-bellied, bigmouth bass is king. Trout? Those are for fly-tossing, Prius-driving, wine-sipping weenies who couldn't thumb a level-wind to save their lives. Pass me something fried. Hold my beer. Now watch this.

I wanted to hate it. I really did. I mean, how else could a Pacific Northwesterner raised on icy, clean rivers and sleek, silver-sided steelhead feel about warm brown water and spiny green fish? "Ditch pickles," as bass are known among certain cold-water enthusiasts, have never been at the top of my wish list. Not to mention the whole high-octane, petro-driven, NASCAR vibe and the very concept of competitive angling, where fish are turned into toys, valued only for their weight and the speed with which we can drag them into the boat. Clearly not my cup of tea. But then again. ...

• • •

You know those sleek, powerful, blindingly fast speedboats with state-of-the-art fish-finding electronics, swivel-mount pedestal seats, twenty pre-rigged rods perfectly arrayed in deck-top racks, huge motors, and custom metal-flake paint jobs that bass pros use to maximize efficiency? We don't have one of those.

Or, for that matter: jumpsuits, racing helmets, suitcase-sized tackle boxes, flippin' sticks, southern accents, or anything else you'd normally associate with tournament bass fishing. Nope. What *we* have is an old brown aluminum jon boat, a handful of fly rods, and a couple of plastic fly boxes full of spun deer-hair bugs. To the seasoned hawg hunters and assembled masses at the starting line, we are, at best, brothers from another planet. At worst, we are commie trout huggers, interlopers here to destabilize the accustomed pecking order.

And yet, the tournament organizers graciously welcome our novelty act and, apparently, take pity on us. In light of our sorely undergunned vessel, they even move us up to "blast off"—their term, not mine, and clearly more in reference to every other boat in the tournament than ours—first. At exactly six o'clock in the morning, as we idle around the starting area, we get the go signal and John puts the hammer down, so to speak. We jump onto plane and begin tearing across the glassy surface at what I, accustomed to my oar-powered drift boat, consider a rapid pace.

Five minutes later, the second flight leaves the marina to a roar of engines and raw horsepower normally reserved for nitro-burning funny cars and monster truck pulls. Glancing back, I see tiny specks of bass boats peeling out of the horizon. I reach down to grab my camera, planning for a cool shot of the water dragsters approaching our stern, and when I look up, they're already flying by. As in eighty miles per hour with hulls completely out of the water, anchored to the surface only by the bottom half of their propellers.

As a side note, here's how it works: Boats leave the starting point in separate flights to avoid mass swamping, crashes, blown eardrums, and/or a complete shattering of the space-time continuum. Each boat has exactly nine hours on the water and must be back for weigh-in at their allotted time. Thus, the faster you can get to and from the fishing grounds, the more time you have to actually fish. The more time you have to fish ... well, you get the picture. In other words, horsepower plus skill and a little luck wins tournaments. Speaking for myself, I'm hoping one out of three is enough. Teams are made up of two anglers per boat who combine for a five-fish limit. Heaviest limit wins the money.

By the time we're halfway to the area we plan to fish, every single boat in the tournament—including those in the last flight who left more than a half hour after us—have blown by, leaving us in a blue haze of exhaust and inadequacy. We are The Little Engine That Could ... *I think I can, I think I can.* Or maybe that's too optimistic. "Slow and steady wins the race, right?" I shout over the wind and motor noise. John hits me with a withering glare from behind his cloth face shield, which incidentally makes him look more crazed terrorist than angler, and grimly tries to push the throttle lever farther forward.

. . .

"The tide's low now, so cast onto the shore and drag the fly into the zone. Got it?" John's at the front of the boat now, running the electric motor as we move along a steep shoreline covered in rip-rap boulders. He bombs out one cast after another, sticking his bug onto the rocks then crawling it into the water. Having spent a lifetime trying to put my flies in water, I can't seem to force myself to cast onto the bank. I strip out more line, fire shoreward, and yet again, something in my subconscious drops the fly right at water's edge. "On the rocks," John says with forced patience. "It's gotta be on the rocks."

I watch him throw it up there on dry land and slither it down. The fly starts swimming and suddenly disappears in a violent swirl. Fish on. As John frantically strips the fish toward the boat, the level of pressure brought on by tournament angling grips me and I scramble for the net. There will be no savoring of the fight or enjoyment until the fish is in the boat. It's just a smallish, greenish fish—one I might normally drag in and toss back—but today, it's money. And as much as I try to fight the rising tide of competitive juices and maintain some level of fly-fishing cool, the whole act falls apart the minute I see the fish. I want it. Bad.

With a quick stab of the net, it's in the boat. Sweet. Yes, it's green. And spiny. And, somehow … beautiful? Sleek lines and clearly defined darker markings run along its sides, the snook-shaped head perfectly designed for aggressive feeding, and. … "Hey! What are you doing?" John shouts, "put it in the live well and keep fishing." He's already got another cast in the air and here I am wasting time. We're on the clock and we need weight.

As we work our way along the bank, John puts another fish in the live well. The straight, featureless levee we're fishing stretches to infinity ahead of us. A hundred feet more and he strikes

again with an undersized bass—they have to be twelve inches to count—that goes back in. Quickly. The dude is a machine. And this little piggie has none.

Slowly, though, I am beginning to get the hang of it. I look at a sixty-foot cast, visualize it as seventy-five, and make myself overshoot. The big hair bug hits the boulders, bounces around, and comes to a rest on terra firma. Emulating John, I crawl it quietly into the weedy water and *bam!* Fish on. Awesome. I nervously horse it out of the tangled reeds, John nets it, and I am now a contributing member of society. Three fish in the live well, two to go, and five hours left to fish. Things are looking up.

• • •

In spite of all preconceived notions—and the sizzling midmorning heat—I am now actually enjoying myself. I'm finally in the groove, chucking it up into the rocks, hitting the little corners, dropping it through holes in branches … just in time for the rising tide and brutal sun to bring everything to a complete halt.

Did I mention the heat? By eleven o'clock in the morning, my rubber flip-flops are getting conspicuously soft on the molten metal deck and my forearms are shiny with sweat. I have now consumed two Gatorades, a half-gallon of water, an iced tea, and a Coke and haven't even thought about taking a leak. Fry an egg on the deck? It would go great with the crispy bacon I now have on the sides of my head where my ears used to be. Having left Seattle's cool, gray skies the day before, my body is not acclimating. Shriveling, roasting, dehydrating … but not acclimating.

Who's stupid enough to be fishing in 105-degree weather? Apparently, us. Along with seventy-four other bass-crazed lunatics. This morning when we launched the boat, I stepped in a candy-colored sticky puddle on the parking lot pavement. While I tried to scrape the mess off my foot, someone walking by said, "That used to be a plastic worm." Now I understand.

An hour passes without a fish. Various assorted Jet Skis, wakeboarders, water-skiers, and other speed-related recreational craft strafe us. Contrary to my normal attitude toward such recreation, I am now thinking these people are actually smarter than the guys getting microwaved to death while fly fishing a bass tournament. Then again, even as I roast, I'm still afraid to touch the tepid brown water, let alone *recreate* in it.

• • •

Others clearly do not share my fear of the water. The Delta is a major recreational resource. Beyond the yahoos ripping up the surface on hurtling implements of destruction, there are striped bass trollers and catfishermen plying the waters. In years past, there would also be a major salmon fishery here, although sadly, populations of the Delta's native, anadromous fish have collapsed. The once-thriving salmon industry was completely closed on the entire California coast for all of the 2008 and 2009 seasons, costing taxpayers $170 million in federal disaster relief.

It's strange. All the healthy fisheries in the Delta, including what is most likely the highest number of bass tournaments on any body of water in the country, subsist on alien, non-native species. The conditions that help largemouth bass, crappie, bluegill, catfish, and sometimes even stripers and shad thrive here have decimated the indigenous salmon and steelhead. There's no doubt these invasive species provide a bulk of the sportfishing value here today, but still, one wonders if that makes it OK.

And now, combatants in the water wars—agricultural interests, municipal water utilities, flood controllers, and conservation groups—are using fish as their pawns. Some claim the salmon collapse is a result of predation by bass and stripers, creating strange bedfellows of water consumers and anti–invasive species conservation groups. Others point out that the imports and natives coexisted for the last hundred years in relative harmony and abundance. Who's right? I really don't know. Predation on juvenile salmon is certainly a factor, but fresh water—or lack thereof—and habitat seem to be the key to survival for all the fish species here.

The banks of the Delta, diked, riprapped, impounded, and channeled, bear little resemblance to the natural, sprawling floodplain that historically nurtured one of the greatest salmon runs on Earth. In fact, by engineering the Delta purely to deliver water and prevent floods, we've effectively destroyed 95 percent of the natural salmon-rearing wetlands here. The proposed Peripheral Canal project, thankfully voted down—at least for now—would have diverted even more fresh water to abate an unquenchable Southern California thirst. Industrial farmers want more water to flood millions of acres of rice each spring and keep corn and tomatoes growing in summer heat. Local residents need drinking water and flood protection … and thus, the modern Delta. But I digress.

• • •

As the afternoon tide begins to roll in, the relentless Central Valley sun beats down on us like a hot iron. Heat shimmers off the surrounding farmland. The rising water lifts nearshore aquatic vegetation and algae to the surface, in some places creating solid chartreuse carpets on the surface. John pilots us directly toward the thickest of these disgusting mats.

In a small cove covered in the yucky green stuff he stops the boat. "Get ready," he says, "this is awesome." It looks decidedly un-awesome. John hands me a huge spun deer-hair bug—known as "The Rat"—featuring an epoxy skid plate on the bottom that keeps the hook point up, allowing the fly to slide over solid scum without snagging. The water here looks more like Astroturf, not an inch of actual liquid in sight. Somewhere under it, though, at least according to John, is water. And bass.

If I thought casting onto the rocks was a strange way to catch fish, this is insane. I've simply never fished on a putting green before. Following John's lead, I cast to where the green stuff goes from flat to steep, indicating water meeting land, and begin to strip the fly across the mat of vegetation. Really? I glance at John to see if I can detect even the slightest sign he's messing with the steelhead guy, but his eyes are glued to the progress of his bug. I'm still not buying it.

I quit casting and watch John's Rat creep across the scum, leaving a distinct, slightly less chartreuse trail behind it. Then the Rat steps on a land mine and a furious eruption of water and grass engulfs the place where it had just been. John rears back and is tight to the fish, which dives and thrashes in the murky water. When it comes aboard, it's more weed than fish, completely encased in vegetation. Four down, one to go. I'm a believer.

At the next spot, I find another fish willing to come up through the crud, and once I recover from the jolting take—and disbelief—I haul it to the boat. Not huge, but a decent keeper which we net, unwrap from its cocoon of algae, and place in the live well. Five fish. Done. Relief washes over me. I sit down on the metal deck … and instantly sear my ass on the broiling surface. I find a seat cushion for insulation, kick back, pop another Coke, and close my eyes.

"What are you doing?" John says. I open my eyes. He's still on the casting deck, firing toward the bank.

"That's five," I say. "We're all good. Limited out."

"Everyone has a limit," he says. "We're not even in the picture with these." Oh. Our five fish are on the smallish side and, as it turns out, the goal is to replace the smallest fish with bigger ones before time runs out. Hence the live well. OK. I get it. Back to work.

Did I happen to mention it was hot? It may have been brutal earlier, but it turns out that was just a little preheat for the full-on, rip-snorting afternoon blast furnace. When I open a fly box, I find the black-plastic shell caving in and the foam inside becoming pourable. I pry a fly loose, wipe off the gooey remains of foam, and start pounding the bank through a haze of heat-induced delirium.

At some point, I hear the sound of a bowling ball hitting the water as another fish tries to destroy John's Rat through the putting green. The semisolid surface quakes like Jell-O and John leans back, pulling hard. Big fish. It dives for the bottom and the fly sails out, landing softly on the other side of the boat. Silence. I don't know if I've ever felt the loss of a fish like this. Another interesting and new aspect to the whole team and competition thing I hadn't anticipated. "That one would've made us respectable," John says quietly. I don't know what to say, so I keep fishing.

Fifty feet farther down the bank, same thing: Another big fish. Another fly sailing through molten air. A deeper slide into depression. "That's the main disadvantage of fly fishing here," John explains. "When the bass comes up through a mat, it gets a mouthful of grass and algae along with the fly. The gear guys have fifty-pound braid to set the hook through all that stuff." That, and they make 50 percent more casts than we can in the same amount of time, and they have boats that triple our speed, and. … Well, if it was easy, everyone would be fly fishing. But we aren't feeling sorry for ourselves. Or at least John isn't. He's already casting again.

• • •

"Five more casts," John says. Forty-five minutes to weigh-in, and we have at least a half-hour run back to the dock. We are fishing a long bank with overhanging trees, dense stands of cattails, and a sudden abundance of life. Bluegills fin along the shore and small bass dart around chasing minnows. It feels fishier than anything we've seen all day, but time is short. Another new sensation: We *need* a fish.

"One more cast," John says for the third time. I'm already stowing gear and getting ready for the run back in. "There it is!" John yells. "Get the net." He strips line furiously and his fly rod takes a deep bend. A broad back wallows into the branches of a downed tree and disappears. John pulls harder and the bow of the boat swings in toward shore. Suddenly, the fish surfaces next to the boat, I make a frantic scoop with the net, and it's money. Right on! Not a world record, but a very nice fish. A heavy fish. A Hail Mary fish. A Doug-Flutie-finding-the-end-zone-with-no-time-left fish.

"What time is it?" John says, suddenly snapping back to reality. We have twenty-five minutes to make it back and miles to go in our slow boat. We drop everything, fire up the motor, and blaze. With high tide, we can cut some corners, and John does his best to shave seconds off at every turn, running tight to banks, churning mud.

And yet, in a virtual replay of our morning start, nearly every boat in the field passes us on the way in, careening wildly off our wake and blowing by in a glittery blur of metal-flake paint and howling engines. John doesn't blink, though. He just keeps cutting corners, glancing at his watch, and slapping the side of the console to urge our old horse along. And amazingly, The Little Engine That Could chugs into the marina with more than a minute to spare.

. . .

It all comes down to this. Most weight wins. Period. Walking to the weigh-in table, heat shimmering off the blacktop and sweat pouring down my face, I am amazed to see people in folding lawn chairs sipping iced tea under an oak tree. An audience of sorts. In this heat! After our brief run-in with Ms. Rottweiler, she leads us to the scales and we are greeted with open arms and respectful curiosity. We put our ditch pick ... er, largemouth bass, on the scales and get a nice round of "way-to-gos" and "good jobs" from the crowd. There is a definite camaraderie here, a spirit of warmth and friendliness that I can only describe as Southern hospitality. Right here in Northern California.

And you know what? I'm good with it. More than good actually. The tournament experience is challenging, addictive, and yes, fun. A lot of fun. I still have concerns about angling as competition, about the footprint of all that horsepower and technology, about the money involved. But listening to the fishing talk and chatter from the crowd, it occurs to me that cultural specifics aside, I understand these people.

All of us—the tournament pro slinging rubber frogs in the Delta, the 7X-match-the-hatch purist on the Henry's Fork, the steelhead bum, the permit junkie—speak "the universal language of fishing." And that, I think, is where hope lies for the Delta, and for that matter, a lot of other places as well. If we can step beyond our prejudices about tackle, technique, and species, and actually work together, we have a chance to force the kind of drastic change needed to save what we love.

And make no mistake, the Delta needs drastic change. If we can't find a better balance between the needs of humans and fish here, fans of introduced spiny-ray species like bass and native salmonids alike will lose. I'm not saying we're all going to hold hands and sing "Kumbaya," but no angler wins when habitat goes down the tubes—or the canal to Southern California, as it were.

It's one thing to lament the loss of someone else's fishery, but it really hits home to see, feel, and fish it in their shoes. And based on my experience here, I'm confident the Delta bass anglers care as much about their resource as anyone.

So, how did we do? OK ... we didn't win. But we didn't lose, either. Let's just say there are currently at least twenty-two hardcore, eighty-mph-boat-owning, state-of-the-art-electronics-using, fifty-pound-braid-chucking, tournament bass anglers currently on suicide watch for finishing behind the feather flingers. Or maybe it sounds better to just say we won the fly division? I wanted to hate it. But now that I've been there? Game on, brother. With the right conditions, I know we'd eventually win. Sign me up for another one. And while you're at it, toss me some hushpuppies and hold my beer. Now watch *this*.

APRIL 2003

On the flight home, I can't let go of it. Over and over again I close my eyes and see the enormous giant trevally disappearing beyond the reef edge, accompanied by the guide's Gilbertese-inflected English in my head, repeating an endless loop: "Eighty feet, two o'clock ... cast now! Cast now! Cast ... ah, never mind." When Stacy picks me up at the airport, I ramble through sun-cracked lips, trying to describe the experience. She listens patiently, then, without a word, hands me a toothbrush-shaped piece of plastic with a small opening on one side. Across the opening runs a faint, pink line. My mind goes blank. "A baby," she says, smiling. A baby! The world spins, and as I begin to grasp the enormity, I recognize that life will be unimaginably different from this moment on. Later, as I drift off to sleep, I try to picture the giant trevally again, but instead dream of a four-inch perch in the hands of a child with a face I already recognize.

FRANKENFISH:
COMING SOON TO A
MARKET NEAR YOU?

In the 1950s and '60s, biologists and dam builders assured us that the threat of lost salmon runs was nothing to worry about. Hatcheries would not only mitigate habitat loss, but could provide salmon runs far beyond what nature produced. We could, in effect, create a bonanza of fish for ourselves. But like almost every instance of humans believing they could out-engineer Mother Nature, that optimism turned out to be nothing more than hubris. Today, we watch as the hatchery runs dwindle, taking the remnants of wild runs with them.

In the 1990s, the international fish-farming corporations told us their activities were no reason for concern; the open-water net pens were a safe alternative to harvesting wild salmon. "The fish are sterile," they said. "Ocean currents dilute pollution. Nothing to worry about." And now, as we find juvenile Atlantic salmon in Pacific coast streams, and watch wild runs ravaged by sea-lice infestations, disease, and pharmaceutical and fecal waste from the fish farms, the head of one of the largest Scandinavian fish farm companies finally admits what many already knew: The net pens are damaging wild fish populations.

Which brings us to the news in the *New York Times* that the FDA is seriously considering approval of the first genetically engineered food animal for human consumption—a GMO salmon that grows at twice the rate of natural salmon. A Frankenfish designed by man to, once again, out-engineer nature. Produced by AquaBounty Technologies, this is an Atlantic salmon with growth-hormone genes from Chinook salmon and a genetic "on switch" from another species, the ocean pout.

We are assured by AquaBounty that the resulting fish is "identical in every measurable way to the traditional food Atlantic salmon." Nothing to worry about. The company also says the federal government has already approved five of their seven data sets demonstrating the AquaBounty salmon is safe to eat and safe for the environment. The remaining two studies are expected to be approved in the not-so-distant future.

This would be the same federal government that approved British Petroleum's deep-ocean oil drilling, and apparently took the company's word for it that adequate safety measures were in place. Both BP and the federal agency tasked with oversight believed the triple redundancy of its blowout preventer was so secure, there was no reason to come up with a plan for what to do if it failed. We all know the results there.

So, when the government and a corporation tell us yet again that there's nothing to worry about, that the Enbridge Pipeline won't leak, that Pebble Mine won't destroy Bristol Bay, or, in this case, that messing with the basic code of life on Earth is not only safe, but will produce something better than Mother Nature, history offers us one piece of advice: Be afraid. Be very afraid.

Postscript 2022
In 2015, AquaBounty's genetically engineered salmon became the first GE animal approved for human consumption in the United States. In 2021, the first crop of these salmon was harvested and sent to market, with approval for sale in the United States, Canada, and Brazil. Yes, I'm afraid.

A CRACK IN THE
DAM REMOVAL

I'm a fisherman and a father, not a biologist or any other kind of real expert, so please bear with me. I think this still qualifies me to raise what I consider an important point as we celebrate the largest dam removal project to date in United States history. After thirty years of extraordinary effort by the Lower Elwha Klallam Tribe and a coalition of conservation groups and individuals, we now have the opportunity to witness more than a hundred miles of pristine wild salmon habitat return to its natural state.

As a lifelong Northwest salmon and steelhead fisherman, I can tell you it's been a long wait. Now that the day has finally arrived, it's hard to describe my excitement. There's so much to look forward to as the Elwha flows freely to the sea for the first time in nearly a century.

There are legends here, of hundred-pound Chinook salmon and mind-boggling abundance of wild steelhead, coho, chum, sockeye, and pink salmon. In my dreams, I see a day in the not-so-distant future when my kids and I can wade the gravel bars and fish for them. Then, the Elwha will be the crown jewel of river recovery, and a stronghold for wild salmon. I think we all hope these dreams and legends can become reality here.

Of course, there are concerns. A lot of us worry the sediment load from behind the dams will prove too much for the salmon to overcome, that natural recolonization will take too long, that we need hatchery supplementation to speed the Elwha's recovery. I've shared some of these concerns.

But I want to turn away from the Elwha for a moment, with a story about another river.

On May 18, 1980, Mount Saint Helens erupted, sending a wall of superheated volcanic ash into the Toutle River watershed. The result was complete and utter devastation of the river as tributaries and the main stem itself boiled in thousand-degree temperatures. If you saw it, or have seen pictures, you know what I'm talking about: All that remained was a desert landscape of blown-down trees and thin trickles of muddy water running over vast stretches of gray volcanic ash. For all intents and purposes, the Toutle River was dead.

Or so we thought.

Turns out, we underestimated Mother Nature's ability to heal herself. Within five years, wild steelhead were back in what was left of the Toutle, finding ways to survive, reproduce, and miraculously, thrive.

According to the Washington Department of Fish and Wildlife, by 1987, there were 2,052 wild steelhead spawning in the Toutle, a number that far exceeded what biologists considered its carrying capacity before the eruption. In contrast, that same year, the nearby Kalama River—completely untouched by the eruption—with its high hatchery production, had a return of just 248 wild steelhead. Somehow, within seven years of complete obliteration, the Toutle River had more wild winter steelhead than any other river in the entire Columbia Basin.

It's an amazing story, but unfortunately, it doesn't end there.

When we saw those numbers, in a river written off for dead, we humans decided to help Mother Nature by resuming massive hatchery plants and building a sediment retention dam. The explosive growth of the Toutle's wild steelhead population responded to our help by stalling and eventually dwindling to match the low returns of all the other hatchery-supplemented Columbia tributaries.

This story shows us that wild fish can and will repopulate a barren river, and much faster than anyone ever imagined. It also shows what happens when man tries to improve on nature.

The restored Elwha has a lot more going for it than the Toutle. There are pure genetic strains of sockeye and steelhead above the dams, a hundred miles of pristine habitat—much of it protected inside the national park—and plenty of opportunity for wild strays to repopulate it. The sediment load coming down from the dams will only affect the lower main-stem river, leaving headwater and tributary spawning grounds untouched.

The wild salmon of the Pacific Ring of Fire have evolved to repopulate themselves in watersheds devastated by volcanic eruptions, glaciers, landslides, and earthquakes. They've been doing it successfully for millions of years.

But because we've somehow lost our faith in Mother Nature and refuse to believe what science shows us in places like the Toutle, we are about to start releasing inbred, genetically inferior hatchery stocks into this newly restored habitat. Despite overwhelming scientific and anecdotal evidence showing that the presence of hatchery fish works as a powerful detriment to wild salmon recovery, we insist, once again, on helping the natural process. If the point of dam removal is wild salmon recovery, why would we spend millions of dollars on something that works counter to the point?

My wish, as a fisherman, and especially as the father of two young children, is that we could somehow find the patience—and the faith—to let Mother Nature do what she's always done.

Postscript 2022

The federal government did, in fact, spend $16 million to build a new hatchery on the Elwha. Thankfully, litigation filed by Wild Fish Conservancy led to a settlement preventing the most inbred stock—Chambers Creek hatchery steelhead—from being released. The new hatchery began operation before the dam removal was even complete, and continues to produce large quantities of coho, chum, and pink salmon. Meanwhile, a state facility on the lower river produces and releases hatchery Chinook salmon.

Hatchery proponents point to the fact that a majority of the salmon repopulating the free-flowing Elwha are of hatchery origin as proof that the hatchery is working. This, though, is nothing more than self-fulfilling prophecy—most of the fish are from hatcheries because they are planting the river with massive numbers of hatchery fish! In scientific study after scientific study, the damaging impact hatchery fish have on wild salmon populations is well documented. Why aren't more wild fish returning to the Elwha? The answer is simply that the prophecy is fulfilling itself.

One bright spot in this story, though, is the sudden and surprising presence of a growing population of wild summer steelhead, a species not currently produced by the Elwha hatchery system. These fish, most likely the result of pure, wild steelhead genes in resident rainbow trout, were protected from hatchery influence when they were trapped above the dams more than a hundred years ago. Today, they are thriving. In 2020, river surveys counted more than five hundred wild summer steelhead in the Elwha Canyon. One can only wish that the other wild salmonids of the Elwha had been given a similar opportunity to naturally repopulate the river.

OCTOBER 2005

Home is perhaps a strange word for the river a thousand miles from where I live, but over the years, that's how I've come to think of the Bulkley. Now, though, with the birth of a child, growing work responsibilities, and a new sense of family—events collectively known as "growing up" to most people—I've missed the last two seasons here. It's good to be back. I fish with great focus, enjoying familiar water and the company of old friends, but tinged now with an awareness of how far away I am from my family. Over the last few days, I've come to realize something new: This river will always be an important part of my life, but it's no longer home. Tonight, fishing through a long, fast tailout with the reflection of golden cottonwoods illuminating the surface, I imagine a future when my daughter will be here with me, the questions she'll ask, the anticipation we'll share. And in that very moment, a twenty-pound steelhead rises up through the current to inhale my waking dry fly.

WHAT ABOUT BOB?

The legend of Bob Clay is already well established: He's one of the finest bamboo rod builders and steelhead fishermen in the world. To cast one of his cane Spey rods is to suspend belief and accept the concept of turning a stalk of giant grass into a high-performance fly rod—which, given the levels of technology and aerospace-grade materials going into most rods these days, boggles the mind. To watch him in his workshop is to grasp the painstaking process and commitment to the craftsmanship it takes to perform this alchemy. To fish with Bob is to catch just a glimpse of the depths at which a human can understand steelhead behavior. But as I mention above, these facts are already known by many through the countless stories published about Bob, or the constant stream of visitors and anglers who've spent time with him during his long guiding and rod-building career. To avoid restating the obvious, then, here are some other ways of thinking about Bob:

Eleven o'clock on an icy night on the Kispiox: A knock at the door of "the Shack," a small cabin on the Clay family property. It's Bob, with ruddy cheeks and a grin that splits his face. "You ready?" he asks with a jaunty cheer in his voice. We, the cabin's occupants, are not ready. We are full of food, half-drunk on good wine, and slipping into hibernation, exhausted from a long day on the water. But now we are up, buoyed by Bob's spirit. Our mission? To capture a flock of semi-feral—and extremely large—chickens, and haul them a couple hundred yards through the dark Kispiox woods to a pen where they will await their demise, to be delivered by Bob in the morning. "Don't worry," Bob says, "if you grab 'em by the feet and carry them upside down, they'll go dormant and make it easy, eh? Take two in each hand. Let's go." My chickens do not go dormant. They do not make it easy. Perhaps, like grizzly bears or mountain lions, they sense fear. Or is it more like sharks smelling blood in the water? I stagger through the dark with fourteen pounds of wildly flailing chickens in each hand, trying not to scream while they peck the shit out of me.

A dinner party in the Clays' kitchen overlooking the Kispiox River: We are getting down to business here. Rick, our host at the Shack, has arranged for an acquaintance from Prince Rupert to haul buckets of giant scallops to the Kispiox. After a quick shucking session in the shed, it's time to make dinner. Colin, the chef, busy with more complicated dishes, assigns me the task of searing the coveted, silver-dollar-sized scallops. Gulp. In an effort to pre-excuse myself for the shortcomings of my imminent performance, I say, "To really make these great, we'd need duck fat to sear 'em in." And Bob is suddenly at my side, digging through the fridge. "Yep," he says, "I thought Kathy saved all our duck fat. Here ya go!" And now, with a soup can full of home-rendered duck fat, I am left without a single excuse.

Near dusk, halfway down one of the great steelhead pools on Earth: Rain pounds out of the sky like liquid bullets. The river is going out. It won't be fishable again until long after I'm back home. For the moment, though, conditions are perfect except for the impending nightfall, my own shaky desperation, and a lone figure fishing below me. I'm casting like a lunatic, charging around in the thickening water, stripping line, making crazy mends. I want a fish so bad I can feel it in my bones. With about an hour of daylight left, the figure below me leans into a fish. When she lands it, Kathy, Bob's wife, lifts it from the water so I can see the enormous slab. I swallow hard and keep fishing. Then she hooks and lands another, while my fly sifts empty water. Then she does it again. And finally, just as darkness brings fishing to an end, she shouts and lifts a fish that's well over twenty pounds before sending it on its way. When I tell Bob what happened, he laughs and says with pride, "She can't be deterred."

Midday at the Shack: Bob's son, Jed, stops by to say hello and fish with us. A top-tier steelheader in his own right, he's also inherited Bob's thoughtfulness. "Hey," he says, "I brought you something." He reaches into his waders and pulls a single, enormous matsutake mushroom from his pocket. He blows the lint off and hands it to me. I show it to Yvon, who grins maniacally and says, "You have to make the matsutake rice tonight." We spend an embarrassing amount of our fishing day talking about the rice we're going to eat and serve to friends who are coming for dinner.

Later that day: The Shack is packed with people—steelheaders and conservationists—drinking, talking, and breathing in the incredible cooking aromas. We've made crispy grouse McNuggets from some birds we shot up by the Babine yesterday. A smoked-lamb soup thick enough to stand a fork in. Broiled, half-smoked black cod. And now, we—especially Yvon and I—are ready for the matsutake rice. I start the prep work while Bob, Rick, Aaron, and Yvon hover around the kitchen. With the first slice, the interior of the prized mushroom is revealed; it's packed with squirming white maggots. More worm than mushroom. Writhing. Wiggling. I recoil in revulsion. Bob and Yvon look around the crowded room and back at the mushroom. I start to scrape it all into the trash. Yvon grabs my arm. "Just cook it," he says, glancing furtively around the room, "nobody will know." I look to Rick as the voice of reason, but he's mysteriously vanished. I turn to Aaron … gone. On to my third choice, Bob. "How good is the rice?" he asks. "*Really* good," Yvon says. Bob nods at the rice pot and disappears into the crowd. It's delicious.

More Bob facts: Bob's family includes a full herd of dogs, including Ootza, who may actually be a small horse. Bob owns one of the original wooden Dean River boats, which he uses to travel the Skeena. Bob is almost always smiling. Bob's daughter Kaili designs waders, jackets, and all manner of fishing gear for Patagonia—her excellent Home Pool fishing gloves are named after the steelhead run she grew up fishing. Bob's son, Jed, is a renowned sketchy-water wader, big-rapids boat driver, and wormy mushroom picker. He also has a unique ability to make steelhead-fighting selfie videos—while fishing solo. Bob's daughter Kateri won the Spey-O-Rama women's distance casting contest at the Golden Gate casting ponds in San Francisco with one of Bob's bamboo rods. Yes, it was against other casters using graphite. Bob's wife, Kathy … well, we already covered her, and I'm still too bitter about that night in the rain to delve any deeper.

But to me, the most important thing to know about Bob is this: Kindness. Not your everyday, run-of-the-mill, hale-fellow-well-met, how-ya-doin' type of kindness, but a soul-deep, authentically human generosity of spirit. The kind that makes you feel better just hanging out with him. The kind that lifts your spirits from even a short chat on the phone. Of the many lessons we can learn from Bob, that's what I aspire to most. Well, that and maybe just a tiny fraction of what he knows about steelhead fishing. That wouldn't hurt either.

RUNNING OUT OF NORTH

This is the spot I've been waiting for all day—a secret midriver bucket that holds fish even when there's a parade of anglers pounding the water ahead of you. I pull back hard on the oars and drop anchor, letting two or three boat-lengths of line trail out before chocking it off. The anchor bounces downstream until finally, it grabs, and we lurch to a halt.

On river left, three-quarters of the flow runs across a broad tailout. On the right, jade-green water moves at walking speed through a narrow trough. Under the boat lies a submerged island of loose cobble—knee-deep here but gradually falling away under ever deeper, faster current. Fish far enough downstream and you'll never make it back to the boat. I scramble over the gunwale, hands shaking with anticipation.

I used to come to this river to escape the conservation battles surrounding our dwindling steelhead returns in Puget Sound. For Pacific Northwest anglers, northward travel works like a time machine—the farther you go, the more years recede. When I first started fishing this great Skeena tributary, it was everything I imagined Puget Sound rivers must have been a hundred years ago. No hatcheries. No clear-cuts. No toxic runoff from suburban sprawl. Just perfect water and wild, free-rising steelhead. I had found the good old days.

My first cast settles on the water and I make a big upstream mend, followed by a shorter downstream mend to make up for slower water eddying along the submerged island. As it starts to swing, my heart pounds. When the line trails below me, I pick up, cast, mend, and take two steps downstream.

Memories float through my mind: the day we found this spot

and discovered we had to turn our backs on the classic tailout and fish toward the bank; the huge chrome hen that rocketed downstream, forcing Nate to ferry me to shore in the boat; Tim blasting elegant single Speys into the wind amid a cadmium blizzard of cottonwood leaves.

This river, though, is changing. The fish politics and destructive forces I came here to escape are creeping in. Or maybe it's just my awareness of them. This is a region rich with natural resources—precious metals, fossil fuels, timber, salmon—and a convenient path to the Pacific from the tar-sand oil fields of Alberta. As long as opportunities for profit exist, threats will hover over the river. Constant vigilance must be maintained. And now, despite the vast amount of money brought into local economies by visiting anglers, the government has closed the river to us foreigners for two days every week. We do not feel very welcome here anymore.

Back in the present, the familiar rhythm of steelhead fishing takes hold and troubling thoughts fade. I work my way down the deepening gravel bar absorbed by the water in front of me. Cast, mend, two steps down. With each swing, the water fishes better.

I don't know when I will be back. Tim sold his house in Telkwa, Nate didn't come this year, and life at home, with two kids in school and a farm to work, has become more complicated. Time is moving on.

Two more steps and the current starts washing gravel out from beneath my feet. Water pushes against my waist, running fast enough to raise a bow wake on my upstream side. But still, it's fishing better with each cast. The line swings through on another perfect arc and comes tight with a soft grab, then nothing. I cast again, but come up empty. I can't stop now. Two more steps and I feel buoyancy taking over and the shocking bite of forty-three-degree water seeping in over the top of my waders. I make the mend with arms above my head. When it starts to swing, I hold my breath.

Where will I fish next season? Am I giving up on this river? There are still major watersheds up the coast worth exploring, and hundreds of smaller rivers, too. But where will we go after that? We are running out of North.

My line comes tight again, solid this time. The fish explodes, streaking downstream, and I understand there is no choice: I have to stand my ground and fight.

JULY 2007

For a three-year-old, it's been a long day. One she's spent patiently waiting for a fish, first in dreamy morning fog and now under brilliant summer sunshine. "Daddy," she says, "why is there a seal on that surfboard?" I reel in our line and turn the boat to investigate. "Are those birds eating lunch?" she asks. "I'm hungry." I toss a cut-plug herring back into the prop wash and hand her another sandwich. "What do you think Weston is doing now?" she wonders aloud, thinking of her baby brother at home. "Do salmon sleep in the daytime?" The rod dips and line starts peeling off the reel. I hand it to her just as the fish takes off, cartwheeling across the surface. Slowly, we work it to the boat together. When it's safely in the net, we hug and slap fishy hands in victory. As our adrenaline fades, though, I can see she is exhausted. I tell her it's time to head home, to check on her brother and Mom, to get ready for dinner. "Daddy," she says, "can we try one more place first?" My heart swells.

BIG IN JAPAN

A week ago, he wasn't smoking at all. Three days later, in the midst of our manic search for the native trout of Japan, it was maybe three or four smokes a day. And now, with the clock ticking and time running out, our gracious host, Shin Katsuragi, is lighting cigarettes back-to-back and sucking them down like a Hoover upright.

Maybe it's the pressure to find fish or better photo ops or a river not blown out by the epic June rains, but I think it's something else. I think it's the extra responsibility our host feels to ensure that his Japanese-American guest, me, gets the most out of his first visit to the Ancestral Homeland. And in perfect Japanese tradition, any attempts on my part to alleviate the pressure or deflect Shin's hospitality only incite more outrageous acts of generosity. That, and having to translate every piece of written or spoken language we encounter. Oh, and driving all over the Japanese Alps on roads that would scare a mountain goat. Safe to say, there's a little pressure building up behind Shin's unwavering smile. Hence the smokes.

I'm not sure what I was expecting upon arrival in the country where my great-grandparents were born. Certainly not Muhammad Ali stepping off the plane in Africa for the first time and gazing out at the adoring masses chanting, "Ali, *Bomaye!*"

OK, maybe a little bit.

But any delusions of grandeur soon evaporated under the greenish glare of fluorescent lights illuminating a deserted Nagoya Airport arrival gate. We quickly—and anonymously—collected our bags, cleared customs, and met Shin and local trout guru Hisashi Suzuki.

As part of a fly-rod company's expedition to test new ultra-light fly rods and explore the alpine headwaters of Central Japan, there was little time to waste in the city. We would be heading west into the mountains in the morning, but first, a hazy, jet-lagged, midnight dinner to talk fish, lay out plans, and get to know our hosts at the local yakitori joint.

• • •

Ten skewers, each impaling some kind of different meat, arrive on a plate. I am hungry, exhausted, and reeling from the trans-Pacific time change. "Chicken," Shin says, "very good here." Upon closer examination, I see it's pretty much the whole bird, artfully divided up and presented with one body part per skewer. One skewer with light meat. One dark. One with five hearts. One with three livers. (The math here remains a mystery.) One with some intestines beautifully strung back and forth along the skewer like a winding mountain road. It's all delicious, and I devour every piece. Except the intestines. To avoid offending my hosts, I dutifully chew a small bit of the rubbery tube until it's at least partially gone. I can deal with rubbery. It's the grit inside that's tough to swallow.

"What do you think of Japan so far?" Shin asks, as I craftily try to disguise the lone unfinished skewer beneath my empty ones. I think of the precise efficiency of the airport, the perfectly maintained highway, even the carefully designed chicken intestines on a skewer, and tell him my first impression is of a country where nothing is "half-assed." He politely inquires what that means. I explain. Then, fueled by the enormous Sapporos that keep appearing in front of me, I continue with an impromptu English lesson: "There's also dumbass, fat-ass, lame-ass, and my favorite, jackass." Shin thoughtfully considers my best *Webster's*

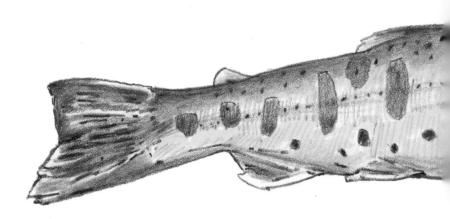

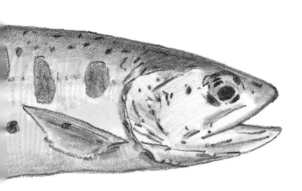

definition of each term, then offers: "You Americans sure like to talk about ass."

We stagger out into steamy, rain-slick streets choked with traffic and bathed in neon, breathing air thick enough to pour on pancakes. I am suddenly so drained of energy I wonder if I can even make it the half-block back to our hotel. Across the street, a giant statue of Ultraman—my boyhood hero—stands sentinel over the scene. This somehow makes me feel that everything's going to be OK. Or maybe I'm asleep on my feet and already dreaming.

• • •

After a sweaty, sleepless night wondering what effect certain parts of a chicken might have on the corresponding parts of my own anatomy, followed by six full hours of twisting, turning mountain roads, we have arrived at a river. Even more miraculously, we are going fishing. And the sun is coming out.

The surroundings are spectacular: vertigo-inducing mountainsides covered in deep-green *sugi* cedar forest plunge to the river, skeins of mist hang in the tributary canyons, and sunlight filtered by lacy Japanese maples dapples the granite boulders and rushing water of the Monami, the "River of Ten Thousand Waves." Every piece of coveted flat land—no matter how small—is planted with geometric rice fields, glowing the luminous spring green of new growth. Ancient houses with thick, straw-thatched roofs stand among the lower hills, surrounded by the ubiquitous flooded rice fields. This is a Japan more beautiful than I ever imagined.

A small, dimpled rise in the first pool announces the presence of feeding *iwana*, the native char of Japan. I feel a pulse of adrenaline and quickly knot a small caddis emerger to 7X tippet at Hisashi's suggestion. Privately, I question the need for such precise imitation and ultra-fine, twelve-foot leaders, but chalk it up to the Japanese culture of perfection. Based on my experience with small trout in remote mountain freestones at home, this is going to be easy. "Get ready for a fish portrait," I tell Dale, the photographer.

I put the fly in the feeding lane and a tiny, five-inch fish materializes beneath it, rising slowly for the take. I tense for the hookset, then watch as the fish calmly inspects the fly and disappears back into the depths. I cast again. No response. Change flies. Same result. This is ridiculous. I keep casting until Hisashi shakes his head in pity and says, "We go now. Try another spot." The photographer rolls his eyes at my ineptitude. Shin sighs and lights the first cigarette I've seen him smoke.

Is this a peek into our own future at home? The inevitable result of intensive human activity and population on limited resources? Will we someday struggle to catch wary fingerlings, even in the remote corners of America? Or are these fish just naturally tough to catch?

Two hours, three river miles, and nine blown chances later, I finally hook an *iwana*—no doubt, the only stupid fish in the river. But I'm ecstatic. The delicate "000-weight" fly rod we're testing dances, bending deeply as the fish flashes around the pool, and when I land it—at nine inches long, an exceptional specimen—I feel the kind of pride normally associated with landing, say, a 150-pound tarpon.

• • •

DIALOG FROM A STEEP ROAD

Me: Smell that? Your brakes are burning up.

Shin: (sniffing) Not brakes … I think, shit of cow.

Me: I'm pretty sure it's the brakes.

Shin: (pumping unresponsive brake pedal, calmly puffing cigarette as the car careens wildly downhill) No, not brakes … shit of cow for sure.

• • •

The old woman dressed in an ornate silk-brocade kimono smiles and shows us into a room devoid of furniture other than a one-foot-tall, black-lacquered table. The floor is woven bamboo, and I understand the dreaded moment—OK, slightly less dreaded than bathing in a small room with three other naked men, but that's another story—has arrived: This is a *tatami* room, and we will sit on the floor to eat. One order of screaming knees with a little aching back on the side, please.

But the food! First, a small plate of *ayu*, a local, finger-sized fish pried from the gullets of captive cormorants, lightly pickled to dissolve the bones, and fried crisp in an airy tempura batter. Then the woman returns and sets small cast-iron grills in front of us and lights them with a flourish. Exquisitely designed platters of raw ingredients arrive—fresh asparagus spears, two kinds of wild mushrooms, and half a dozen perfectly cut one-inch cubes of *Hida* beef. The locals proudly proclaim *Hida* beef to be far superior to the better-known Kobe variety, and it does not disappoint. More creamy fat marbling than red meat, the cubes of steak sizzle on my personal grill. A quick dip in seasoned sea salt and the beef melts away in my mouth like a pad of meat-flavored butter.

When the table's cleared, the chef—a local fishing fanatic—comes out and kneels to talk with Shin and Hisashi. Shin reaches into his shirt pocket, removes a pack of cigarettes, and lights one. I sprawl out flat on my back like a beached whale in what is surely an egregious violation of etiquette, but I simply cannot help myself. And unbeknownst to us, somewhere in the mountains towering above, a heavy rain begins to fall.

• • •

Shin knocks on my door at exactly six o'clock in the morning. In Japan nobody is ever late for anything. Except me. I've somehow forgotten to set my alarm, and in the mad scramble to exit my closet-sized room, I also fail to recall that the top of the door-jamb is exactly five-feet, six-inches high. *Bam!* Down goes Ali. Or Gulliver, as it may be. To the crew waiting for me in the hall, this is probably the best moment of the entire day.

Outside, the Tateyama Range looms above the coastal city of Toyama, looking steeper and more imposing than even the Front Range of the Rockies. Under clear blue skies, Shin points the van toward the mountains and we begin our search for *yamame*, a resident form of the cherry salmon that once filled local rivers. As we drive, Hisashi hands me a fourteen-foot leader tapered to 8X and says, "*Yamame* much smarter, much more harder to catch than *iwana*."

We push up into the foothills past small villages surrounded by precise, parallel lines of new rice plantings, and finally wind our way down through dense bamboo forest to the Shiraiwa River, "the River of White Stones." At the first bridge, we pile out of the van with growing anticipation, peer over the railing, and see that, today, it's the River of Brown Water. Completely blown out. Flood stage. Shin drums his fingers on the railing and lights a cigarette. Hisashi's shoulders slump in disappointment. Dale puts his camera gear away and we pile back in.

Arrival at the next small stream; another chocolate torrent. Next river, same deal. As the old-timers back home would say, too thick to drink, too thin to plow. When we stop for gas, Shin strolls out of a convenience store with a full carton of cigarettes under his arm.

Plan D: The Joganji River, a broad tailwater running through a huge, open valley. Not exactly photo-worthy, but here at least the dam should hold back some of the floodwater and give us a shot at *yamame*. Looking at the huge pools and boulder-strewn tailouts, I switch from the ethereal triple-ought rod to a more reasonable two-weight. I also can't help but imagine where steelhead and salmon might hold in these waters. I ask Hisashi if he fishes for cherry salmon here. "Yes," he says, smiling, "very much. Good year this year. I fish twenty-seven days and catch three cherry salmon."

All the water in all the gorgeous rice fields has to come from somewhere. The Joganji, like many Japanese rivers, is dammed, diverted, and pumped along its entire length. During growing season, it never even reaches the sea. That there are any salmon here at all is something of a miracle, and local anglers are left, for the most part, with land-locked smolts—*yamame*. They have traded salmon for rice. It occurs to me we might be making a similar trade at home for timber, minerals, oil, agriculture, and development. Would you trade a steelhead for a shopping mall? Apparently, a lot of us would.

All wouldas, couldas, and shouldas aside, the fishing is completely engrossing. We cast tiny, precise mayfly imitations on diaphanous leaders into pockets the size of a kitchen sink surrounded by swift currents, seams, and eddies. Any drag whatsoever results in emphatic refusals. These fish are tough. And beautiful, with smooth, nearly translucent amber sides and distinct vertical parr marks. A light sprinkling of black dots completes a clean, precise beauty that perfectly fits this country's design ethic. Nothing half-assed about *yamame*, that's for sure.

...

DIALOG FROM DINNER AT A KOREAN BARBECUE

Me: Man, I'm starving. This smells great, what is it?

Shin: How you say, bo ... bow ... bowl?

Me: Bowl? Yeah, I can see it's in a bowl. But what is it?

Shin: Not bowl ... animal part. Here, (points to abdomen) ... goes back and forth.

Me: Bowels? Really? Again?

Shin: Yes! That's it. Bowels. From cow. Very tasty.

Me: Funny, I'm not as hungry as I thought.

...

Dale needs more photos. I just want to fish a river that isn't blowing chunks. And Shin will stop at nothing to make both happen. Even if it means yet another long, torturous drive through countless switchbacks and hairpin turns clinging to sheer mountain walls. After all, what's another half day in the car? Especially when it involves utter terror for Westerners not used to left-lane driving or Shin's Speed Racer velocity. But that's what it takes to reach the pristine, sparkling headwater streams that run through the highest mountain range in Japan. And of course, that's what we do.

When we reach our destination, I pry my sweaty fingers from the door handle and step out into crisp, dry air and a scene of unimaginable beauty. Above, white-capped mountains send waterfalls cascading down granite chutes to the valley floor through ancient *hinoki* cypress forest. Wild chrysanthemums and knotweed grow head-high along the river, and we look for monkeys among the gnarled branches of broad-leafed chestnuts. Before we even make the first cast, I know that this place makes everything—not just the drive, but all the travel and time and effort—worthwhile.

Hisashi beams. "Here," he says, "is my favorite place." Indeed. Of course, even in this remotest of rivers, the fishing is no easier. But we're learning, adjusting, and maybe even—dare I say—getting better at this game. My flies land closer to the sweet spots, the mends prevent drag for just an instant longer, and predictably, the *iwana* seem just a bit more cooperative. More importantly, Hisashi doesn't have to struggle to conceal his disappointment quite as frequently.

In a deep, emerald pool beneath a grotto of giant, moss-covered boulders, a fish is working the far seam where a twisted maple shades the water. I flick my wrist, reach the rod to the left, and the fly settles and begins to drift. Money. The fish appears, tips back, and in the last possible instant before drag sets in, takes the fly.

The fish surges away and I let line run through my fingers until I have it on the reel and the clicker buzzes loudly. When it tires, Hisashi carefully nets my trophy, and we gather to shoot some photos before making a careful release. Shin slaps me on the back and laughs with relief. Hisashi shakes my hand vigorously. At a full eleven inches long, this is the fish of the trip, if not a lifetime. I break down the rod and sit back, surprised by the joy I feel from landing a fish less than a foot long. How easily the tectonic plates of our baselines shift.

• • •

There is no sign outside, or, for that matter, any indication at all that this might be a restaurant. There aren't even any windows. Just an anonymous black door in a quiet neighborhood of modest storefronts and low-rise apartment buildings. To the uneducated eye—mine—it looks like a most inauspicious place to celebrate our last night in Japan. I think we must have the wrong address.

Shin strides confidently to the door, opens it, and we step into a warmly lit room packed with people. Behind a polished wooden bar, three men dressed head to toe in immaculate white uniforms stop slicing fish and shout a guttural greeting in unison. If you've ever seen an old samurai movie—or for that matter, Belushi's imitation of one—you know what it sounds like. We are quickly seated, and after an animated conversation between Shin and the head chef, the magic begins.

First, freshly grated wasabi root, pickled wasabi greens, and sliced ginger are placed in neat piles directly on the bar in front of each of us. This is when I first notice that the bar's inset granite surface is refrigerated. This is serious. A trio of sushi arrives, each oval ball of rice wrapped in a sheet of *nori* seaweed to create a cup-shaped parcel, one holding deep-red salmon roe; another, ochre sea urchin; and the third filled with hundreds of nearly microscopic, raw, white shrimp. Incredibly, someone has removed the shells from every single nano-shrimp.

And we're just getting started. I find each successive serving better than the last: fresh *unagi* eel, basted in light, gingery soy and broiled crisp around the edges; a single, sugar-sweet, local shrimp tail still quivering with life; crunchy, briny clam neck; smooth, buttery strips of the local yellowtail, called *buri*.

Then, the one bite of devastating perfection: a thick, rectangular slab of pale, heavily marbled tuna belly. In fact, it looks remarkably like the decadent *Hida* beef we had back in Toyama. I dip it quickly in soy, pop it into my mouth, and reality warps. It is the single greatest bite of anything I have ever eaten. By far. The luxurious texture and incredible flavor create such an overwhelming sensation that it literally brings tears to my eyes.

"How do you like the *toro*?" Shin asks, smiling broadly at my reaction. I snap back to reality and immediately begin the mental gymnastics of dealing with Japanese hospitality—if I tell him how fantastic it is, he will immediately buy another round of what must be absurdly expensive fish. But if I lie to save him the money, he will be crushed. "That was amazing," I say, "but …" and before I can finish, he's already ordered another. I cringe at what it must be costing him, but my guilt is quickly washed down by the next delectable bite. "How do you like it this time?" he asks, lighting a cigarette. I consider my answer carefully again before speaking. Then I remember, with relief, what my mother always taught me: It's not polite to lie.

• • •

In my time here, I have learned to appreciate the wonders of miniature trout on wispy fly rods. To slurp my noodles loudly. To accept the overwhelming hospitality and relentless good cheer of Shin and Hisashi—although I find myself secretly hoping they never come to visit me, as I could never, ever reciprocate in kind. To understand more deeply the impacts of human activity— from agriculture, industry, and even the consumption of that magnificent *toro*—on our fisheries.

On a personal level, the visit has made me feel both more and less Japanese than ever. The food is a definite comfort zone, as is the culture of perfectionism. (I always assumed my fanatical attention to detail—maddening to most who know me—was some kind of OCD affliction. Now I can blame it on genetics.) On the other hand, the language, impenetrable to my Western eyes and ears, the sitting on the floor and diminutive living spaces, the centuries-old social traditions, have frequently turned me into a clumsy, lumbering American giant.

Looking out my rain-streaked hotel window at the streets of Nagoya, I can, once again, see the Ultraman statue there, standing tall, inscrutable, invincible ... and I know this foreign land is somehow a part of me, no matter how awkward the fit.

• • •

Just outside Nagoya, under a humid, dingy sky, four lanes of traffic have come to a halt. We inch forward at an agonizingly slow pace, Shin checking his watch, drumming his fingers on the wheel, smoking cigarettes one after another. "What time is your flight again?" he asks. When I answer, he frowns, shaking his head.

Finally, we can see flashing lights and flares up ahead. Another fifteen minutes and we reach the scene of the accident. A large Jet Ski has slipped off its trailer and now lies across two lanes of traffic, a jagged gash torn in its fiberglass skin. A Jet Ski. Figures. I have to refrain from making a sweeping generalization about the universal character of personal-watercraft owners. Police in powder-blue uniforms and white helmets direct traffic while highway workers scramble around trying to clear the wreckage. The owner of the Jet Ski, a young man with a dyed blond mullet and *Flashdance*-style sleeveless sweatshirt, sits on the trailer, head in hands, clearly distraught.

As we crawl past him, Shin veers closer, rolls down the window, leans out, and yells, "Jackass!" Then he looks at me with a satisfied grin, lights another cigarette, and steps on the gas.

MAY 2008

*It seemed like such a good idea earlier. But now that I'm
actually taking both kids fishing together for the first time,
maybe not so much. To minimize disaster potential, I have
chosen a small pond close to home and hauled enough snacks
to feed an army of sumo wrestlers. Still, things go sideways
quickly. The little guy, despite his sister's pleas for stealth,
cheerfully applies himself to whacking sticks, splashing into
the water, and tangling lines. She watches her bobber intently
while dirt clods and rocks rain down around it. "Alright," I
say, giving up on any semblance of fishing, "who can hit that
log with a rock?" Rods are tossed to the ground and forgotten.
We throw rocks. We watch eagles. We laugh together about
nothing at all. When I look back at the pond, I notice one of
the bobbers is missing, just as a rod starts skidding toward
the water. "Dad," they shout, "we got one!"*

THE WEATHER WILL DECIDE

I wake to the steady drip-drip of rainwater leaking through the hatch cover above my bunk. My sleeping bag is soaked. Last night, we fell asleep to the soft rhythm of waves sliding along the hull and a light mist falling on deck. Now I can feel the boat straining and bucking against a tight anchor line. Ten-year-old Skyla and seven-year-old Weston, warm and dry in their lower bunks, sleep on. But I need dry clothes, caffeine, and a new plan.

Up in the wheelhouse, Bruce and Gerald already have coffee on and charts spread across the table. The plan was to make the white-sand beaches and bountiful urchin beds of the outer islands today; we would eat *uni* for dinner. But the glass-calm bay we anchored in yesterday is gone now, replaced by whitecaps and driving rain. Shreds of mist hang in the avalanche chutes of dark, spruce-covered mountains towering above the sea. When I ask Gerald, the Haisla elder, what he thinks we should do, he says, with wisdom earned through a lifetime of working these waters, "The weather will decide for us."

The radio crackles: "Small craft advisory for Hecate Strait, wind fifteen to twenty-five knots, rising to twenty-five to thirty-five in the afternoon, wind waves three to five feet ..." So much for urchin diving.

Here in the Great Bear Rainforest, where you can look up to see driftwood logs caught in tree branches a hundred feet above the waterline, this hardly even qualifies as weather. But it's enough to force us to recalibrate.

We will not make our planned destination tonight. We will not have *uni* for dinner. Our best, and really, only, option: Fish here. The kelp beds lining this shoreline teem with quillback and black rockfish, snapper, greenling. Door-sized halibut lurk in the depths. Several million salmon—Chinook, coho, sockeye, chum, and pink—are, at this moment, migrating through the water around us, drawn like iron filings to the magnet of their birth rivers. For the kids and me, conditioned as we are by more austere harvest opportunities in our Puget Sound home waters, this feels like an embarrassment of riches.

After breakfast, we pull anchor, our ears filled with white noise from a million raindrops strafing water. Another squall barrels toward us from the channel. We'll have to fish tight to the shoreline, tucked into the lee of the land wherever possible. The kids huddle under a tarp we've jury-rigged across the back deck. Porpoises, seals, salmon, and more seabirds than we can count obliterate the boundary between sea and sky, gorging on acres of herring.

"The tankers will come through there," Bruce says, pointing to a narrow gap between islands. He's talking about the ships that will haul away crude oil piped here from the tar sands. The Enbridge Pipeline, if approved, will carry up to seven hundred fifty thousand barrels of oil per day. The ships, some more than fourteen hundred feet long, won't arrive empty, either. They'll come in loaded with condensate—a toxic, explosive by-product of the Indonesian oil fields used to dilute thick tar-sand bitumen—for the two-hundred-thousand-barrel-a-day twin pipe going back to Alberta. That the pipeline will traverse headwaters of both the Fraser and Skeena Rivers—two of the most important salmon watersheds in North America—through torturous, slide-prone terrain, or that two-hundred-plus oil tankers will have to negotiate these narrow fjords every year, means little to those who measure such things only in terms of profit.

Weston shouts, "There's a fish! There's a fish!" We look around, seeing salmon leaping in every direction. "No," he says, "on the line!" Skyla leaps to the rod, sets the hook, and the reel's clicker chatters as line pours out. This is not another little pink salmon. The fish dives, then streaks to the surface, launching its thick, deep-shouldered body into the air. King salmon! Skyla's knuckles tighten on the reel handle.

Suddenly, just off the starboard side, an explosive whoosh of air and water—a humpback whale gulping herring and air. Skyla loses focus, distracted by the whale's immense size and close proximity. But she keeps cranking. A collective cheer goes up when Weston and I scoop the fish into our net. The whale, a bit farther off now, continues feeding.

We won't have urchins for dinner tonight. But we're already looking forward to grilled king salmon steaks dripping with savory fat. This happy surprise won't be a result of our plans, but rather, what the weather decided for us. That's how it works here; Mother Nature sets the conditions, and humans adjust. It's how Gerald's people have survived, and until relatively recently, thrived, here for ten thousand years.

In the evening, with wind still whistling through the rigging and the open channel engulfed by the chaos of rolling five-footers, we seek shelter in another small bay shielded from the weather by a nearly circular wall of precipitous mountains. We will eat dinner, then the kids and I will take the skiff ashore to a small cabin built by Haisla fishermen for nights like this. We are looking forward to sleeping under a dry roof on solid ground. Gerald fires up the grill and when I drop the salted belly strips from Skyla's king salmon and thick steaks from the halibut Weston caught yesterday onto the grill, the sizzling, popping fat makes my mouth water.

With the addition of piles of Dungeness crab boiled in sea-water and dipped in melted butter, it's an epic feast. We eat until we're stuffed to the gills, as they say, then retire to the covered back deck for fresh air and a brief flash of warm, low-angled light as the sun ducks under the cloud cover. Bruce brings out his guitar and picks the melody of "Long Black Veil," a song I grew up hearing my dad play. After days of the kids begging him to tell the Bigfoot stories he mentioned before we set out, Gerald says it's time. The kids pull their chairs in close around Gerald and he tells a chilling tale of one of his relatives who accidentally wounded a Bigfoot while hunting. The hunter was chased by a family of Bigfoots through the forest, across the beach, and into the water, where he was rescued in the nick of time by his partner in their fishing boat.

Gerald finishes the story just as full darkness sets in, leaving the kids—and I will admit, me—with wide eyes and goose bumps. In an attempt to lower his level of fear, Weston prods Gerald for a bit more information. "But that was a really, really long time ago, right?" he asks. "No," Gerald says, "it was just recently. Probably only 140 years ago."

The kids are relieved. Not relieved enough to find any remaining appeal in the idea of a dark cabin on the dark shore, but relieved. We will sleep on the boat. And, with rain once again dripping onto my bunk, I have hours to think about the concept of time, and Gerald's view of it versus my own, not to mention most of the modern world's. It's an important perspective, something I turn over and over in my mind while listening to the wind and feeling the boat rolling in the chop.

Outside our little bay, in the main channel, the weather intensifies through the night. Clearly, we made the right decision to stay put today, and will most likely need to do the same tomorrow. It's OK, though, the fishing is plenty good here in the lee of these islands, and we have the luxury of not needing to be anywhere anytime soon. We'll let the weather decide.

But I wonder, in the boardrooms and stockholder meetings of distant financial centers, will anyone care about a storm front on some distant coast? In the corner offices of skyscrapers, will they have the patience to adjust shipping schedules with seven hundred and fifty thousand barrels of crude pushing to the coast every day and quarterly projections looming?

If we allow Enbridge to build the pipeline, there will be surprises. But they won't be happy ones. For that matter, on this coastline of tight, twisting channels and extreme weather, they won't really be surprises, after all. And when the inevitable happens, what will I tell Skyla and Weston?

APRIL 2009

Way up here on the northern coast of British Columbia, just across a stormy, inland sea from Alaska, things are not going well. Our spring steelhead expedition has stalled because, contrary to the calendar, spring has not arrived. Eight-foot ice walls line the riverbanks. The 34-degree water runs winter low, exposing a bony riverbed and leaving little enticement for migrating fish. The VHF says another front is bearing down on us from Haida Gwaii, and at this moment, we are stuck. High-centered on exposed rocks four miles up a nameless river in a sixteen-foot jet sled, which, full disclosure, I was driving. I think of Weston asking, while I packed for this trip, if he could "come to Tanada" with me next time, and feel a sharp pang of missing the kids. As we try to jam an alder-log lever under the bow, with near-freezing water pouring over the tops of our waders, Tim looks up and starts to laugh. And then, inexplicably, I'm laughing too, our voices echoing out into the vast northern night.

THE MYTH OF HATCHERIES

The appeal is undeniable. I get it. If we just put enough money into building fish hatcheries, we can make up for all the damage we've caused to our rivers. The idea that man can do better than nature, that technology can triumph over any adversity, is just part of our pioneer mindset. On the once-mighty Columbia, the efforts to make up for all the cheap electricity our dams produce have, according to the Northwest Power and Conservation Council, cost citizens $12.4 billion (as of 2011) in salmon mitigation efforts. As noted previously, not long ago, a single harvested spring Chinook born and bred in the Upper Columbia's Entiat hatchery cost more than $68,000 to produce. Ridiculous, sure. But it's easy to discount such programs, along with the hundreds of hatcheries up and down the West Coast that see their returns dwindling year after year, as relics of a bygone era.

Today, as a growing percentage of our country seems intent on ignoring scientific fact, the support for hatcheries remains. Like our youthful belief in Santa Claus and the Tooth Fairy, we need to outgrow the myth that hatcheries can save us from ourselves. In most cases, they simply don't work—especially where wild fish are involved. A mountain of published, peer-reviewed scientific studies shows that the mere presence of hatchery fish works as a powerful detriment to wild fish recovery. The mass release of hatchery smolts displaces naturally produced juveniles and outcompetes them for resources. According to studies by biologist Mark Chilcote and many others, when the hatchery adults return, they mingle and spawn with their wild counterparts, adding their domesticated genes to the pool and reducing the survival rate of the offspring by up to 30 percent. In fact, the National Oceanographic and Atmospheric Administration (NOAA) cites genetic pollution from hatchery steelhead as the primary cause for listing eighteen of the twenty-one distinct Oregon coastal wild steelhead stocks as either "depressed" or of "special concern."

Science and negative impacts on wild fish stocks aside, anglers know hatcheries don't work either. We see the failure almost everywhere we fish. If hatcheries are supposed to mitigate the loss of wild fish—even though we now know they actually contribute to the loss—the resulting sport fisheries are hardly a viable substitute. Hatchery salmon and steelhead, inbred for generations and lacking the constant pressure of natural selection as juveniles, return in compressed time frames and race to their hatchery-terminal holes without pause.

After decades of harvesting the biggest hatchery fish and those most prone to lingering in the lower river or biting, we've selected for a race of fish that are both smaller and less aggressive. For example, on the Deschutes River in Oregon, where hatchery steelhead far outnumber their wild cousins, a majority of the fly-caught steelhead are still the naturally more aggressive wild fish. In Puget Sound, the average historical size of an adult Chinook salmon was nearly twenty-five pounds. Today, after decades of heavy hatchery production and the associated harvest, the average size is less than ten pounds. And in most rivers where hatchery salmon and steelhead return, the primary sport fishery exists at the hatchery outlet hole, creating a poor angling experience and increased opportunity for snagging and other illegal activities.

It's not like hatchery fish keep coming back in huge numbers, either. Based on published hatchery return rates from a broad cross-section of West Coast hatcheries, when a hatchery first starts production, there are typically spectacular initial runs, with up to a 12 percent return rate. Then, after a few generations, as the genetic pool weakens, the spiral of diminishing returns sets in. Within a decade or two, most hatcheries get returns of half or less than their initial rates. In another decade or two, it's cut to half or less yet again. And so on. The pattern is clearly a steady and continuous decline, trending toward zero.

According to hatchery records and harvest reports published by the Washington Department of Fish and Wildlife (WDFW), the North Fork Nooksack River is a prime example. The best return rate in recent years was 1.7 percent in 2002. In 2009, it was 0.07 percent. That year, the combined tribal and sport fisheries harvested fifty-nine hatchery steelhead from a release class of one hundred sixty thousand smolts. If we make a low estimate of $1 per smolt raised, which doesn't even include the cost of building or maintaining the hatchery, a little simple math shows it cost the general tax-paying public $2,712 for each harvested adult fish. Bill McMillan, a biologist recently retired from Wild Fish Conservancy, wonders, "Does a recreational angler who catches one of these Nooksack hatchery fish need a $2,700 gift from his fellow taxpayers? What if he catches three or four?" If you were lucky enough to land one, imagine asking your nonfishing neighbors how they feel about paying for your recreation. What about an out-of-work teacher or public-health worker? Or a college student who can no longer afford the skyrocketing tuition at a state university? When you look at the high cost of hatchery production and combine it with ever-diminishing returns, low recreational quality, and the heavy toll it takes on wild fish, it would be difficult for the recreational angler—or any tax-paying citizen, for that matter—to call hatcheries a success.

One day you wake up, look at the facts, and come to the difficult conclusion that maybe the big guy with the white beard isn't really hauling a sack full of gifts in an airborne sled driven by flying reindeer. It's tough to swallow. Some call it a loss of innocence and lament the day, but we all accept the reality and move on.

Or, maybe we don't. Here in Washington State, a part of the country renowned for its environmental consciousness, we are proving otherwise.

• • •

The city of Seattle, that bastion of municipal greenness, where organic food, recycling, and hybrid cars are a way of life, recently announced completion of a $31 million salmon hatchery on the Cedar River. Its purpose? To more than double the number of artificially produced juvenile sockeye salmon released into Lake Washington, and thereby increase recreational and tribal fishing opportunities. In order to open the popular Lake Washington fishery to recreational angling, a run of three hundred fifty thousand adult sockeye is required. On average, this fishery occurs about two-and-a-half times per decade. At every level, attempts to further invest in this fishery are a serious mistake.

Let's start with the money: Thirty-one million dollars of municipal funds at a time when the city struggles to maintain decent student-to-teacher ratios, mental healthcare, or housing for the poor, or even drivable roads, is pretty tough to swallow. Even if the hatchery was a success, it's a gross misuse of funding when so many other critical services are disappearing. I doubt the average taxpayer would consider this a good investment of their hard-earned money.

Even worse, as numerous biological studies demonstrate, the reason for poor returns of adult sockeye has little to do with the number of juvenile salmon released. In fact, the bottleneck occurs in the lake itself, where a wide range of factors—most significantly, the high concentration of predators—decimates the juvenile sockeye population in its first year of life. According to most scientists who studied the problem, the lake is at carrying capacity and the influx of more baby salmon will not increase the number of returning adults. If the lake follows a common trend found in other hatchery programs—including the North Fork Nooksack cited earlier—the addition of more hatchery juveniles may in fact cause fewer adult salmon to return.

Another limiting factor is water quality. The major creeks running into Lake Washington are so loaded with toxins from various urban sources—including failing septic systems, lawn chemicals, and car brakes—the water is lethal for 50 to 100 percent of the entering salmon during stormwater events. While the creeks remain earmarked for major cleanups in the coming years, a century's worth of accumulated toxins sits trapped in the lake itself. While this will surely impact Lake Washington's ecosystem for decades into the future, even more troubling is the potential effect eating these fish might have on the humans who harvest them. And the city wants to increase this fishery?

Finally, the Lake Washington sockeye run is a largely artificial fishery. What native sockeye population that may have existed before the hatchery introduction was small at best. There were, however, once-robust runs of native Chinook, coho, and steelhead, all of which can now be found on the Endangered Species List. The effect of the sockeye introduction on naturally occurring fish stocks is unknown, but one thing is certain: Their presence is at best neutral, and there is a high likelihood that because of the competition for resources and attraction of predators, it's probably negative. Given this, wouldn't it be a smarter investment of taxpayer dollars to work on habitat restoration or other efforts to recover populations of fish that are actually supposed to be here?

• • •

Out on the Olympic Peninsula's Sol Duc watershed, another battle is currently underway. Here, the Snider Creek hatchery brood-stock program produces a run of "nearly wild" steelhead for the sport fishery. Each year, volunteer anglers take fifty or more live, wild steelhead from the river and deliver them to the hatchery. These wild, naturally produced, native steelhead are then spawned in captivity, and their offspring raised in a safe, sterile, predator-free environment.

On the surface, it seems like a good plan. The wild fish genetics pass along to a larger number of offspring, and the sport fishery gets a boost during the normally slow season between the early hatchery run in December and the late wild fish run in February and March.

But this is, once again, the same old man-can-do-better-than-Mother-Nature hubris. And in this case, it's the safe hatchery environment itself that creates the primary problem. Tinkering with the critical process of natural selection turns wild fish into genetically weak hatchery fish within a single generation. When Snider Creek steelhead spawn with their wild cousins, the genetic impact is immediate and clearly detrimental to the wild population. Furthermore, the brood-stock concept removes fifty healthy, viable spawners from a wild Sol Duc steelhead population that's dropped nearly 40 percent in the last twenty years.

There's also another complicating factor. The increased sportfishing pressure generated by the January return of Snider

Creek fish has a negative impact on depressed early run wild steelhead stocks. Historically, wild Sol Duc steelhead returned in great numbers in December and January, but with the traditional hatchery-steelhead kill fishery centered around these months, the early returning wild component has been nearly extirpated as bycatch. Increased sportfishing—even with catch-and-release regulations implemented for wild fish—cannot help the least-healthy segment of the wild steelhead run.

From a purely economic standpoint, the Snider Creek hatchery is also a disaster. Based on records from the WDFW, releases of Snider Creek hatchery smolts over the last twenty years, ranging from fifteen thousand to one hundred twenty thousand in number, result in one of the lowest adult return ratios in the state. Most years see less than 1 percent returns, and it sometimes falls as low as 0.22 percent. Can we really afford to take fifty wild, spawning steelhead out of natural production for such paltry returns? Dr. Nathan Mantua, a NOAA scientist, notes that, "Relatively healthy wild steelhead populations in watersheds with relatively good habitat, like we have in the Sol Duc, have become increasingly rare. They don't need hatchery programs, they need protection." And the Sol Duc needs every last wild fish spawning in its gravel that it can get.

I don't begrudge my fellow recreational anglers' desire to have a viable steelhead fishery in January. I'm even more sympathetic to the guides who need the income. But I do believe that as users and stewards of the river, we all need to look at the bigger picture here. If guides and anglers invested the same amount of time and effort in habitat restoration that currently goes into the Snider Creek program, the end result would be a healthier, more sustainable run of wild fish. Which, of course, would mean better fishing and more business for the guides.

In 2014, the Snider Creek hatchery is up for review by the state. Both sides of the issue are lobbying intensely, and officials should make a decision later this year. It's a tough situation. A number of Olympic Peninsula anglers and guides who I count among my friends support the Snider Creek program. But I hope they can see the forest for the trees, as it were, and understand not only the negative impacts of the Snider program, but also the potential positives that come from eliminating it.

• • •

On Northern California's Eel River, a steelhead hatchery was built and began operation in 1964. That year, the run of wild steelhead to the Eel was eighty-two thousand fish. After continuous hatchery planting for thirty years, in 1994 the combined hatchery and wild run came in at two thousand fish total. Which is to say, thirty years and millions of taxpayer dollars later, the steelhead run was eighty thousand fish fewer than before the hatchery was built.

At that point, the wild Eel River steelhead were deemed endangered, and the hatchery was closed. Fast-forward twenty years without the hatchery, and in 2014 the run of wild steelhead returning to the Eel was estimated at more than forty thousand fish.

This would be a shocking story if it weren't almost exactly the same as what took place on Washington State's Toutle River, where, following the eruption of Mount Saint Helens, the hatchery was closed and wild steelhead repopulated the devastated river to levels higher than what the state considered maximum carrying capacity *before* the eruption. In fact, seven years post-eruption, there were more wild winter steelhead spawning in the Toutle than in any other Lower Columbia watershed.

The Skagit River in Washington was once the crown jewel of Pacific Northwest steelhead fishing. It sustained wild steelhead harvests between ten thousand and thirty thousand wild fish per year—for decades. After a steelhead hatchery was built to supplement the already robust wild run, the wild population, and then later, the hatchery fish themselves, dwindled, resulting in an annual harvest of fewer than four hundred combined wild and hatchery fish. For recreational anglers, that meant a complete closure on the spring wild fish catch-and-release season. This, after spending millions of dollars to build, maintain, and operate the hatchery.

In 2014, the WDFW settled a lawsuit brought by Wild Fish Conservancy, agreeing to stop hatchery operations on the Skagit for twelve years. The results of this action remain to be seen, but I'm confident that if the Skagit follows the remarkable recoveries we've seen when hatchery operations were stopped on the Eel, the Toutle, and other rivers, the wild fish will come back.

. . .

With millions of dollars already invested and hatcheries operating across the country, are we past the point of no return? I really don't know. But our collective belief in hatcheries is not slowing down, even with all the scientific, financial, and anecdotal evidence pointing to their failure. In fact, taxpayers invested $16 million to build a hatchery on the newly dam-free Elwha River, in spite of the pristine habitat and pure wild genetics from salmon and steelhead that had been trapped above the dams.

I believe that everyday citizens and taxpayers would be outraged if they understood how their money was spent and the negative return on investment the hatcheries provide. I think we need to reach beyond the angling community. We need to spread the word to friends and family, write letters to editors, and more importantly, contact our elected officials and let them know how important these issues are to us. We need to demand they stop throwing good money into wasteful programs that work as a detriment to their stated goals.

And we need to hope that recreational anglers and guides, tribal nations, and decision makers at the state and federal level can see that the long-term benefits of healthy wild fish runs— more fish for everyone, sustainable fisheries, no cost—outweigh short-term needs. Hell, in most cases, hatcheries don't even come close to meeting our short-term needs anyway. Sad as it may be, it's time to stop putting cookies out on Christmas Eve and tucking teeth under pillows. We have to grow up and face the facts: Hatcheries don't work.

Postscript 2022

On the Columbia River, the Bonneville Power Administration continues to spend hundreds of millions of dollars per year on fish and wildlife mitigation, with hatchery costs representing the largest percentage of those expenditures. As of 2021, the esti-mated total amount spent is now over $18 billion.

The City of Seattle's $31 million hatchery, completed in 2011, has failed to produce a recreational sockeye fishery in Lake Washington. In 2021, the hatchery managers requested additional funding for "improvements" to the project.

The Snider Creek brood-stock hatchery, like similar, well-documented programs on the Hood River, the Deschutes, and Sheep Creek, continued its negative impact on wild steel-head recovery on the Sol Duc River. In 2012, after the previous nineteen years produced an average of 129 harvested adult

Snider Creek fish per year for the tribal and recreational fisheries combined, the WDFW announced the cancellation of the program and the establishment of the Sol Duc as the only wild steelhead gene bank on the Olympic Peninsula. Not surprisingly, in 2021, when wild steelhead runs on every other major river on the Washington coast were projected to barely meet or come in below minimum escapement numbers, the Quillayute system—of which the Sol Duc is a major tributary—projections were nearly double the escapement goal.

On the Skagit in 2014, after years of wild steelhead returns too low to open the spring catch-and-release season, Wild Fish Conservancy sued to stop the WDFW from planting the highly inbred Chambers Creek hatchery winter steelhead. The state settled by agreeing to close the Skagit hatchery for twelve years. As the number of wild fish rebounded, the long-lost catch-and-release fishery reopened in 2019, and again in 2021. While the openers were controversial, the fact that the state and tribal comanagers deemed the recovery strong enough to provide recreational fishing opportunities shows how quickly wild fish populations can rebound when the limiting factor of a hatchery program is removed.

As hatchery stocks continue to dwindle due to inbreeding and domestication, a distinct regional push to move toward integrated or brood-stock hatchery programs—where instead of using returning hatchery fish, wild fish are captured and taken to hatcheries for spawning—is gaining momentum. While this may temporarily reinvigorate hatchery genetics, it also removes natural selection for survival in the wild, resulting in more examples like the failed Snider Creek program. In other words, wild fish are taken from their spawning beds, and their offspring are turned into hatchery fish, with all the attendant problems. Worse, as the science has become clear that the presence of hatchery fish leads wild fish populations to trend toward zero—and hatchery fish themselves eventually trend toward zero from inbreeding—brood-stock hatchery programs bring us closer to extinction for both hatchery and wild stocks.

Recently, as I was looking at real-time fish counts for various fish hatcheries online, I discovered that the state was taking wild steelhead from the South Fork of the Skykomish to their hatchery facility at Reiter Ponds. I immediately called Wild Fish Conservancy to find out how, or if, this was even legal. The resulting litigation is currently pending, but I think this provides a window into the way many states are thinking about reviving their hatchery programs.

It's been estimated that, given the huge numbers of hatchery pink salmon coming out of Prince William Sound, the recent increase in hatchery production in the Pacific Northwest, and expanding hatchery programs in Korea, Japan, and Russia, there are now more juvenile salmon in the Pacific Ocean than ever before. At the same time, there are fewer adult salmon surviving to ascend rivers around the Pacific Rim than at any other time in history. According to the work of Greg Ruggerone and other scientists, the Pacific Ocean is likely at or beyond carrying capacity for salmon. Which is to say, there isn't enough food to support the massive numbers of hatchery fish we're pouring into the sea. On years with high releases of juvenile hatchery salmon, the average size of adult Bristol Bay sockeye, a 100 percent wild run, is significantly smaller. Coinciding with the historical growth of hatchery programs, the average size of adult Puget Sound Chinook salmon has gone from more than twenty pounds to about ten pounds. And the overall returns of wild and hatchery fish alike continue to fade.

In 2018, as the population of southern resident killer whales, which rely on Chinook salmon as a key part of their diets, shrank to just seventy-three animals, the Washington State Orca Task Force recommended increased production of hatchery Chinook to feed the starving whales. Salmon and whale experts alike protested this recommendation, citing scientific findings that showed the killer whales need larger, wild Chinook salmon in order to survive. The influx of additional hatchery salmon would also further hinder wild salmon recovery, making the situation worse. But the task force took the easy way out, the way that requires little to no sacrifice by any of the other stakeholders. Today, in an action that further endangers both southern resident killer whales and Puget Sound wild Chinook salmon, the hatcheries are increasing production to "feed the whales."

While recreational anglers often view hatchery programs purely in relation to their own interests, it's important to remember that hatcheries also now serve as the primary method for the United States to satisfy treaty obligations with sovereign tribal nations of the Pacific Northwest. I fully support meeting these obligations, and in all honesty, would give up my own fishing if that's what it takes to ensure treaty promises are kept. After years of studying the situation, though, I believe there is a better path to what we all want—more harvestable numbers of salmon and steelhead for tribal and recreational fisheries alike. I'm hopeful that we can find common ground on the subject of hatcheries by making science-based decisions—which are well supported by real-life anecdotal evidence—and look forward to a time when thriving, sustainable runs of wild fish return for everyone's benefit.

When I wrote this story, I thought all we needed to do was "grow up and face the fact that hatcheries don't work." That the overwhelming number of scientific studies demonstrating the negative impact hatcheries have on wild salmon recovery would make the point clear. That the failed economics of hatcheries alone would move voters to demand that we stop wasting money on a concept that creates a negative return on investment. That the stories of remarkable recoveries of wild fish populations in places where we stopped planting hatchery fish would win the day. But clearly, I was wrong. Now more than ever, we need to double down on efforts to highlight the destructive impact of hatcheries. We need to use every available tool—legal, political, and media—to change this narrative. If you care about fish, or orcas, or just fiscal responsibility, I'm asking you to join me.

SEPTEMBER 2011

*The ringing sound of steel hitting concrete echoes down
the canyon and spills into town. The dams are coming out.
The Elwha River is about to run free and unimpeded to the
sea for the first time in more than a hundred years. I am
in Port Angeles to give a talk at the celebration with Yvon.
Standing outside the auditorium, we watch as hundreds
of people stream in from the parking lot. My already high
anxiety flies off the Richter scale. Yvon looks around calmly,
hands in pockets. Earlier, when we first arrived, Yvon had
suggested we do something fun to kill time. With stress levels
climbing, I told him I was fine with anything. He chose to
calm my jitters with flu shots at Rite Aid. Back at the event,
seeing my growing distress, he points toward the bathroom,
muttering something in Spanish. "Piss of fear," he translates,
"bullfighters do it before entering the ring." "Oh," I say,
feeling a glimmer of hope, "to calm their nerves?" "No,"
he says, "so when they get gored by the bull, their bladder
won't explode."*

A RIVER REBORN

Three minutes into our float, the V-wakes of submerged rocks in the tailout begin to move, creasing the glassy surface as they peel away from our approaching raft. Skyla and Weston lean forward, scouting ahead. "Are those all fish?" Skyla asks, then, with rising urgency, "They are! Look!" Weston climbs up onto the bow, afraid to miss out. Chaos ensues. I yell at him to keep his feet on the floor; he ignores me and scrambles for position. "There's one over there!" he hollers, "and two more over there!" Our raft accelerates into the riffle, the glare shifts, and now I can see for myself: king salmon. Lots of them.

The final remnants of the upper dam came down last week; the lower dam was cleared more than a year ago. And we are here to experience the newly free-flowing Elwha River. Despite dire predictions of sediment choking the river with mud, today, the water flows with startling clarity, colored only by the faint blue-green hint of its glacial origins. Clean cobble—from fist- to basketball-sized—covers the bottom; new logjams and gravel bars line the banks.

And in every tailout and flat terrace, there are fish. Descendants of the king salmon we've watched for years banging against the lower dam have finally reached their ancestral spawning grounds. While I am sad and disappointed that the continued hatchery operation most likely contributed many of these fish, it is, nonetheless, uplifting to see them here, doing what they were meant to do. I wonder, though, how much stronger and more sustainable this run would be if we'd only had the patience to let Nature repopulate the river on its own. Still, that there are fish here at all feels like a miracle. We watch a thirty-pound female king tip onto her side and, with great tail-flapping exertion, excavate a new redd, or nest. Several males with fearsome, hooked jaws and ragged fins hover nearby, while cutthroat and bull trout hold just downstream, waiting to snatch a salmon-egg meal. The ancient conveyer belt is back in business, delivering rich ocean nutrients to the sterile interior in the form of salmon.

Even as we float the Elwha, I can't help but imagine this kind of resurgent life on the once-mighty Snake River. There, four enormous, salmon-killing dams have outlasted their useful lifespan and now stand only as grand monuments to hubris. Is it asking too much to want something more than stagnant, warm-water reservoirs and empty tributaries for the Snake? I don't think so.

We pull over to stretch our legs on a broad gravel bar. While the kids run the shoreline looking for more fish, I stare into the choppy surface at the head of the pool. Perfect steelhead water. As I mentally work through the mends needed to fish the inside seam, I can almost feel my fly swimming through four feet of blue-green water, the line tight on my fingers. When the Elwha reopens to anglers, I will be here in this run—or, given the shifting nature of a new river, one like it—swinging a sink tip with crazed anticipation. In the deepest part of the pool, I can just make out the shadows of pale, chrome salmon, fresh from the sea.

Our afternoon falls into the typical rhythm of a coastal river float: riffle, pool, the occasional joy and adrenaline jolt of small rapids. The kids remain absorbed by their quest to spot fish. Weston keeps count, as is his nature, and loses track when the number reaches triple digits. We are buoyant.

When we reach the takeout, the kids aren't ready to give up the river just yet. Neither am I. We shed our float gear and pile into the car. Where the Elwha meets the Strait of Juan de Fuca, we walk to the beach. For longer than I can remember, the mouth of the Elwha was a straight, sediment-starved channel pouring abruptly into salt water, but now we find acres of fertile delta—a complex maze of tidal pools, flood ponds, sloughs, and sandbars littered with driftwood.

Tiny salmon, flashing silver in the evening light, leap for insects and create intersecting rings across the smooth surface, a natural Venn diagram of wild salmon survival. We sit in silence, watching baby salmon feed and the new river pushing against the tide. On the far side, an adult king explodes into the air on its way upstream. "Dad?" Weston asks, "can we come back here to fish sometime?" I'm way ahead of you, buddy. Way ahead.

GIANTS LIVE FOREVER

Through the years, I've talked to Bruce Hill on the phone more times than I can count, often at odd hours, about subjects big and small. Recipes for teriyaki sauce and salmon caviar. Conservation campaign strategies. Guitar techniques. Family. Personal issues and challenges. For so many reasons it's been a steady comfort in my life to know that I could pick up the phone any time and he'd be there with wisdom, compassion, and pure, big-hearted kindness.

When I was going through my divorce, he was there, knowing when to keep it light, when to sympathize, and when to make suggestions. He offered me the couch at the Hill house, which I have slept on many times, saying, "Just come up and we'll fish and eat. If you start driving now, you'll be here tomorrow. I'll have dinner ready."

Yesterday I woke up feeling the need to talk to my old friend Bruce, as I have so many times, and it finally hit me that he's gone.

When I met Bruce, he was already a giant, a legendary figure in the conservation world for the campaign to protect wild steelhead in British Columbia, and for working tirelessly—often desperately—to save the Kitlope, the largest intact temperate rainforest in the world, from destruction. Along with his Haisla brother, Gerald Amos, he continued an incredible run of work, helping to stop Royal Dutch Shell in the Sacred Headwaters of the Skeena, Nass, and Stikine Rivers; to keep the Enbridge Pipeline and its oil out of the Skeena; and most recently, to prevent Petronas from building a natural gas plant that would destroy vital salmon habitat in the Skeena estuary.

As a father, I've always tried to make sure my kids spend time with the mentors who've helped me along the way. Perhaps it's lazy parenting on my part, but my hope is that their wisdom would rub off on the kids. Four years ago, I brought Skyla and Weston to meet Bruce and Gerald. We took the *Suncrest*, an old, converted halibut boat, to explore the Inside Passage. We fished, hiked, snorkeled, cooked epic meals, fought the weather, gathered prawns and crabs, listened to and told stories, laughed, and sang. We made lifetime memories, and the kids learned valuable, early lessons on what it takes to protect the world we love.

When I think of Bruce, I see him playing guitar and singing with the kids on the back deck of the *Suncrest*. I think of him holding court at the Hills' legendary kitchen table with friends and activists of all kinds gathered around. I think of countless long drives, boat rides, and fishing trips, and the stories that filled them. I remember the time Bruce, Yvon, and I consumed an entire mixing bowl full of salmon eggs in two days. I think of his life's work, how he taught us to kick ass and butt heads, but to remember the human side of conservation. I think of how he could get angry and rage, then let it go and laugh and hug you.

Bruce has left the building, but he isn't gone. The untouched Kitlope, now protected forever as a Provincial Park; the pipeline-free Skeena flowing pure and clean from headwaters to sea; the eelgrass beds teeming with salmon on Lelu Island, all stand as monuments to his work. His wisdom and teachings have fueled the next generation of ass-kicking conservationists, the Shannon McPhails, the Greg Knoxes, the Caitlyn Vernons of the world. His presence flows through his wife, Anne, and their two children, Aaron and Julia, who follow in his footsteps with a ferocious commitment to protecting our planet. And yes, his spirit rubbed off on my kids, Skyla and Weston, who carry the fight forward as budding activists.

He's with us and all around us in the wild places that remain wild, in the rough-and-ready conservation spirit of the North, in the meals we cook and share with friends and family, in the kindness and generosity that made hundreds, if not thousands, of us who knew him want to be better human beings. I still need to come to grips with knowing I can no longer pick up the phone and hear his big laugh and welcoming voice, but I am happy—and honored—to have been his friend. Giants live forever.

WHAT IS FLY FISHING?

It's that ice-cold Belikin on a sweltering tropical night. The sweet scent of wet alders and the pungent odor of low-tide mangroves. The 4:00 am alarm clock. Endless drives on dark Canadian highways. Rivers coming in and going out. Muddy trails. The Bucket. Insomnia and exhaustion. Nearly crashing every time you cross a bridge. A twenty-inch brown sipping duns and the rattling explosion of tarpon. Roosters crowing at dawn in the Keys.

It's the sun coming up over the Absaroka Range, going down across the wide-open Pacific, or circling the horizon in the Russian Arctic. It's albies crashing bait off Harkers, six-inch *yamame* in the Japanese Alps, and finding good water at the end of a long hike. Cheap hotels and soggy tents. Cuban sandwiches. Freeze-dried chili mac. Gut-busting asados. The crunch of caddis in camp-stove spaghetti.

It's telling lies around the woodstove. Singing along to road music. Spelling your buddy on the oars or taking a turn on the platform. Fishing first water and following someone through. Too much rain. Not enough rain. Snow. Heat. Humidity. Wind chop and swell. Tide rips. Nervous water. Seams, eddies, riffles, and pools. The little pond up the road and the Gulf of Mexico.

It's teaching and learning. Twisting feathers and chewing the fat. Parents and kids. Responsibility to protect what we love. The empty place in the bow where a dog named Madison used to sit. Sunburn. Mosquito bites. Line cuts. High fives and back slaps. Old friends and new. Elation and despair. Memories. Hopes. Dreams.

What is fly fishing? Everything.

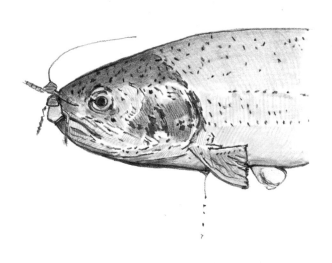

JULY 2014

We ducked into this shallow, mud-bottomed bay to avoid the white squalls and vicious chop pounding the coast. Now I'm standing at the tiny stove, frying bacon in the wheelhouse. Out on deck, Weston is fishing, although I've already told him that he probably won't catch anything here. I'm on the North Coast of British Columbia again, this time to write about a pristine wilderness endangered by a proposed oil pipeline. I've brought Skyla and Weston for an adventure that I hope might soothe their worries about my divorce from their mother, and to soak up the wisdom of Bruce and Gerald. Now Weston is shouting that he has a fish on, that it's "pulling really hard." I shout back that he's just snagged on the bottom and the boat is swinging on anchor. He insists it's a fish. In frustration, I turn off the stove and step outside. And there he is, sitting in a lawn chair, feet braced against the gunwale, his little trout rod bent double. Line smokes off the reel. The crew gathers around, cheering. After nearly an hour, his face streaked with sweat and rain, Weston pulls back one more time and Gerald scoops a thirty-pound halibut into the boat. "See, Dad," Weston says, "I told you it was a fish."

THERE IS NO PLAN B

Day Six 7:05 pm

We explode out of the mist a hundred feet off the deck, roaring up River X, careening around skeins of cotton-candy fog snagged on old-growth sentinels, banking hard, skidding through empty air to charge up River Y, rocks, trees, all reality blurring beneath my feet. A mostly gone bottle of Crown clutched between Kate's knees and hammering rotor slap tearing at our ears. We cut the corner on a sweeping oxbow and rise, the carpet of model-railroad spruce and incandescent yellow cottonwoods zooming past, racing darkness back to camp now. Rick in the back seat hunched over his video camera, peering into the playback screen, his voice crackles over headset static—"Dude, I double punched it!"—followed by rising, maniacal laughter.

Day Six 6:27 pm

If a camera adds fifteen pounds to its subject, I'm going an easy 260 in the film. Red lights blink. A drone zooms past, hovers, then shoots away, its robotic eyeball pivoting to devour the scene. A school of GoPros swims past the radiant quicksilver fish in our hands, snapping pictures like starving piranhas. Kate and I climb out of the river hugging and dancing. We all are. A voice from my self-conscious subconscious: *Get a grip! Act like you've caught a freaking fish before!* But actually, who cares? We got our fish. Give me another hug, give me some knuckles, give me a drink of that Crown and throw away the cap. Todd looks up at the darkening sky and mouths something that looks a lot like "Thank you."

Day Six 6:15 pm

The arc of sky-blue line slows, my fly swimming into the seam for the ten-thousandth time … and then it isn't. A bathtub of river water churns and boils, a broad tail slashes the surface, shards of chrome flash in the center of chaos. Line shoots through my fingers. Blood drums in my ears. Behind me on the riverbank, the clatter of stones and pounding feet. Line sails away downstream, trailed by yards and yards and yards of hot-orange backing slicing through cool green water. The edges of vision darken and blur; heat surges through my gut.

Day Six 6:09 pm

I quit. Bail. Tap out. The wet, the cold, the … deflation win. My casting has fallen apart—not that it was ever really together, but now we're talking catastrophic failure. Tailing loops. Crap timing. Wind knots. I try to fix my stroke midcast and duck to avoid a #4 Tiemco 5262 sailing through the space where my head just was. Time to reel up and get outta Dodge. Rick says, "No, no … keep fishing. The light's really nice. Perfect for shooting a fish." Then, looking me right in the eye, "What? Yeah, I'm serious. C'mon, man." I strip out line and step back into the run, my every exaggerated movement dripping with sarcasm.

Day Six 10:43 am

Caffeine, nicotine, ethyl alcohol, the great equalizers of misspent time and futility. Cast, mend, step, swing. Repeat the same action over and over again, expecting a different outcome—the definition of me. Cast, mend, step, swing. Three feet of vis, dropping and clearing, rocks the size of toaster ovens. And still, there are no fish. How long have we been doing the dance in this Valhalla of uncut old growth, pristine water, and wolf tracks in the sand? A boat appears out of nowhere, its bow pointed directly at me. Sunglasses, hat, hood ... right into my water. I prepare to deploy my standard one-finger salute when an arm extends, an unopened fifth of Crown Royal gripped in finger-less gloves. "For luck," the figure says, and suddenly, it's Steve, a good friend I haven't seen in more than a year, bearing gifts in the middle of Neverland. And then he's gone. No conversation, no explanation, the bottle in my hand the only proof. Cast, mend, step, swing ...

Day Six 8:01 am

There is no Plan B. "Without a fish, we don't have a movie," Todd, the producer, mumbling over his untouched plate of congealing eggs and cold toast. Todd the producer, the organizer, the dreamer behind this collapsing, fishless fish film, shoulders crushed under the freight of hopes slipping through fingers. "Do you hear me? No Movie!" Forehead veins bulging, eyes bloodshot, brain short-circuiting in an endless internal loop of *What will I tell the sponsors? Will we have to give the money back? What money? It's all been spent.* A not-insignificant conservation career streaks toward oblivion.

Day Five 9:37 pm

Rick the camera guy: "I can't believe steelhead fishing is even an ... activity."

Day Five 5:48 pm

The film guys, once tense and coiled as herons ready to strike, now stare into space and examine their fingernails. Shivering, soaking wet, their rain jackets sacrificed to keep waiting cameras dry. How many days has it been? How many casts into this perfect, empty river? They've shot enough B-roll to fill a Terrence Malick feature—morning dew on blades of grass, shimmering golden cottonwood leaves, ancient spruce forest—and now slump into the excruciating cadence of paint drying. Still, every time I row to shore, our fishing sessions are bracketed by the snap of Pelican cases opening and closing on gravel bars, the metallic glide of tripod legs extending. Nobody wants to miss The Moment, should one of us actually hook a steelhead. Or worse, be responsible—amid the chaos of unpreparedness—for the dreaded double punch of the record button. The Cardinal Sin. The ultimate cameraman screwup. Curly telling Moe he locked the door twice, "once this way and once that way."

Day Four 4:20 pm
Knee-deep in rushing water, line swinging arcs across the head of another perfect run. Kate wades out to chat. I keep casting, swinging, hoping. On the hang down, brief resistance, the fly touching rocks in soft water. I lift to cast and as the fly skids to the surface, a swirl and heavy pull on the line. My heart leaps. *Fish.* I rip the rod back from near-vertical to beyond vertical. Nothing but empty water streaming past my hook. Kate's all over me like the proverbial hobo on a ham sandwich. "Dude, you trout set!" I start to explain, "I was casting ... what was I supposed ..." Never mind. Kate's already stomping back to the bank in disgust. The amplitude of fraying nerves rises another notch.

Day Four 3:45 pm
McGuane once said there are only two requisites a good steelheader must possess: a big arm and a room-temperature IQ. But it occurs to me, on what must be the thousandth cast of the day,

that the advent of modern Spey rods has rendered the former obsolete. Leaving only the latter. Which I clearly qualify for, as demonstrated by the utterly unrealistic belief that I am about to catch a steelhead on this very cast. This water is too damn good not to get a fish. I open my fly box yet again and stare into its contents with contempt and befuddlement, "a chimpanzee," to quote McGuane again, "defeated by shoelaces."

Day Three 9:01 pm

"All we need is one fish! That would be enough for the film. Is one fish too much to ask for? Don't answer that." Todd, dark circles under eyes, and the beginning of what appear to be veins pulsing at his temples. The river's just coming into shape now. Conditions, perfect. We'll find more than a few fish. Easy. A day or two of drawing blanks? No problem. It's steelhead fishing. We just have to stick with it, the big wave of fish will arrive anytime now. We'll bail on River Y and go meet them in the big water of River X tomorrow. No worries, Todd. Have another piece of pie.

Day Two 3:52 pm

High water, but good; clear enough to fish, all that rain filtering through acres of forest primeval. Cast, mend, step, swing. I am about to catch a fish, I just know it. And this river! A fully intact watershed; no clear-cuts, no roads, no dams, no hatcheries. Just a perfect steelhead river with a well-documented run of big, wild fish. I am stoked. And I'm about to catch a fish right now. Cast, mend, step, swing. Clean water pours off a long, sweeping riffle and slows, gliding into the trough at walking speed. Four-feet deep, choppy on top, big rocks bank-to-bank. I'm going to catch a fish on this cast. Cast, mend, step, swing. OK, this cast. ...

Day One 7:34 pm
"So maybe we don't need a ton of fish. Just enough to get the movie shown and keep fishermen interested … I can live with that." Todd, the producer, with a little expectation management to relieve pressure from the crew. Or allay his own fears. But really, what's a four-hour fishing session without a fish? Hell, we just got here. And the water's still high from last week's flood. When it drops, fishing's going to be off the charts. And it's not like someone else is going to catch 'em … we have the whole river to ourselves. Unbelievable. There is only one minor smudge on our glossy shell of optimism: Kate.

Day One 2:05 pm
Kate staggers from the helicopter door, shoulders slumped and feet shuffling with exhaustion. Kate, the optimist, the energizer, the spirit lifter … looks slightly less than stoked. A lot less, actually. The guests she's been hosting this week pile out with the same shell-shocked expression on their faces. Kate hugs me a bit harder and longer than expected, as if trying to draw some kind of fresh sustenance. She takes her glasses off, revealing a frayed, worn look around her eyes. "Eighteen days," she says, "eighteen effing days without a single fish." And as she trudges away, under her breath, "Welcome to the suck."

Day One 2:01 pm
The River Y runs through this pristine valley like a jeweled necklace, a succession of perfect steelhead pools strung together with sparkling riffles, runs, and pocket water. A trail winds from lake to river mouth for easy access to miles of the best steelhead water in the world, and there's not another soul fishing it. I know I've had this dream before, but now, here we are. I don't even know

where to start. Upstream? Downstream? Right in front of camp? I wader up, my hands shaking with anticipation as I try to tie a fly to my leader. But wait. Why hurry? The fish aren't going anywhere. I will wait for Kate, who's on her way to meet us now, having already been here and fishing for a couple of weeks. She'll have it wired. Then the two of us can hang out, catch up, and chew the fat between all the fish we're about to hook. Awesome.

Day One 3:52 am
Geeked on equal parts anxiety and stoke, I writhe under twisted sheets in a stuffy hotel room in the Far North. Dr. Yoram Bauman, the University of Washington's economist-slash-standup comic, looms in my imagination: "You know you're a climate-change economist if you spend a lot of time flying around on airplanes telling other people to spend less time flying around on airplanes." I flew here on an airplane. We will be flying in helicopters in the morning. And while we are making a film about climate change, we'll be leaving a pretty decent carbon footprint. Thus the anxiety. I think this film can help fishermen understand the value of pristine watersheds, the importance of wild salmon and steelhead unpolluted by hatchery genetics, the necessity of cold, free-flowing rivers on a rapidly warming planet. Will it make a difference? I have no idea. But we have to try. And anyway, we are going to catch a ton of steelhead. Thus, the stoke.

Five Months Earlier
"Hey, Dylan, this is Todd. How'd you like to help us make this film. It's about climate change and steelhead. We need to get anglers engaged in the climate-change battle, and this film can do that. We just need to catch a lot of fish for the cameras so

people will watch it, you know, the spoonful of sugar to help us deliver our message. We're already booked for River Y, prime time, untouched watershed, no other anglers ... just us. What d'ya think? I know, I know ... planes, helicopters ... but we aren't telling people not to drive or fly. This is bigger stuff ... policy-level stuff, major changes in government and industry, that's what's going to make a real difference. What d'ya think? Want to help us catch a bunch of steelhead? Hello? You there?"

No worries, Todd. River Y? September? No other people? I'm in. We'll catch tons of fish. Tons of fish.

A SMALL OFFERING

Crouching behind a car-sized boulder, I look upstream into the tumbling, rock-strewn current of a gorgeous mountain stream I won't name here—mostly because I can't pronounce it, let alone spell it. Somewhere in the translucent water above me, I am told, *iwana*, the native Japanese char, scan the surface for insects. From where I stand, the stream looks much like the high-gradient mountain creeks we fish back home, the ones that are stuffed with hundreds of little cutthroat trout that race upward to grab any fly we choose to cast. This should be easy, but I know this drill. I've fished for *iwana* before and came away humbled.

The small, black, parachute-style fly given to me by local fishing guru Junichi Nakane sails out into dappled light filtering through streamside maples. I make a quick mend, and achieve, at least to my eye, a perfect, drag-free drift. A small, trout-shaped form materializes beneath my fly, where seconds before, there'd been only water and rock. For a brief moment, the fish hovers, floating downstream with the fly, then turns and disappears back into the depths. Yep, I know the drill all too well.

The night before, at the Japan premiere of *Artifishal* in Shibuya, I stood in front of a sold-out crowd and talked about human arrogance, and the mistaken idea that we could some-how, in the face of all our habitat destruction, engineer our way to abundant trout and salmon. Someone in the audience stood and asked what he could do to help wild fish in Japan. I struggled to answer.

Again and again, in cities across Japan, as we screened the film, I was amazed by the interest and concern of the audiences.

In Fukuoka, I was honored to meet Shoko Tsuru, the brave activist behind Japan's first—and so far, only—successful dam-removal campaign, on the Kuma River. In Nagoya, I heard from fishermen craving a way to protect the remaining wild *iwana* and *yamame*. In Hiroshima, I spoke with a group working to preserve their local watershed. At the Patagonia Japan offices in Yokohama, I looked out into a sea of bright, eager faces and when I asked who would lead a campaign to stop buying farmed salmon, every single person raised a hand. And everywhere we went, I heard fishermen and nonfishermen alike say that they were ready to help, they just needed to know how.

But what could I offer the concerned citizens of a densely populated island nation, where resources are increasingly scarce and the landscape has been engineered by thousands of years of civilization? Where rivers are so diverted to rice fields that many no longer reach the sea. Where even on the pristine mountain stream we fished, there were impassable retention dams every couple hundred yards blocking any kind of migration. What did I have to offer here?

Back on the water, as the warm afternoon dissolves into evening, Junichi, Reo, Manabu, and I sit on a six-foot dam, dangling our feet in the water and eating our *onigiri*. We recount the day, the Japanese fishermen happy with the single eight-inch *iwana* we landed and a handful of similar-sized fish that rose but refused our flies. Then, in the shallow water below us, a shadow slides out from under a rock. A big *iwana*. Huge. Easily two feet long. A seemingly impossible fish for this austere alpine water. How could it grow so large, limited to this small stretch of plunge pools between dams? We watch in awe as the great fish swims around the pool, then disappears beneath the rock again. Nature finds a way.

What do I have to offer here? A push for wider acceptance of catch-and-release fishing, no small feat in a culture built around the eating of fish; a request to stop buying farmed salmon; encouragement for those working to remove dams and preserve habitat. If we're successful, as recreational harvest declines and wild fish habitat improves, a move away from reliance on hatcheries. There is much work to be done in Japan, and the solutions feel very far away from where we are today. But I know that wherever we live, we need to start now. And I know that if we do our part and give them half a chance, wild fish can recover and thrive. What I can offer here turns out to be the same thing I offer my own countrymen at home. It's not much, but for me, it's enough: Hope.

AUGUST 2016

Skyla has fallen into the cold waters of the Madison, filling her waders and bruising her arm, not to mention her pride. When she sits back in the riverside grass to dry off, she is stung by a hornet. I ask if she wants to keep fishing. She shakes her head. Later, after a restorative elk-burger dinner at Craig and Jackie's, I cautiously ask if she's ready to fish again. She says yes, but without her usual enthusiasm. On the river, a blizzard of caddis swarms in the warm evening light. Weston and I wader up and walk downstream, leaving Skyla to fish with Craig. Just before dark, on the way back up, we pass two anglers huddled together, dejectedly looking upstream. "Doing any good?" I ask. "Nope, but that girl up there is crushing," one says, his voice thick with envy. "Goddammit, now she has another one on!" When I peer around the willows, I can see her silhouette against the blue-black sky, rod bent and laughing, just as an eighteen-inch rainbow launches into the air.

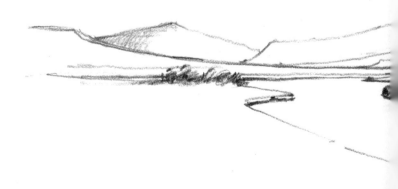

THE GRAND SALAMI

To be honest, I don't really care one way or the other about permit. It's not that I actively dislike these overgrown pompano, I just don't have enough experience or context to elevate them, as many anglers do, to Holy Grail status. Besides, as Tom McGuane has pointed out, if you mention these fish to your nonangling friends, they usually think you're talking about your fishing license. And yet, here I am, on the bow of a skiff staked out on the ocean-side drop-off of an enormous flat in Jardines de la Reina, Cuba, during what has been billed as the prime permit week in one of the best big permit destinations on Earth.

We'd been poling along the deep edge of the flat when our guide, who I will call Señor Holler, spotted three permit off the starboard bow. This, after four solid days in which nobody in our group had even hooked, let alone landed, a single permit. Now, my friend Mauro and Señor Holler are on foot, about a quarter mile away, stalking the elusive fish that seem intent on leading them on a wild-goose chase. I watch the receding figures walking with exaggerated stealth. From time to time, they pause, crouch, cast, then continue walking until they become tiny dark silhouettes in the blinding glare of tropical light.

I wait and watch, killing time. I look at clouds building into towering thunderheads. I wipe sweat off my brow. And then, about a hundred feet off the transom, I notice a small patch of muddy water. Interesting. With the boys still stalking, now even farther out, I slide over the gunwale and walk toward the growing area of murky water. At about sixty feet, I can see some kind of fish swimming around in circles, swirling up the marl. I cast my

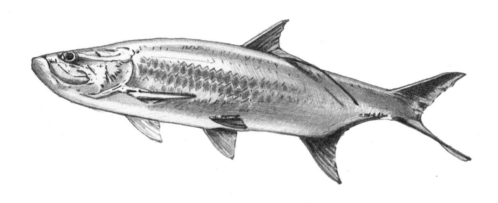

bonefish fly into the disturbance, make a couple of strips, and watch two permit materialize in clear water about where I think my fly should be. One fish races ahead of the other, tips down, and opens its mouth, gills flaring. I keep stripping until the line tightens, then I come back hard against the resistance. The shallow water detonates with an explosion like a rooster pheasant flushing from heavy cover.

The fish careens across the flat leaving a contrail of cloudy water behind it, zooming around at a speed I can barely fathom. I watch the fish growing ever smaller in one direction, while my fly rod and line still point at a place where the fish was seconds earlier. By the time I've recovered all that backing, and given a diminishing amount of it back on several occasions, Mauro and Señor Holler are back at the boat, defeated by their quarry.

My fish makes a short run back toward the skiff, and Señor Holler sees it flashing through the water. "Permit! Permit!" he yells. "Don't lose it!" He jumps out of the boat and splashes to my side, just in time to tail the fish. Mauro snaps some photos and I release the fish, which shoots out of my grasp and hightails it over the edge of the flat into blue water. Señor Holler hails the fleet on VHF, shouting into the handset in rapid-fire Spanish, of which I can only decipher my name and the word *palometa*, Spanish for permit. Congratulatory messages come back from the other boats. During one of the replies, I hear Yvon in the background saying, "Oh god, the guy who cares least always catches the best fish."

· · ·

Yes, it was a boondoggle. But who am I to turn down a free trip to Cuba? Bruce McNae, a generous and longtime benefactor of wild-salmon conservation, was hosting a week aboard a mother ship, flats skiffs in tow, in search of permit. The idea was to gather a handful of conservation leaders—and me, feeling something like an imposter or perhaps someone's little brother—from around the world for a meeting of the minds and to foster collaboration. We would fish in pairs during the day and figure out how to save wild salmon over outrageous dinners at night. The whole thing seemed a bit over the top, but like I said, who am I to turn down such an offer?

"Just get yourself to Miami," Bruce said. "We'll fly private to Nassau from there, and meet the yacht in Cuba. I'll cover all your costs."

"Private jet, luxury yacht, guided skiffs ... um ... this doesn't involve me taking off my clothes, does it?"

"What? No ... are you ... OK, whatever. Look, some of your friends will be there, Yvon and Mauro are in, and Kurt from Wild Fish Conservancy. Then there's the salmon advisor to Prince Charles, and the guy who's developing closed-containment salmon farms, and ..."

"We're going fishing, right?"

"Yeah, for permit, but I mostly just want to bring all you guys together and kick ideas around, come up with some new ways to save wild salmon."

"And, just to confirm, I can keep my clothes on? OK, I'm in."

• • •

When our G5 landed at the small, rural airport in Cayo Coco, Cuba, we were greeted by armed guards in full military uniform. They were not happy to see us. Trying to be helpful, I unpacked my trusty Spanglish, and eventually learned that they didn't know what to do with us—a private jet from the United States had never landed in Cayo Coco before.

We milled around on the tarmac while our pilot, the head Cuban military officer, and the airport manager conferred. Without saying anything to us, the military man and the manager abruptly walked back into the building. Our pilot said he didn't know what was going on, but that they needed to call someone. If worse came to worse, he thought we probably had enough fuel to make it back to Nassau.

The rest of the military contingent, a half-dozen stone-faced, AK-47-toting troops, stood at attention, staring straight ahead. When I stepped forward to attempt some small talk, the closest soldier put his hand on the pistol holstered at his waist.

An hour's worth of increasingly tense seconds—thirty-six hundred to be exact—passed. The airport manager returned with news: We were not allowed to land here without a special visa. We looked first to our pilot, then to Bruce, our fearless leader. Both shrugged. I asked the manager when and how we should've obtained the visas. He brightened. "Oh," he said in English, "I have them right here."

"How much do they cost?" I asked.

He slowly looked from one to another of us, then over to the soldiers. He cast his eyes upward, brow furrowed in concentration. His lips moved silently, while he unconsciously touched his thumb to the tip of each finger, counting. His eyes shot furtively left, then right, then, his math complete, he broke into the kind of gleeful expression one associates with lottery winners.

"I am very sorry for the expense," he said, "but it will cost each of you … five dollars."

· · ·

By the third day, nobody had hooked a permit. We'd seen plenty, but all the usual factors that keep anyone from catching a permit

had come into play: blown casts, standing on the line, long follows with the inevitable refusals, fish that simply didn't see the fly
or care enough to react to it. The one constant? Señor Holler's
growing frustration, which he expressed through increasingly
abusive yelling.

The day Yvon and I fished with him, Señor Holler shouted
at us about the permit that wouldn't eat our flies; about the
bonefish we—mostly me—couldn't see until they were too
close; about casting at and hooking a barracuda—again,
me—that he had to deal with. Finally, Yvon had enough and
told the guide we just wanted to fish on foot, to let us out
at one end of a sprawling, mangrove-strewn flat, and pick
us up several hours later at the point on the far side. Señor
Holler seemed to take great pleasure in explaining, in very
loud and condescending tones, that it was impossible, that
we were stupid to even try fishing on foot there. The bottom,
he explained, was too soft to wade; we would need to stay in
the boat with him.

Yvon calmly reached into his pack, produced a couple pairs
of small snowshoes, which we strapped to our flats boots, then
bailed over the side. "See you at the point in three hours," he
said, addressing Señor Holler. Then Yvon and I proceeded to
enjoy a quiet, stress-free walk through the marl and low mangrove shrubs, spotting bonefish here and there, and catching
enough to keep our interest.

Clearly, when we fished from the boat with Señor Holler spotting fish from the platform, we had more shots at fish. But you
can't discount the value of not being yelled at, and fortunately,
my limited fish-spotting range matched my casting abilities perfectly. Of course, I'm simply not going to say how much time
I spent casting to elongated coral clumps, fish-shaped sand

patches, and occasionally, complete hallucinations. But nobody yelled all afternoon.

•••

Back on the permit flats, I hand my bonefish rod to Mauro, telling him I know it's not the right gear, but that it worked. Having just landed a permit, I feel as though I've accomplished something, even if I'm not really sure what. In any event, it seems that we have, for once, stumbled into the right time and place to actually catch these fish. Now I want to watch Mauro give it a shot. He slides into the water and starts walking, head up, scanning for signs of life. With the tide coming in and good numbers of fish around, I figure he's going to get one any minute. And even if not, it's only eight thirty in the morning, yesterday's wind has fallen out, and the whole day stretches out ahead of us.

Señor Holler jumps overboard with very little stealth, marches up to Mauro, and snatches the rod out of his hands. "You are not fishing!" he shouts. "We go now!" He climbs back into the boat and starts the motor. "Hey," I say, "there's permit here, Mauro should fish."

"No! Only you. Grand slam! Grand Slam! Now is time for tarpon!"

"Really, it doesn't matter."

"No! You must catch tarpon now! Grand slam!"

Mauro climbs aboard, looks at me, and shrugs. Señor Holler jams the throttle forward, the skiff jumps up on plane, and we're running wide open, the mottled coral bottom streaking past, wind whipping our faces. If I am too ignorant to fully comprehend the significance of permit, I care even less about the grand slam—catching a permit, tarpon, and bonefish by a single person in a single day—something I've read about but only vaguely registered in my consciousness. Mauro waves his hands in a dismissive gesture, rolls his eyes, and laughs, telling me not to worry about it, he doesn't care either. But we're going tarpon fishing anyway.

• • •

Each night, we gathered in the yacht's air-conditioned salon to live like royalty. Icy mojitos and frozen towels to wipe our sweaty, sunburned faces greeted us the second we stepped off the skiffs. Then, fresh tropical fruit salads. Snapper and humongous lobsters caught by the chef while we chased inedible sport fish all day. Flan, fine rums, and cigars for dessert. Yes, it was a boondoggle, and for me, almost-unimaginable luxury. The Cuban crew and guides—excluding my nemesis, Señor Holler—were kind, thoughtful, and open to answering all the questions we had about life in this last outpost of communism. In the rural areas where they lived, the crewmembers assured us, there was very little property crime because everyone owned the same stuff, which meant there wasn't anything worth stealing. Everyone in the country except doctors drew the same salary, about nineteen dollars a month. With no incentive or pressure to get ahead, and few options for entertainment, citizens were free to spend their days making good food, music, and love. Propaganda messaging for the tourists, perhaps, but it sounded utopian anyway. Lest we start making plans to move south, though, there were also subtle reminders of the authoritarian regime. Each night, the captain of the mother ship had to radio the government to report that nobody had taken a flats skiff and headed for Florida. Citizens were not allowed access to the beaches for the same reason. The guides hungered for our monofilament tippet material, modern fly lines, and wading boots.

I still felt a strange mixture of gratitude for being invited along on a trip I could never afford and a kind of low-grade embarrassment, not to mention a skeptic's view of the real value of what we were doing there. But true to Bruce's word, we occupied our evenings, often long into the night, with salmon conservation: technological breakthroughs for a closed system of dry-land salmon farming; ancient selective-fishing techniques that could allow thriving runs of fish to be harvested without harming depressed stocks; an idea for a gathering of international salmon experts to create a new global management paradigm; a rough outline for a film that could show taxpayers how their money is being wasted on hatcheries and their public waters polluted by fish farms. Just talk, sure, but we all dove into it with sincere effort, happy to talk with our counterparts from different countries and trade thoughts and ideas.

• • •

And now, the tarpon. We make a hard turn into a long, wide channel of murky water walled in on both sides by impenetrable mangrove forest. Señor Holler cuts the motor and we drift in thick, humid heat. Señor Holler yells at me to get my tarpon rod. I don't own a tarpon rod. He yells at Mauro to give me his tarpon rod. Mauro, gracefully maintaining his naturally upbeat demeanor, laughs and hands me his tarpon rod.

You know the really cool part about tarpon fishing? That adrenaline surge, the dry mouth, your knees quivering as you watch a string of hundred-pounders finning and gulping in crystal water as they come into range? That doesn't happen here. Señor Holler, in what passes for a stealthy whisper from him, tells me very loudly to strip out all the sinking line, cast as far as I can, and count slowly while the fly descends into dark waters.

I pile the line on deck, reach back, and let it fly. The heavy lead-core line shoots out, straightens, and splashes down. Señor Holler starts counting, loudly: "*Uno* ... pause ... *dos* ... pause ... *tres* ..." At *veintisiete*, he motions for me to start my retrieve. I make two strips and it comes up solid. I strip set again, and while the rod tip is ripped down toward the surface, the far end of the line, way out there, starts rising to the surface. Fast.

Seventy feet off the bow, water tears open and a twisting, rattling blur of silver vaults into the air as if shot from a catapult. Three more explosive leaps, a hundred yards of backing, and a slowly descending tail walk tire the fish, and when it pauses, I am able to gain line and move it toward the boat. Then, on a short line, another flurry of crazed—and, I will admit, slightly frightening—jumps right next to the boat and the fish is out of gas. It swims in a wide circle, pumping its tail to dive, but slower each time it passes around the boat. Finally, I pull the tarpon alongside and Señor Holler grabs it by the lower jaw, leaning the fish's big head against the gunwale. I pull the hook out, lift it for a photo, then feel it power away into the murk.

One cast, one tarpon. Not exactly how I picture tarpon fishing, but still, there must be a bunch of them under the boat here. I hand the rod to Mauro, crack a Cristal, and sit back against the ice chest.

"No fishing for you!" Señor Holler shouts, jabbing a finger at Mauro. "Only him! Grand slam! Bonefish now!"

"Come on," I say, as a creeping déjà vu sets in, "the fish are here, let's fish."

Señor Holler throws his arms in the air and stomps his foot against the floorboards. "Grand slam! Grand slam!" he yells, "Only you fish!" He snatches the tarpon rod from Mauro, furiously winds up the line, then points it at me, shouting, "Only you!"

For Señor Holler, the coveted grand slam is now a slam dunk. It's only ten o'clock in the morning, which leaves eight more hours for me to catch a bonefish. While the permit seemed impossible, and the tarpon doubtful and random, bonefish here are a dime a dozen. Señor Holler poles us through a narrow cut hidden by mangroves and into an open saltwater lake. The glassy surface is pierced by dozens of bonefish tails and backs glinting in the sun. With the grand slam now within easy grasp, Señor Holler has taken it down a notch, confident in his success. He hands me my bonefish rod, extends his arm horizontally, and with palm up, gestures magnanimously to cast in any direction.

I hand the rod to Mauro and Señor Holler boils over. "Grand slam!" he screams, spit flying and neck veins bulging. "No fishing for Mauro! Only you!"

I sit down on the cooler and look up at Mauro. Then I extend my arm horizontally and, with palm up, indicate that he should cast in any direction.

• • •

Yes, it was a boondoggle, a week of incredible opulence and comfort in a spectacularly beautiful place with good friends. An extravagance I could never even imagine, let alone deserve, and one I soaked up and savored. But "boondoggle" also carries a connotation of bogus intent or lack of results, and here's the thing: That closed-containment salmon-farm technology? In the months since we talked about it, it's grown into a viable business, with several of the group investing in the rollout. The World Salmon Forum, the first-ever gathering of salmon activists, scientists, and managers from around the globe, became reality, with the inaugural three-day symposium in Seattle. A comprehensive, coast-wide strategy for saving wild Pacific salmon started with a fully operational selective-harvest fish trap on the Columbia River. The idea for a film about the cost of fish farms and hatcheries turned into the documentary *Artifishal*. Add it all up and boondoggle or not, at least in my book, it beats a grand slam any day.

SEPTEMBER 2017

The West is on fire. From California to Alaska, our tinder-dry forests, desiccated by drought, are burning, filling even our usually fresh coastal air with smoke. A fine layer of ash covers the boat and swirls into the air as we motor out of the harbor under an eerie, midday twilight. We are going to protest the net-pen salmon farm off the south end of the island where we live. The kids made signs and carry air horns. Because I am also working on a film about threats to wild salmon, Smarty trails behind us in his own boat loaded with camera equipment and crew. We join a fleet of other boats, all carrying signs, and circle the net pens. An armada of kayakers arrives. The Coast Guard arrives. The media arrives. Our film crew launches a drone. My eyes sting from the smoke. This all feels so absurd, so far away from actually fishing, that I wonder: How did I get here?

STEELHEAD, LOVE, AND
OTHER MYSTERIES

Fly fishing for steelhead is an act of faith, a practice entirely dependent upon belief in the existence of an unseen force responding to your prayers. Most other forms of fly fishing are visual—you cast a dry fly to a rising trout, place a shrimp imitation in the path of a cruising bonefish, toss a baitfish pattern into the frothing whitewater of blitzing stripers. But steelhead fishing is different. There is no proof, no empirical evidence, that somewhere beneath the river's surface, there are fish present. You are left, then, to perform a kind of liturgy, a ritual of cast, mend, step, and swing, and hope that your devotion will be enough.

We agreed to part ways a month ago. After a lengthy period of intense long-distance dating, fishing, and adventures, and the past seven months of more intense, but good, day-to-day life, we're calling it quits. Danielle's clock is ticking too loudly to ignore any longer, and after countless deep and sometimes painful hours of introspection, I've come to two conclusions: One, I don't think I can live up to the future she envisions, and two, I can't let myself stand in the way of the life she wants. In many ways, it's my fault; when she packed up her life and moved west to be with me, I believed—we both did—in the possibility of a different outcome. I'm the one who dropped the ball. And now, we are enjoying each other's company so much, neither of us knows what to do. A hovering, opaque sadness waxes and wanes between us. On a long drive to fish the Columbia one September afternoon, we finally accepted it was time to let go.

But first, a steelhead. We've caught king and coho salmon, five species of trout, grayling, Dungeness crabs, razor clams, and spot prawns together; hunted crystals, antlers, morels, and chanterelles; and along the way, we learned to live with each other. Our first real date was a long weekend spent fishing the Clearwater in Idaho. Our second date was ten dark, wet days spent swinging flies on the Olympic Peninsula in bitter February weather. She's learned to Spey cast, to mend her line so the fly swims across the current, to read the water, and step her way down a run at the right pace. She's hooked steelhead, too, but so far, each encounter has ended only in heartbreaking loss.

In retrospect, that second date to the Olympic Peninsula probably wasn't the most auspicious way to kick off a budding romance. After seven days of dark-to-dark fishing, much of it spent submerged waist-deep in thirty-nine-degree water while battling rain, wind, snow, and the awkward, unfamiliar Spey rod, I could see more than a little doubt creeping into Danielle's pale-green eyes. I hoped the twelve-pound buck I landed behind her would lift her spirits, but it only raised her frustration and boosted her resolve. A kind of grim determination set in. She'd pause to wring freezing rainwater out of her long braided ponytail, pull a knit cap down over her ears, and start casting again. I could feel myself falling in love.

Long before dawn on the eighth day, we cleared a skiff of fresh snow off the car and drove down to the Hoh through the muffled silence of snow-shrouded rainforest. At the river, we rigged up under the tailgate light. When I reached to tie a new fly onto her leader, she stopped me, saying that it was time for her to do it herself. Then she waded out into the dark river to wait for daylight.

My friend JD's old truck came crunching onto the frozen gravel bar and parked alongside. He and I sat on the back bumper, drinking coffee, watching as Danielle started fishing her way into the run. In the grainy gray light of what passes for dawn on the Olympic Peninsula in winter, we watched her pull more line off her reel and step downstream. "She's almost to the sweet spot," JD said.

Then Danielle's line pulled tight and she stepped backward, her rod bending deep into the handle. The fish shot upstream and just as it cartwheeled into the air ten feet in front of her, her rod sprung straight. The worst kind of straight, the kind where all the pulsing, adrenaline-pumping energy that momentarily brought it to life is suddenly gone. "Did you see that?" she screamed, running out of the river toward us, empty line trailing behind her. When she reached the truck, she held up her leader and discovered a curled end where the knot had unraveled. JD, the grizzled guide, took the leader, held it up to the light, and said, "I bet that's a mistake you won't make again." She cried on the way home.

And so it went. For all her success trolling for king salmon, casting dry flies for trout, and pretty much everything in between, steelhead eluded her. We fished hard, started early, and quit late, made long predawn drives fueled by fast-food drive-through breakfasts and murder-mystery podcasts. We returned home in darkness again, our eyes gritty with exhaustion and car windows fogged from rain-soaked gear. Whenever I landed a fish, she cheerfully took pictures and celebrated with genuine happiness. In the deepest, coldest days of winter, her enthusiasm was often the only thing that kept us going. I would say the weather sucks or the river's still rising, and she'd reply, often too brightly for my taste, "You don't know if you don't go."

Danielle's steelhead became a mission, a pilgrimage of faith we were making together.

So now we're on the Kispiox, working our way through the Home Pool on our first day in the North. The water is on the high side, but dropping and clearing. It's October fifth. When we arrived last night, Bob said the river was just coming into shape, that we should get up early and fish first water. So we rolled out of bed in the dark and, shivering, slid down the steep, muddy trail by the bright cones of our headlamp beams. Above us, between black silhouettes of spruce and birch, pinpricks of stars wheeled through cold autumn air.

We wade by braille, sliding our boots around algae-slick boulders, searching for solid footing. With headlamps off, it makes no difference whether our eyes are open or closed. I've already promised myself not to fish until Danielle catches one, so I'm mostly just here for moral support. And to act as a human wading staff as we feel our way into the rocky top end of one of the great steelhead pools on Earth.

At home, when I look at the night sky, I always search first for the Big Dipper, then follow its lines to find Polaris, and dream of this place. At least for the moment, I don't even feel the need to fish. Just being here is enough. It helps, too, that Danielle is fishing well. I watch her line straighten on long casts, we talk through the mends, and I hold my breath each time it comes tight and starts swinging across the current. She gets mad at me for over-coaching—a bad habit left over from my guiding days, or perhaps a personality defect—then gets mad at me for staying silent. After some unknown duration, when the dream state of steelhead fishing has, as usual, warped all sense of time, we are about two-thirds of the way down the run, right in front of the big birch. Danielle, this kick-ass fish woman from Idaho, who's killed elk and antelope, who can bust brush and climb rocks like a mountain goat, is running out of steam. I can tell her faith in the idea of steelhead on the swung fly—in me, really—is fading.

Without warning, the curved arc of her line straightens and leaps from the water. A flash of pink and silver out in the main flow appears under an enormous boil of water. The raspy click of her drag accelerates. The fish bulldogs, fighting to stay in the trough the way big bucks often do. Danielle pulls back, reeling, and the line goes slack. The color drains from her face. I tell her there's probably another one in there, to keep fishing, she's just getting to the Bucket, the water's perfect. She finds no solace in my words. I don't think she believes anymore.

But she sticks with it, mechanically now, a born-again atheist still going to church on Sunday. Our friends Rick, Colin, and Aaron, who took the raft upstream earlier, arrive up at the head of the run. Thinking Danielle could use some space, I get out of the water and walk the trail back up to the top for a report. The guys are pulling the raft up a steep bank, and I jump in to help. A scream cuts through the sound of rapids and echoes off the far bank. Oh god, grizzly bear, I think. But there's a pealing timbre of unchained elation in the screams, like the hysteria of teenage girls overcome by the Beatles in old newsreel clips. "You better run," Rick says.

I haven't moved this fast since … I can't remember ever running like this, let alone in waders and boots. At an all-out, full-tilt, leg-churning sprint, I cover the ground between us, skidding to a stop only to grab the net Bob left leaning against a small spruce. The screaming continues, filling the riverbed with equal parts fear, joy, and dread. I slide down the bank and plunge into the water. She's deep in the heavy current, leaning back against the fish, which, hearing my splashing entry, streaks away across the tailout like a skipping stone. Every time the fish jumps, Danielle shouts something, but I can't make out any actual words.

As I've heard said, if I was a praying man, I'd pray. I'm not, but I do anyway. And eventually, the fish stops running, holds for a moment way out there on the far side, then begins to yield. Danielle gains ground, pulling back and reeling down, her jaw clenched now in silent concentration. The knuckles on her right hand, the one holding the cork grip, turn white.

One more moment of chaos: At this water level, there's no beach to speak of, just a steep bank covered with overhanging willow saplings and thorny brambles. Danielle is backed all the way up against the brush with nowhere left to go. She can't reel in any more line; most of her sink tip is already in the guides and pulling the rod back further would tangle it in the brush. The fish, though, is beat. With one half-hearted little run and a wallowing leap, it tips over and allows me to slip the net under it. Danielle lets out a howl—part war whoop, part cathartic release—and reaches to touch the ghost we've been chasing for so long. She cradles the fish in the water, running her fingers along its flank as if to confirm its existence. A small miracle has been granted. When it revives, the fish shoots away, disappearing into the moving green depths as if it never existed.

Danielle hugs me so hard we stumble and almost fall into the river. She raises her arms like a referee signaling a touchdown and exhales a long, sighing breath, eyes closed and face turned up to the sky. In a few months, she'll be gone. I will miss her more than I could've known. We will both move forward into a future different from the one we imagined. But this fish, this moment, and the seasons that led up to it, will always be there—beneath the surface, perhaps, but no less real because they can't be seen. I have faith.

SALMON DREAMS

At night I dream of salmon gliding through stormy seas, turning streamlined noses toward a faint scent of distant birth rivers; in brackish bays feeling the pull of lunar gravity and a taste of sweet water; beneath swirling canyon pools, rain spackling the surface and silver bubbles streaking past like shooting stars.

Under high-summer sun, I think of salmon in more calculating terms. Where are they on this tide? How deep? What will they take? But I have waking dreams as well, of the Elwha's legendary one-hundred-pound Chinook salmon, of sockeyes spawning sixty-five hundred feet above sea level in the Sawtooth Mountains of Idaho, of the staggering numbers of fish that once filled Puget Sound.

I think of deep-ocean elements found a thousand miles from the sea, carried on Mother Nature's conveyer belt—migrating salmon—high into sterile interior mountain ranges. I think of traditional First Salmon celebrations, and an eleven-thousand-year story of humans and fish evolving together. I think of my own life, from early memories of fishing with my father, to the places and people I've come to know in the years since, all measured in terms of salmon. And of course, I think of my children and our shared connection to these fish.

Such thoughts and dreams, though, do not come without concern. Or maybe it's fear. Will my generation bear witness to the last wild salmon? Our growing population appears relentless in its destructive powers. We harm salmon through neglect, with shopping malls, resource extraction, and our need for energy. And we harm them out of love, with misguided hatchery programs, indiscriminate fisheries, and industrial net-pen fish farms. Salmon conservation often feels like plugging one leak in the dam—a fitting, if ironic, metaphor—only to see two more spring up just out of reach. Some days, the enormity of the task—this continuous fight against the unwavering currents of progress—becomes overwhelming.

But then, I think of my kids again. And I remember the way salmon move upstream, resting in pools and eddies to summon strength for the next push into seemingly insurmountable flows. My mind wanders back to dreams of enormous Chinook salmon powering up through free-flowing Elwha rapids, of sockeye schools cruising the air-clear waters of high alpine lakes, of wave after wave of chrome fish pouring into Puget Sound. And I dream of my kids, and theirs, returning to meet them.

JULY 2020

We've been at home for almost five months, locked down by the global pandemic. We've traded our annual fishing trip to Montana, the eighth-grade state basketball tournament, volleyball camp, and the joys and comfort of people we love, for isolation. It has not been easy. Today, we are an hour from home, searching for tiny native trout in the headwaters of a small mountain stream. I crouch on the mossy bank in a shaft of warm, summer light. Just downstream, Weston releases an eight-inch rainbow that rose to his fly in the shadow of a moss-covered granite boulder. Upstream, Skyla kneels in the current, taking pictures of a brilliant, pink-spotted bull trout fingerling that ate her Parachute Adams. Weston gestures toward the tailout, "Dad, look." A wild summer steelhead as long as my arm, its translucent fins glowing in the sunlight, holds for a brief, miraculous moment before dissolving into the shadows. The kids and I look at each other in wonder. And then I understand, perhaps for the first time ever, how I got here. And more importantly, why.

STORY NOTES

NOVEMBER 1969–JULY 2020
Sage Catalog

The short, chronologically ordered vignettes sprinkled throughout the book started as an assignment for the *Sage* catalog as part of the fly-rod company's thirty-year anniversary celebration. I was going to put them all together as a single chapter in this book, but in the course of creating the manuscript, I realized that it made more sense to expand the timeline and use them as snapshots to create a lifetime (so far) story arc that overlaps the twenty-year arc of my fishing writing.

CONFESSIONS OF A STEELHEAD BUM
p. 16, *Fish & Fly*

After many failed attempts at writing and submitting stories to fishing magazines—one of which memorably came back from the editor with a note saying, "At (unnamed magazine) we publish stories. This is not a story."—I finally made it into print with this one. About a month after it was published, I was in Smithers, British Columbia, when someone I didn't know came up to tell me how much the story meant to him. I later related this incident to friend and mentor Tom McGuane. He said, "That's really the only reason to do any of this." His words still ring true today.

TROUT FISHING AT THE END OF THE EARTH
p. 32, *Fish & Fly*

The first of many adventures set up and made possible by Tim Pask, whose fantastic photos accompanied most of my early stories.

SILVER LINING
p. 44, *Patagonia Catalog*

WAY DOWN SOUTH TO THE OLD WEST
p. 48, *Fish & Fly*

LUCK
p. 60, *Fish & Fly*

HUNTING GIANTS
p. 66, *Fish & Fly*

This story was originally written on assignment for a French fly-fishing magazine. The publication went out of business sometime between the writing and the printing, and Tom Pero at *Fish & Fly* bailed me out by publishing it.

THE WORST GUIDE IN THE WORLD
p. 72, *The Flyfish Journal*

The publication of this one story pretty much ensured limited employment opportunities in the fly-fishing industry, not to mention everywhere else.

THE SEARCH FOR ATLANTIC STEELHEAD
p. 78, *Fish & Fly*

COMMITMENT
p. 96, *Sage Website*

THE LITTLE THINGS
p. 99, *Patagonia Catalog*

STATE OF THE STEELHEAD
p. 104, *Wild on the Fly*

My first attempt at serious conservation writing came out of a dinner conversation with *Wild on the Fly* editor Joe Daniels,

Yvon Chouinard, and Casey Sheahan in Ventura, California. It started with a discussion about the farmed salmon on the menu and ended, after months of research, with Joe publishing the story. At the time, I was feeling increasingly desperate about the dwindling numbers of fish and what that meant to my life. With a young daughter and newborn son, I also experienced the first inklings of responsibility to future generations. I believed at the time—and still do—that the best contribution I could make was to collect and translate some of the growing body of scientific evidence into easily digestible words to arm my fellow anglers. I think I was also feeling some guilt around my latecomer status to the hard work others had been doing for decades.

CRASH

p. 124, *The Drake, The Flyfish Journal*

This story is the source of one of the biggest screwups in my publishing career. I sent it to Tom Bie at *The Drake* and, having not heard back from him, I actually forgot about it. A year later, I ran across it in a file and sent it to Jeff Galbraith at *The Flyfish Journal*. Jeff said they'd publish it immediately. At that same moment, unbeknownst to me, Tom decided to publish it. When the two magazines sent out their next issues—you guessed it—this story was in both. I actually still cringe about it. So I will take this opportunity to say, Jeff, Tom, I am truly sorry. My bad.

A RECIPE FOR CADDIS CARBONARA

p. 127, *The Flyfish Journal*

WHY CAN'T FLY FISHERMEN BE WATERMEN?

p. 132, *Fly Fisherman*

HIDDEN GOLD IN THE DEEP BLUE SEA

p. 135, *Sage Catalog*

For eleven years, under the guidance and encouragement of Sage Vice President of Marketing Marc Bale and the support of HL2 Creative Director Dale Lantz, I was given the opportunity to write editorial-style fishing stories with the financial security of commercial work. I still consider myself lucky, and remain thankful for the experience.

THE HIGH COST OF KOLA CHROME

p. 140, *The Flyfish Journal*

Sometime in 2008, I received a call from Jeff Galbraith, publisher of *Frequency* and *Ski Journal*. He said he was starting a new fly-fishing print magazine that would sell for $12.95 per copy. I laughed. He then listed some of the writers and photographers who would be involved, and I stopped laughing and started scheming to join the crew. When the gorgeous inaugural edition—Volume One, Issue One—came out, this story, along with "A Recipe for Caddis Carbonara," made the pages among stories and images from many of my heroes. The fact that the brilliant designer Jessie Lu used a photo of my Russian hotel room and blue prom-dress bedspread to open this story, in a fishing magazine of all places, sealed the deal— I've been a huge fan and proud contributor ever since.

TROUBLE IN PARADISE
p. 160, *The Flyfish Journal*
Given that this piece was first published in 2010 and the situation on the Olympic Peninsula is, if anything, worse now than it was then, it's hard for me to think of it without a little bit of heartbreak. I still believe there's reason for hope, but the factors updated in the postscript make it abundantly clear that we need serious change. And fast.

WRATH   GLUTTONY
p. 166   p. 169
The Drake
These two stories were part of a theme concept from *The Drake* editor Tom Bie. The concept? The seven deadly sins of fly fishing, with different writers each assigned one of the sins to cover. I liked the idea so much, I requested, and was given, two of the sins. This probably says something about me as a human being, but I don't want to dig into that too deeply.

OPERATION DITCH PICKLE
p. 174, *The Flyfish Journal*
Two fly guys infiltrate the high-octane world of tournament bass fishing? I credit publisher Jeff Galbraith with the idea, which I resisted for months, and long-time fly-fishing sales rep—and seasoned warm-water fly angler—John Sherman for making it happen. It turned out to be a blast, and the unusual subject matter pushed me to what I consider a shift for the better in my writing.

FRANKENFISH: COMING SOON TO A MARKET NEAR YOU?
p. 190, *The Flyfish Journal*

A CRACK IN THE DAM REMOVAL
p. 192, *Unpublished*
This is essentially the text of a talk I gave at the Elwha Dam Removal Symposium, which later appeared, in part, in the film

DamNation. I was originally just supposed to introduce the keynote speaker, Yvon Chouinard, but shortly before the event, he called and said he thought we should monkey wrench the event by talking about the elephant in the room—the hatchery that was being built to mitigate the effects of dam removal. I immediately thought of a story researched and written about by biologist Bill McMillan, and figured the parallel was too good to ignore. In my anxiety about the speech—it was a huge crowd—I forgot to credit Bill that night for what was the major part of my talk, a mistake I regret to this day.

WHAT ABOUT BOB?
p. 198, *The Flyfish Journal*
Jason Rolfe, editor at *The Flyfish Journal*, asked me to write a piece to accompany a photo essay about British Columbia steelhead legend Bob Clay. I was planning a standard profile piece, but when I saw the beautiful photos that were going to be published, I realized they pretty much said everything I was going to write about, and more. So we decided I should describe Bob in a more unexpected light.

RUNNING OUT OF NORTH
p. 202, *Patagonia Catalog*

BIG IN JAPAN
p. 208, *The Flyfish Journal*
A fourth-generation descendent of immigrants visits his ancestral homeland for the first time? The proverbial offer I couldn't refuse.

THE WEATHER WILL DECIDE
p. 224, *Patagonia Catalog*
Of the many difficult aspects of my divorce, the toughest was dealing with the fact that I would no longer be an everyday dad. As I pondered the implications of only physically being with the kids for half of every week, I realized I needed to change my perspec-

tive on parenting. Spending a week aboard a small boat in the Far North with the kids and two of my mentors somehow turned out to be a good way to start our new family dynamic.

THE MYTH OF HATCHERIES

p. 232, *The Flyfish Journal*
This story, coauthored with Bill McMillan—yes, he graciously forgave me for forgetting to credit his work in my Elwha speech—and published in *The Flyfish Journal* in 2012, formed the basis of a talk I gave in locations all across the Pacific Northwest. At some point in my speaking tour, as I lectured in front of four octogenarian fly-fishing-club members at some small-town VFW clubhouse, or perhaps it was the Sons of Norway Hall, I realized that I wasn't exactly creating a tidal wave of change. Around that time, I was fortunate to be peripherally involved with the Patagonia film *DamNation.* The experience showed me the power of film and the impact with which it could deliver complex messaging. Long story short, this story became a talk, which, years later, became the film *Artifishal.*

A RIVER REBORN

p. 248, *Patagonia Catalog*

GIANTS LIVE FOREVER

p. 251, *Unpublished*
I wrote this for Bruce Hill's memorial service, but when I tried to read it at the podium, I was so choked up I don't think I actually finished. Or if I did, I'm sure nobody could understand a word. So … Bruce, if you're out there, this is what I was trying to say.

WHAT IS FLY FISHING?

p. 254, *Patagonia Catalog*

THERE IS NO PLAN B

p. 258, *The Flyfish Journal*
Everyone knows how fish stories work: First, there's a long struggle, and if it's a good story, doubt and challenging situations crop up and must be overcome. Eventually, the angler triumphs by catching a fish. Knowing this story would be published after the film it's based on, *Chrome*, came out, I figured it would be more fun to reverse the narrative.

A SMALL OFFERING

p. 266, *The Cleanest Line*

THE GRAND SALAMI

p. 272, *Unpublished*

STEELHEAD, LOVE, AND OTHER MYSTERIES

p. 286, *Unpublished*

SALMON DREAMS

p. 292, *Patagonia Catalog*
My friend, the poet Cameron Scott, says I can claim this one as poetry, but I'm doubtful. I think it's really just a very short essay that took an excruciatingly long time to write.

GRATITUDE

In my experience, the very different worlds of fishing, conservation, and literature share at least one common virtue: an extraordinary number of people who are willing to lend a hand. This book as a whole is, in many ways, a culmination of the generosity I've received from so many, and my attempt at thanking all who helped along the way.

First, to my dad, who sparked an early obsession, bought me my first fly rod and tying materials, and took me fishing whenever he could. To my mom, for spending every Sunday waiting in the car while I fished, and for the very definition of unconditional love. To my brother, Adrian, the toddler who sat in the back seat with his comic books and stuffed animals on all those rainy Sundays, and grew up to inspire me with his commitment and well-deserved success in the art world. And to Andy Landforce, who took a fish-obsessed kid under his wing and offered much-needed wisdom on how to be a good fisherman, and more importantly, a good human being.

As my fishing world expanded, so too did my list of fishing buddies. These are people who've provided more than just companionship and adventure, they've shaped who I am today: Nate Mantua, Dan Sweeney, Steve Perih, Tim Pask, Mike Kinney, David Smart, Neal McCulloch, Kate Crump, Rick Koe, Bob Clay, Craig and Jackie Mathews, Del Martin, Brian Horsley, Sarah Gardner, John Larison, and the Alagnak Crew: Jeff Brunzell, David Franklin, Carson Stevens, John Nestande, Marvin Orwig, and Matt Miller. Fishermen are often thought of as ne'er-do-wells and slackers by the civilized world, but when our family owned a blueberry farm and we suddenly found ourselves in need of serious help, it was the anglers who dropped everything and showed up ready to work.

Then there are the friends who've guided my conversion from selfish, fish-obsessed fisherman to selfish, fish-obsessed conservation advocate: Nate Mantua; Yvon Chouinard; Craig and Jackie Mathews; Bill McMillan; Bill Bakke; Gerald Amos; Bruce, Aaron, Julia, and Anne Hill; Matt Stoecker; Kurt Beardslee; Nick Gayeski; Conrad Gowell; Emma Helverson. Also Hans Cole, Ron Hunter, and Lisa Pike, who continue teaching me how to actually get things done. These are some of the smartest, most dedicated human beings I know, and my minimal scribblings on the issues pale in comparison to their lifelong commitment. When the politics and struggles of fish conservation beat me down, I look at what they've accomplished and what they're working toward, and my sense of hope is renewed.

To my "Bachelor Dinner" family—David Smart, Neal and (occasionally) Matt McCulloch, Pete Berg, Helene Smart, Morgan Smart—who make Tuesday nights the highlight of every week. Remember: Just say no to Uncle Ben's.

To my comrades in conservation and the fish industry, Brian Bennett and Dave McCoy, who provide friendship, great times, and more support—emotional, creative, intellectual—than anyone could hope for. You guys make the hard work fun. *Viva los tres hermanos!*

To the Monday Zoom call crew, Craig Mathews, Rick Koe, Mark Harbaugh, Mike Thompson, Mauro Mazzo, Oggy Fox, and Yvon Chouinard, plus Malinda, our IT specialist who makes it all work. Sage advice, fishing reports, fly patterns, food notes, and general bullshitting lifted my spirits throughout the long months of social distancing. Next up: Going back to actually hanging out and fishing together again soon.

It is difficult to quantify the profound effect Yvon and Malinda Chouinard have had on my life. Their friendship has fundamentally changed how I look at the world. Not by teaching, per se, but purely through example. I've been lucky to share time on the water and many memorable meals with Yvon, from Cuba to British Columbia, and at Yvon and Malinda's home in California. Every time we fish, talk, or just hang out, I gain new perspective and renewed energy to protect what we love. More importantly, the Chouinard lessons have taken hold of the next generation as well, helping my kids develop a fierce sense of responsibility for the world they're inheriting.

The writers, editors, artists, and publishers who set the bar just high enough to let me in, gave me a shot, and encouraged me to keep at it: John Larison, who generously provided many close readings, sharp suggestions, and the foreword for this book; Tom McGuane, Dave Guterson, Ted Leeson, Kate Crump, Cameron Scott, John Dutton, Vincent Stanley, Karla Olson, Tim Pask, Dale Lantz, Marc Bale, Steve Perih, Tom Pero from *Fish & Fly*, Tom Bie from *The Drake*, Joe Daniels from *Wild on the Fly*, Jeff Galbraith, Steve Duda, and Jason Rolfe from *The Flyfish Journal*. And to Frances Ashforth, for all the gorgeous art—including in this book—that captures the spirit of our planet's essential elements.

Special thanks to Danielle Dorsch, whose faith in the idea that these stories paint a bigger picture together than they did on their own kept the project alive. Your years of cheerful pressure to make this book a reality ... made it a reality.

A big thank-you to my agent, Valerie Borchardt, for looking out for me, hand-holding, and answering my calls at all hours. I understand this is rare. Also, to Karla Olson, John Dutton, Christina Speed, and Sonia Moore at Patagonia Books for believing in this book, for investing in it in so many ways, and for making it beautiful.

You will notice that a number of the names here appear in more than one category. I think this is a result of fishing, travel, conservation, and literary matters converging in what I consider to be an exceptionally fortunate life.

And finally, to my kids, Skyla and Weston, my favorite fishing buddies of all, for motivation to put my thoughts on paper and keep fighting to protect this world. In one way or another, I wrote all of this for you.

Thanks, everyone! Now, let's go fishing.

Photo: Tomine Family Archives